Military Memories

Military Memories

Draft Era Veterans Recall Their Service

Edited by Donald Zillman

Anthem Press
An imprint of Wimbledon Publishing Company
www.anthempress.com

This edition first published in UK and USA 2024
by ANTHEM PRESS
75–76 Blackfriars Road, London SE1 8HA, UK
or PO Box 9779, London SW19 7ZG, UK
and
244 Madison Ave #116, New York, NY 10016, USA

First published in the UK and USA by Anthem Press in 2022

© 2024 Donald Zillman editorial matter and selection;
individual chapters © individual contributors

The moral right of the authors has been asserted.

All rights reserved. Without limiting the rights under copyright reserved above, no part of this publication may be reproduced, stored or introduced into a retrieval system, or transmitted, in any form or by any means (electronic, mechanical, photocopying, recording or otherwise), without the prior written permission of both the copyright owner and the above publisher of this book.

British Library Cataloguing-in-Publication Data
A catalogue record for this book is available from the British Library.

Library of Congress Control Number: 2024941596
A catalog record for this book has been requested.

ISBN-13: 978-1-83999-252-0 (Pbk)
ISBN-10: 1-83999-252-2 (Pbk)

Cover Image : The Cover Photo is the USS Enterprise nuclear aircraft carrier on which Author Arne Salvesen served as a nuclear engineering officer.

This title is also available as an e-book.

The authors dedicate this book to their wives, children, parents, and siblings who shared the challenges and accomplishments of their military experiences.

CONTENTS

Bios of Contributors   ix

Section I	Introduction	1
Section II	America Raises Its Military Forces	3
	Bibliography	24
Section III	Personal Recollections	27

A. Eugene R. Fidell   29

B. Tom Mackie   37
   Family Background and Experience   37
   High School and the Path Forward   40
   University Life   42
   Active Duty   44
   Post-Active Duty Life   55

C. Mick McBee   59
   Ancestral and Immediate Family Military Experiences   59
   Early Experiences   60
   Selective Service System and College ROTC   61
   Active Duty Military Career   63
   Post-Active Duty Military Connections   66
   Military Service and Civilian Career   66
   Other Observations   70

D. Arne Salvesen   73

E. Leif Salvesen   87
   Ah—But Let Me Begin at the Beginning   88
   My Time at Naval Oceanographic Facilities   92
   Some Thoughts on My Active Duty Life in the Navy   94

	My Life after Active Duty	95
	Some Reflections	96
	Let Me Conclude with the Following	97
F.	Paul Strieby	99
G.	John Tewhey	107
	My First Air Force Assignment	110
	My Second Air Force Assignment	110
	My Third Air Force Assignment	111
	My Fourth Air Force Assignment	112
H.	Donald Zillman	115

Section IV Perspectives on Today's Military — 153

A.	The Draft and the All-Volunteer Force	155
	The Draft Eras	155
	The All-Volunteer Force Era	156
	The Next Fifty Years	157
B.	Our Shared Experiences	159
C.	The Contemporary American Military	163
	The Need for a Larger Force to Fight Conventional Wars	164
	Today's More Sophisticated Military Needs	167
	A Need for Shared National Sacrifice and Greater Citizen Familiarity with the Military	168
D.	Decisions for the Government about a Renewed Draft	171
	The Legality of the Draft	171
	Gender Classification	171
	Mandatory Public Service Beyond the Military	172
	Conscientious Objection to Military Service	172
	Administering the Draft	173
	Popular Views on a Return to the Draft	174
E.	The Extraordinary Events of 2020–22	177
	The COVID Pandemic	177
	Climate Change and Natural Disasters	178
	Race Relations	179
	Political Disruption	179
	International Affairs	180

Index 183

BIOS OF CONTRIBUTORS

Eugene R. Fidell was commissioned in the U.S. Coast Guard following graduation from Harvard Law School. In uniform, his duties included military justice, merchant marine suspension and revocation proceedings, the adjudication of in-service conscientious objector applications, and fisheries law enforcement. His subsequent career has combined private law practice with public interest activities, including co-founding the National Institute of Military Justice, a non-profit organization he headed for 20 years. He has also taught law school courses on military justice and a variety of other subjects, and is currently a Senior Research Scholar in Law at Yale and Adjunct Professor of Law at New York University. He is a leader in domestic and international efforts to reform military justice.
eugene.fidell@yale.edu

Thomas Mackie is a graduate in engineering from the University of Wisconsin where he was a member of Navy ROTC. Following further officer training he opted for service in the United States Marine Corps. His Marine service included Vietnam War duty as a combat artillery officer and stateside service in California and Chicago. Captain Mackie's Chicago service involved leadership of one of the largest midwestern Marine Recruiting offices at a time that the military draft was ending. He helped shaped new recruiting initiatives for the Corps. His Marine experiences shaped a career in corporate leadership around the United States and overseas. Mr. Mackie worked at Parker Hannifin Corporation for 33 years retiring as Operations President, Corporate Vice President in 2006. He earned an MBA from Case Western Reserve University in 1977. He resides in Vero Beach, Florida with Cheryle, his wife of 53 years with three children and five grandchildren.
twmackie@icloud.com

Mick McBee is a graduate of the University of Wisconsin and the Navy ROTC Program. His experiences as a helicopter pilot on active duty included encounters with Soviet Union naval units and work in tracking Soviet submarines. Following his active duty he received a law degree from Arizona State University. Mr. McBee put his experience to work in litigating aviation and other vehicular crashes with an emphasis on survivability and post-crash fire prevention and safety techniques. After two decades of successful law practice, Mr. McBee has served in a wide number of public service leadership roles.

mickmcbee@sbcglobal.net

Arne Salvesen Arne Salvesen is a mechanical engineering graduate of the University of Wisconsin. He earned his commission in the Navy via the Naval ROTC program to which he was selected when he was a high school senior. Arne had a rich experience in the Navy, first as a midshipman for four years and then as an officer for four years of active duty. His primary area of service was in the Reactor Department of the nuclear-powered aircraft carrier USS Enterprise during the time the ship was deployed with the Sixth Fleet in the Mediterranean.

After his naval service Arne worked as an engineer for two years before earning an MBA from Harvard Business School. Thereafter and for 26 years he held general management positions with several publically-owned companies. In 1996 he purchased Tronex Technology, Inc. a California manufacturer of precision tools. Arne managed and grew the business before selling it in 2019 and retiring in Fairfield, California.

arnesalvesen3@gmail.com

Leif Salvesen is a graduate of the University of Wisconsin and has an advanced degree from Thunderbird School of Global Management now a part of Arizona State University. He completed Navy Officer Candidate School and spent his full active duty career at two Navy Oceanographic School bases, one in the state of Washington the other in California. While described to the public as research facilities, the then confidential mission of the bases was the tracking of Soviet Union submarines. The Soviet submarines of the 1960s were capable of carrying nuclear weapons that needed to be located close to their targets, hence the importance of the Coastal NOS bases. Leif served in a variety of leadership roles at the two facilities. He brought those skills he developed in the Navy to his 30 years plus civilian career with Wrangler Jeans and Red Kap Industrial wear in posts in Wisconsin and Texas.

Paul Strieby is a graduate of the State University of New York. He had 26 years of active service in the United States Air Force. His specialty in foreign languages led to his postings and leadership around the world and his elevation to the highest enlisted rank of E-9. His multiple assignments included presence in Southeast Asia in the last days of American military presence in South Vietnam in 1975. Paul's excellence and diversity in foreign languages began with expertise in Albanian language and extended to a wide range of other languages and other postings that included leadership positions and close connection with Operation Desert Storm in 1991.

John Tewhey is a graduate of Colby College and holder of a doctoral degree from Brown University. John was an Air Force ROTC graduate from Colby. His science and engineering studies shaped his Air Force career at bases in the United States and overseas. His military experiences prepared him for post-active duty career work where his leadership experiences in the military allowed him to undertake leadership positions far sooner than persons without military experience would have done. John's specialization in the military was aircraft fuel issues. Special focus was on avoiding and correcting fuel spill errors with their potential for fatal harm to individuals and considerable damage to planes and surrounding properties. Among his significant military postings were an assignment in Korea at a time of high tension between North and South Korean nations.

Donald Zillman is a graduate of the University of Wisconsin undergraduate (BS) and Law School (JD) and the University of Virginia (LLM). Following service as a Law Clerk to Federal Court of Appeals Judge James M. Carter he was commissioned as a Captain in the Army Judge Advocate General's Corps. Following JAG School basic training he was assigned to the JAG School at the University of Virginia in Charlottesville. There he served as the Editor of the Military Law Review and as a faculty member in the Civil Law Division. Don's JAG experience led him to a career in Law Teaching at Arizona State University, the University of Utah, and the University of Maine School of Law in Portland. He served as Dean of the Maine Law School, Interim Provost at the University of Maine, Interim President at the University of Maine at Fort Kent, and President of the University of Maine at Presque Isle. He continued as an active scholar of military law at all civilian schools. One of his most stimulating experiences was at the United States Military Academy (USMA) at West Point. He served as Distinguished Visiting Professor at USMA during the months leading up to the 1991 Desert Storm campaign against Saddam Hussein's Iraq.

Section I
INTRODUCTION

For 35 years of the twentieth century, US armed forces relied on the draft (also called required military service, conscription or Selective Service) to fight World War I, World War II, the Korean War, the Vietnam War and the Cold War with the Soviet Union. Men coming of age in 1917–18 and 1940–73 faced compulsory military service as they reached young manhood.

In the early 1970s, the unpopularity of the Vietnam War and changing public attitudes towards mandatory military service caused Congress to end the draft. The one remaining legacy of the draft was the requirement for young men to register with the Selective Service System in case Congress might again need to rely on conscription to staff its armed forces.

America now approaches 50 years during which all-volunteer military services have served the nation. The great majority of the current population probably view themselves as having "done their military duty" by putting "We Support Our Troops" stickers on their vehicles and paying taxes to support the world's strongest military force. A wide gap exists between the present military and the large majority of the civilian population.

In the last few years, however, world circumstances have changed. America continues to have the world's strongest military. But, its numbers are modest. Its strengths may not be suited to many of the challenges America is likely to face. It now faces potential conflict with China, Russia, North Korea and Iran.

The young men who faced the draft are now in their late 60s at their youngest. Most of the World War II "greatest generation" who are still living are in their 90s. As we eight authors look back from our mid-70s and early 80s on the draft and military service in our lives, many memories come to mind. As we have visited among ourselves and with other fellow veterans over half a century, we are reminded how varied the military (or non-military) experiences of the "draft generations" were. But, we also reflect on common experiences of military life shared by combat veterans and desk-bound soldiers, officers and enlisted personnel, career and single term soldiers. All of us wish that the rest of the nation not touched by military experience had some understanding of those experiences as the nation faces the challenges of the 2020s.

Our book examines the experiences of military service from three perspectives. The first examines American history in the raising of military forces for over 250 years. The major focus is on the laws enacted by Congress from 1916 to 1973 that mandated military service.

With that background, the eight of us examine our personal experiences with the draft and with military service. We start with family experiences with military service that shaped our personal responses to military service during the Cold War and Vietnam War eras. We then review our personal experiences through high school and our first exposure to possible military service. Those years had sometimes obvious and sometimes subtle influence on the decisions we made regarding military service.

The final section of the book then looks back on how military service shaped our lives and the nation at large. We give special emphasis to lessons learned and decisions facing America in the 2020s regarding its armed forces and foreign policy. One issue is whether a return to some form of mandatory public service, especially military service, is needed in the third decade of the twenty-first century.

Section II

AMERICA RAISES ITS MILITARY FORCES

America began four centuries ago with the settlement of what would become thirteen colonies by British settlers at Plymouth Rock in Massachusetts and Jamestown in Virginia and the arrival of the first black slaves from Africa. They joined longstanding Native American tribes and settlements in French and Spanish colonies to the north, south, and west of the British colonies.

America at the beginning of the Revolutionary War in 1775 had changed little over the last century and a half. Transportation was by horse or other animal on land and by sailing ships on the water. The railroad, the automobile, steam propulsion on the water and the airplane were 75 to 150 years in the future. Electricity would not be harnessed for a century. Rapid exchange of information—telegraph, telephone, radio, television, the internet and social media—was more than a century in the future.

Weapons of war were primitive by modern standards. But they included pistols, rifles and artillery that allowed fighting at distances beyond hand-to-hand combat. And, combat was a concern to most colonials. Native Americans, defending their homelands, could pose a serious threat to white settlers. So could the threat of slave revolts in the southern colonies. The other European colonial powers, France in Canada and Spain in Florida, offered militaries that could match British forces. The equivalent of modern police forces did not exist.

Cities, towns and rural communities responded with the creation of militias. The militias were modeled on Britain's actions in the 1600s in response to British kings assertion of control over all military actions inside and outside the British Isles.

The British experience gave rise to several precepts that would shape the American approach to raising armed forces. A first concern was to keep direction of the army away from the exclusive control of an executive (the British king). The major challenger to the King was the national parliament. One element of legislative control by parliament was the bitter opposition to standing armies, particularly in times of peace. The counter to the standing army was a more locally based militia. The standing army was seen as a body of men whose primary dedication was to a national military establishment and to a command structure governed by a powerful executive.

In practice, the local militia had aspects of both voluntary and coerced service. However, the militia typically promised service with neighbors, leadership selected from those neighbors and limited military duties that allowed the soldier to be a part of the local farm or business community. Any higher loyalties were to colonial government, not to a national leadership.

The Revolutionary War brought military exposure to most citizens of the colonies. Most saw some military combat take place within fifty miles of their homes. Many of the men who would form the new government in 1787 either served in combat or as legislators or governors in their colonies where military issues were a major portion of their work. Colonial forces achieved just enough victories to keep the war going and to gain the support of the French who were happy to assist in a victory over their British rivals.

Allan Millett's study of The Constitution and the Citizen–Soldier observed: "Although all the English North American colonies with the exception of Pennsylvania established the principle of universal military obligation and citizen based defense, they also immediately modified these charters to limit their application." The militia obligations applied only to white males of what today would be the upper or middle classes of society. Further, the "system was designed for training, not active service." What active service there was, was limited to local actions. "Real war in North America—and there was plenty before 1775—had little to do with the militia."

Performance of the militias in the Revolution ranged from excellent to poor. When capably led and fighting close to home, militia forces won significant victories. When more was demanded of them, George Washington's comment that relying on the militia was like "relying on a broken reed" was accurate.

During the war and then afterwards to the drafting and ratification of the Constitution, the new states (the former colonies) weighed the military needs of the new nation. A constant theme in all discussions was the dislike of the "standing army" with its potential for terrorizing citizens with tyrannical rule. However, the founding fathers also recognized that some military capability was needed to deal with local rebellions, Native conflicts, and potential European intrusions.

The Constitutional Convention of 1787 compromised. The new national Congress was given the power to create, fund and regulate a national army and navy and to declare war. Funding of the army was limited to two years. A new act of a new Congress was required to renew that funding. Congress was further authorized to call forth the militias of the states "to execute the

Laws of the Union, suppress insurrections and repel invasions." Congress was given the power for "organizing, arming, and disciplining" the militia and governing them when in federal service. The states retained the power to appoint militia officers and to train the militia in accord with Congressional laws.

For most of the next 130 years this structure provided sufficient military strength to serve national needs. The dream of "no standing armies" was rejected by regular legislation funding modest-sized federal forces to man fortifications around the country, to operate the United States military and naval academies, and service a War Department in Washington, D.C. When necessary, parts of the militia could be called to federal service or additional volunteers could be recruited to provide larger national forces. This mixture of forces fought the War of 1812 with Great Britain, and wars with Mexico in 1846 and Spain in 1898.

The great conflict of the 130-year period was the Civil War of 1861–65. Initially both North and South relied on volunteers (often state militia members). Officers of the national regular army of 1861 were divided in their loyalties. Many natives of the Confederate states violated their oaths of office to fight against the national government for the cause of their native states. Almost no enlisted soldiers deserted the Union cause.

Expectations of a short and relatively bloodless war were not realized and new waves of volunteers grew scarce. The Confederacy first adopted conscription to sustain their war effort. By mid-1863, the national Congress imposed conscription on northern young men. Or at least some of them. The statute excused certain categories of men from conscripted service. One category of exemptions allowed a potential draftee to purchase a substitute. Jean Strouse's biography of J. P. Morgan noted that Morgan "had paid a substitute $300 to go in his place. Other draft-age Northerners who did not see military service included Theodore Roosevelt, Sr., John D. Rockefeller, Andrew Carnegie, Elihu Root…Brook and Henry Adams stayed home, as did William and Henry James." Historian Shelby Foote's The Civil War reported that at the height of the war in 1864 "the Harvard-Yale boat races were resumed…and not a member of either crew volunteered for service in the army or the navy."

The unpopularity of the exemption for the rich and the general dislike of the draft gave rise to riots in the summer of 1863 in New York City. Overall, the draft provided only a small percentage of the union soldiers who fought the War. Many of the leaders of the next decades avoided military service. Shelby Foote summarized: "86,724 individuals escaped by paying the $300 commutation fee, while of the 168,649 actually drafted, 117,986 were hired substitutes, leaving a total of 50,663 men personally conscripted, and of those only 46,347 went into the ranks."

After the Confederate surrender at Appomattox in 1865 both the northern and southern armies rapidly demobilized. However, the Regular Army of the United States grew from its pre-War strength for policing duties in the Confederacy and continued conflict with Native tribes in the West. A cadre of military professionals based in Washington, D.C., and elsewhere made clear that a "standing army" had become part of America in war and peace.

The War with Spain and its empire in 1898 marked the beginning of a new American military. Army and Navy service ranged from Cuba to the Philippines. Historian Eliot Cohen, in Citizens and Soldiers, The Dilemmas of Military Service (1985) estimated that 112,000 well-trained volunteers served in the Philippines from 1898 to July 1901. Like it or not, the United States was becoming a world power with some of the military expectations that accompanied that stature.

In the first decade of the twentieth century, Congress addressed some of the consequences of the military challenges facing the nation. There was general agreement that while some permanent Regular Army was essential to the nation, its size should be kept small. If a larger force was needed for war, debate centered on whether primary reliance should be placed on a reserve force under clear federal control or upon the National Guards of the states with their joint obligations under state and federal law as defined by the Constitution. Legislation in 1902 and 1905 preserved the powers of the National Guards but strengthened federal control when national needs arose. Legislation also advanced federal control by providing federal dollars for equipment, training and salaries of Guard units.

No American better personified military issues than Theodore Roosevelt, Jr. As Roosevelt rose in political prominence in New York State and Washington, D.C. he agonized over his beloved father's avoidance of drafted military service in the Civil War. His son's national prominence began with his appointment as Assistant Secretary of the Navy. That combined with his admiration of military virtues prompted his volunteering to organize the volunteer Rough Riders for combat in Cuba during the Spanish–American War in 1898. His leadership at the Battle of San Juan Hill against Spanish troops shaped a national reputation that led to his election as Governor of New York and, in 1900, selection by the Republican Party as William McKinley's Vice President. One year later McKinley's assassination made Roosevelt the youngest President in American history at a time that many Americans were embracing a new role of world leadership.

After almost eight years of service as President from 1901 to 1909, Roosevelt chose to honor George Washington's precedent of a two-term limit on Presidential service. He supported his friend William Howard Taft for the position and moved to a very visible status as former president that included close attention to European political and military developments along with hunting and wilderness travels.

By 1911 Taft's conservative domestic policies had destroyed his friendship with Roosevelt. TR was persuaded that he was needed back in the White House to lead a progressive agenda combined with well-informed attention to developments in Europe.

Developments in Europe did suggest that a century of European peace after the end of the Napoleonic Wars might be coming to an end. Great Britain, Germany, France, Russia, Italy and the Austro-Hungarian Empire each had objectives that supported or conflicted with those of the other powers. Incidents around Europe and Africa (often involving control of European colonies) from 1900 to 1914 threatened war but were settled peacefully. At the start of Summer 1914 most nations assumed that diplomacy would control any risk of a continent-wide European war.

George Washington's cautions against "entangling alliances" with European powers spoke for most of the American people. The substantial portion of the population who were recent immigrants also made it uncertain where American allegiance would lie in a European war. Germany, Russia, Ireland, and Italy had supplied thousands of new Americans. Many of them retained allegiance to their ancestral homes, or at least to kinfolk who remained behind in the "old country."

The American election of 1912 was like no other. William Howard Taft made clear his desire for a second term. A considerable portion of the Republican leadership promised their support. Teddy Roosevelt made clear his desire to return to office on a strongly progressive platform. The Republican Convention backed Taft. Roosevelt then announced he would lead a third party under the wonderfully Rooseveltian title of the Bull Moose Party.

The winner would be the Democrats, who had elected only Grover Cleveland, since the Civil War. They nominated one-term New Jersey Governor Woodrow Wilson, an eminent scholar of American government and the former President of Princeton University. To Roosevelt's misfortune, Wilson also brought strong progressive credentials to the contest. In November, Roosevelt solidly outpolled Taft. But he could not defeat a Democratic Party united behind Wilson.

Woodrow Wilson assuredly did not assume the presidency to advance bold foreign or military policies. His foreign policy experience and enthusiasm was minimal. One of his leading cabinet members was three-time Democratic presidential candidate William Jennings Bryan, a strong pacifist. Wilson's first two years saw the enactment of bold domestic progressive legislation. His foreign and military record was limited to uneasy dealings with Mexico including sending American troops to Mexico to control rebel leader Pancho Villa.

Then on June 28, 1914, Austrian archduke Franz Ferdinand and his wife were murdered in Saravejo, Serbia. A horrific six weeks of diplomatic blundering turned the Balkan tragedy into a war in which Austria–Hungary and Germany lined up against France, Britain and Russia. By early fall both the eastern and western fronts had seen heavy casualties and a World War was under way.

President Wilson reflected American sentiment that the United States should stay neutral in the War and be ready to serve as a neutral peacemaker. By early Spring of 1915, however, the War was impacting America. The British Navy, the strongest in the world, imposed a surface blockade on goods being shipped to Germany. That harmed American trade. Germany responded with submarine warfare that included the sinking of the British liner Lusitania on May 18, 1915 off the coast of Ireland with the loss of 128 American lives. That removed any prospect of America joining the German war effort. However, support for American neutrality remained strong heading into the 1916 election. Congress and the President, however, recognized that further European developments remained uncertain and that the American Army needed to be increased.

The result was the Hay Bill enacted in June 1916 after months of vigorous debate over the nature of a new American Army. The bill was named for Representative James Hay of Virginia, Chairman of the House Military Affairs Committee. Representative Gordon spoke of Hay as knowing more about the military establishment than "any other living man." In presenting the unanimous repot of the Military Affairs Committee, Hay called the bill a "general preparedness bill" whose focus was "a peace proposition and not…a war proposition."

The crucial issues for Congress in the debate were: (1) the size of the Regular Army; (2) the need for volunteer reserve forces should war demand a larger force; and (3) the role of the state National Guards in providing the larger federal force. The considerable majority of Congress agreed that hard facts shaped a resolution of the crucial issues. First, volunteers alone could probably not supply promptly a quarter million men for a peacetime army or a wartime force of any description. That would require statutory conscription. Second, the National Guards offered the benefits of trained troops ranging in quality from poor to excellent. But state control of the Guards threatened uniform control of the federal force by career Regular Army officers. A volunteer army of reserves drawn from volunteer training programs, college training programs, prior service soldiers, and some National Guardsmen could avoid worries over dual loyalties.

Two other issues inspired considerable discussion. The first was the prospect of "universal military training" (UMT) for all young men regardless of their immediate active service. Numerous civilian and military leaders argued for the value of UMT and advancing physical conditioning, commitment to national service, and preparedness for civilian careers. A stated and unstated premise was the need to accustom new immigrants to such American virtues. A second issue was racial. The prospect of large numbers of militarily trained black citizens frightened many southern legislators.

The Hay Bill approved a modest expansion of the Regular Army to 175,000 men; the rejection of any peacetime conscription or universal military training; the rejection of creation of a significant volunteer army; and the expansion of the National Guards with a clarification of when they could be called to national service. Representative Hay bluntly answered Representative Longworth's question: "Suppose a governor ... had called out the militia to suppress a very serious riot, and on the same day an invading force was landed in the country. Would the President ... then have the right to call on the forces which was in the process of quelling the riot to suppress that invasion?" "Undoubtedly," responded Hay.

Shortly after the enactment of the Hay Bill, the presidential election of 1916 moved into its final stages. Republican Charles Evans Hughes former Governor of New York and a United States Supreme Court justice and Democrat Woodrow Wilson faced off in one of the best-credentialed presidential contests in American history. A remarkably close contest may have been decided by Wilson's slogan: "He kept us out of war."

Wilson began his second term hopeful that America could continue its war-driven economic prosperity and its hope to serve as a neutral mediator in the War. By early April, 1917 the latter hope had vanished as Germany resumed unlimited submarine warfare against American shipping and Germany appeared to offer Mexico the opportunity to join it in the war against the United States in return for the return of Texas, New Mexico, and Arizona to Mexico. President Wilson asked Congress for a declaration of war against Germany. Congress approved, and on April 6, 1917, America entered the war against Germany.

The 65th Congress then moved to address some of the most consequential legislation in American history. One of the first bills returned to the debates in the 64th Congress over the Hay Bill. The military establishment had endorsed a bill to approve conscription to allow a major growth in the Army. Several factors supported the decision for conscription. The first was a recognition that America might need to supply more than just expansion of the Navy and financial assistance to the Allied nations. Reliance on volunteers might not be sufficient. The second was advice from British military leaders that reliance on volunteers alone at the start of the War in 1914 had been a catastrophic error. Thousands of young men from upper class families with little or no military experience had volunteered in the early days of the War. They died by the hundreds in the first months of combat in France and Belgium. These young men were better needed as junior officers and trainers of the large forces that would shortly be needed to compose the British Army.

A third argument for conscription was the continued enthusiasm for UMT beyond just participation in the European War. UMT advocates included many leaders of the business and professional communities. They perceived immigrant "new Americans" as reluctant to adopt traditional American values and to abandon old world habits. Training in military virtues were seen as a strong counter. Author John Chambers II saw the advocates as believers that the military training camps would teach immigrants American values and teach rich and poor to understand each other and work together for the benefit of the nation. It would build better men, physically as well as morally, and would fashion superior workers "who were mature, obedient, and productive." (John Chambers II, Conscripting for Colossus in The Military in America (Peter Karsten, ed. 1980) at 279.) Among advocates for the draft were Army Chief of Staff Hugh Scott, former Presidents Teddy Roosevelt and William Howard Taft, and the New York Times.

President Wilson and Army Secretary Newton Baker initially favored raising new forces exclusively from volunteers. But, by April 1917 they had become advocates for conscription with men chosen "on the principle of universal liability to service."

Debate over the Army Bill continued for two months in April and May. Many provisions had nearly unanimous support. Among those were the need for considerable expansion of the size of the Army and recognition that the entire National Guard could be called to national service despite the objection of the states of Guard members. The role of volunteers, the adoption of conscription, universal military training and the appropriate ages of draftees were more controversial. Army Secretary Baker rejected UMT and substantial reliance on volunteers.

A fascinating part of the debate involved Teddy Roosevelt's offer to raise at least one division of volunteers with himself in a leadership role. These heirs of the Spanish War Rough Riders could serve as the first American combat troops in France with Roosevelt's presence as a powerful message to the French, British, and Germans. Roosevelt made clear his continued support for UMT and his willingness to take only volunteers outside the age limits for the draft. However, it was soon clear that the Roosevelt division(s) was not just a public relations statement. Recruiting offices for Teddy's volunteers indicated they might be able to enlist 200,000 men in the Draft Act debate. The Roosevelt volunteers became one of the most contentious issues.

President Wilson and Army Secretary Baker made clear their opposition to the Roosevelt volunteers. The goal of the Bill was to "mobilize a nation" and this was to be "no war for amateurs." Despite opposition to the draft from House Speaker Champ Clark, a bill passed the House by the end of April by vote of 397 to 24. The Senate agreed by vote of 81 to 8. Nonetheless, support for the Roosevelt volunteers continued and a provision to allow with presidential approval one or more volunteer divisions was included in the bill that went forward for President Wilson's signature on May 18, 2017. Wilson and Baker then made clear that further delay "might have serious consequences." Senator Hiram Johnson, a supporter of Roosevelt, probably did not help the cause when he noted that Roosevelt was "in the twilight of his life."

Racial issues also returned to the congressional debate. Southern legislators made clear their objection to black draftees being trained in the south. Congressmen wanted to make clear the black draftees should be expected to be treated as black residents, not as honored members of the armed forces or even as black civilians in northern cities.

Chapter 15 of the Acts of the 65th Congress was "An Act to authorize the President to increase temporarily the Military Establishment of the United States." Section one raised the Regular Army to its full authorized strength. Section two drafted all members of the state National Guards into national service "for the period of the existing emergency." Section three approved "[t}o raise by draft ... an additional force of five hundred thousand enlisted men." Section four gave the President discretion to draft an additional five hundred thousand men. Section seven made clear that if the Regular Army and National Guard enlisted enrollment could not be satisfied by volunteers, they would be raised by "selective draft exclusively."

The Act then detailed procedures for the draft. After considerable debate Congress agreed to apply the act to males between 21 and 30 years of age. Attempts to lower the minimum age to 18 or to increase the maximum age to 40 or even more were rejected. The statute exempted from the draft government officers, "regular or duly ordained ministers of religion, Divinity students," and members of "any well-recognized religious sect or organization...whose existing creed or principles forbid its members to participate in war in any form and whose religious convictions are against war or participation therein." However, such conscientious objectors could be assigned to military duties that were declared to be noncombatant. The President was also authorized to exempt local government officials, civilian workers in arsenals and navy yards and other businesses "found to be necessary to the maintenance of the Military Establishment...or the maintenance of the national interest." Further exemptions could be issued to persons who had "persons dependent upon them for support", and those "found to be physically or morally deficient." A separate section forbade the objectionable Civil War practice of paying bounties to induce enlistment or allowing a draftee "to furnish a substitute for such service."

Selection of draftees was assigned to over 4,600 local boards of citizens not "connected with the Military Establishment." The goal was to have draftees selected by their neighbors. Decisions of the local draft boards could be reviewed by District Boards. All eligible males were "to present themselves for and submit to registration." Failure to do so was a federal crime punishable by one year's imprisonment and forced registration.

Further provisions of the Act set minimum draftee pay at $36 per month, authorized the President to bar "alcoholic liquors in or near military camps," and authorized the Secretary of War "to suppress and prevent the keeping or setting up of houses of ill fame, brothels, or bawdy houses" near military installations.

President Wilson signed the Bill on May 18, 1917. He described the enactment as a "selection from a nation which has volunteered in mass" and set registration day for June 5, 1917. He turned down Teddy Roosevelt's volunteer force with a description that the "business now at hand is undramatic, practical and of scientific directness and precision." Congress itself felt the impact of its legislation when Representative Augustus Gardner, a leader of the campaign for mobilization and military training, resigned from the House to assume his officer's rank in the Army.

Two anonymous quotations in the New York Times captured the events of June. The first marked the arrival of General John J. Pershing and members of his Regular Army command in Paris. High ranking American and French leaders commented enthusiastically. But an anonymous Frenchman at the Invalides summarized the larger significance of the celebration. "Behind [Pershing] there are ten million more."

The second captured the spirit of the June 5, 1917 national registration. Despite the Administration's enthusiasm for "volunteering in mass" it remained to be seen whether that would happen. The Civil War draft experience had not been a happy one. A considerable portion of the potential draftees were of German or Irish (and anti-British) ancestry. Numbers of potential registrants had also seen their Congressional representatives oppose the declaration of war and the choice of the draft over volunteering. Various groups had already made clear their resistance to the draft. What would be the impact on the American and Allied war efforts of a widespread refusal to register for one or more of the reasons mentioned? Wilson Administration leaders publicly expressed optimism but quietly prayed for success.

On registration day, the optimists felt vindicated. The Times quoted an anonymous New York City registrant: "It was the thing to do; everybody was doing it." By June 24, 1917 the Times reported that 9,650,382, 95.9 percent of expected registrants, had enrolled for selection. However, half of all registrants were ready to claim an exemption from service provided by statute. The 4,600 draft boards and the military medical personnel would have plenty of work to do.

The next visible event was the July 20, 1917 ranking of the registrants. Decisions moved to Washington as a blindfolded Secretary Baker drew the first of 10,500 numbered capsules (that corresponded to individual registrants' assigned numbers) in a public ceremony in the Capitol. The selection of number 258 began 16 hours and 30 minutes that would tell every registrant what their chance of conscripted service was.

By early September the first draftees were ready for mobilization and assignment to training camps (called "concentration camps" in Times articles). Suitable ceremonies and parades marked their departures from home. Most selected registrants were treated as part of the new national army. Others were assigned to Regular Army or National Guard positions to fill those units to their necessary strength.

In January, 1918 Provost Marshal General Enoch Crowder reported on the first draft. A total of 3,982,949 men were called to possible service. 1,057,363 were accepted, and 730,756 served. Crowder also reported that another 700,000 men would turn 21 each year.

On January 7, 1918 the Supreme Court of the United Sates sustained the constitutionality of the Draft Act in a relatively brief 9–0 opinion that sustained numerous lower court opinions. Congress' power under Article I of the Constitution to "raise and support Armies" provided ample authority for the draft. Chief Justice White wrote for the Court: "As the mind cannot conceive an army without men to compose it, in the face of the Constitution the objection that it does not give power to provide for such men would seem to be too frivolous for further notice." The Court further contemptuously dismissed the claim that the XIII Amendment's prohibition of "slavery or involuntary servitude" had application to the case. The Court was "unable to conceive" the terms of the Act applied to the "exaction by government from the citizen of the performance of his supreme and noble duty of contributing to the defense of the rights and honor of the nation."

By February 12, the last draftees were off to training camps. A New York City crowd of 500,000 watched Camp Upton trainees march down Fifth Avenue en route to active-duty training. A second draft for April or May was predicted as developments on the European battle fronts made clear that the Allies would need more reinforcements to defeat a German Army that had just defeated Russian forces and were ready to concentrate its forces on the Western Front. By late March, Germany had begun the first of a series of major offensives that would threaten to end French participation in the War.

Congress continued discussion of the new Draft Act in the face of nervous worries that the United States might be coming to the War too late. By May of 1918 Secretary Baker was asking for as large an Army as possible and suggesting a maximum age of 55, with men over 40 limited to non-combat assignments. On May 20 Congress enacted a joint resolution for the registration of men turning 21 since the first draft. In the same week, the National Army's 77th Division became the first unit to provide draftees to take over a combat sector in France. On July 9, 1918 Public Law 193 gave the President the power to increase the drafted armies to "the maximum number of men who may be organized, equipped, trained, and used" for the rest of the War. Debate over draft ages recorded that approximately three million men were between 18 and 21 and ten million, six hundred thousand were between 31 and 45.

A new Draft Bill was introduced in both houses. Debate centered around the appropriate ages for service and the need to induct "slackers" who had avoided service for a variety of frivolous occupational activities. A request to exempt American League baseball players was greeted with contempt and various citizens' groups circulated in public areas to identify draft dodgers. On August 31, 1918, Public Law 210 amended the first Draft Act. Men between "eighteen and forty-five both inclusive" were liable to service in the Army, Navy, or Marine Corps. It was estimated that 13 million men would be required to register. On September 12, registration day saw such prominent citizens register as opera singer Enrico Caruso, composer George M. Cohan, and John D. Rockefeller, Jr. On September 30, President Wilson drew number 332 to begin 20 hours of number selection. Two weeks earlier the Times reported an epidemic of influenza at Camp Devens and that Assistant Secretary of the Navy Franklin D. Roosevelt had caught the flu returning from Europe.

American forces saw their most serious combat and suffered the considerable majority of their war casualties in September, October and November of 1918. Gary Mead's The Doughboys, America and the World War I, summarized the brevity of the American combat experience and the shortcomings of the American forces. "Yet the reality is that most doughboys did not hear a shot fired in anger. The average doughboy who saw any battlefield action at all was under fire for a total of just seven days…there is no avoiding the fact that the green AEF divisions thrown into the battle were revealed as grievously inexperienced and sometimes poorly led." The inexperienced Americans suffered high casualties for their inexperience but did drive German forces back towards Germany and removed any doubts that Americans would fight with vigor. Most importantly, the prospect of "10 million more" American troops by 1919 persuaded Germany that they had lost the War. Mead summarized: "The important question in assessing the part the United States played in the First World War has a much broader focus: could the Allies have defeated Germany without the financial, economic, military, and psychological backing of the United States? Unquestionably not." Germany asked for an armistice and on November 11, 1918 at 11 a.m. combat ended.

Secretary Baker promptly ended the draft. The Times reported a trainload of draftees headed for training camp was halted three minutes before departure. The men were released and honorably discharged. By early December, 1,151,000 troops had been mustered out of service.

By February of 1919 draft officials reported that 24,234,025 men had been registered for the draft. A total of over 2,700,000 were inducted into military service. As of November 11, 1918, America had 4,791,172 in some aspect of military service. General Crowder estimated that 3.6 million eligible draftees never entered the system at all and of those who registered and were declared eligible for service, 2.8 million dodged the draft. A total of 192,688 civilians had been involved in some part of draft work. Local board officers totaled 13,416. District Board members were another 1089.

By early March 1919, total American casualties were reported as 274,760. Meirion and Susie Harries, *The Last Days of Innocence*, America at War 1918–19, listed American dead at 75,658. Killed in action totaled 34,249. Another 13,691 died of wounds. Most of the rest died from disease, the majority from influenza.

Public Law 309 of February 28, 1919 authorized the "resumption of voluntary enlistment in the Regular Army." The Act removed the freeze the Draft Acts had imposed and indicated Congressional and popular sentiment towards continued mandatory military service and overseas involvement.

Despite Woodrow Wilson's enthusiasm for American leadership in the League of Nations, Congress rejected American participation. In 1920 Republicans Warren Harding and Calvin Coolidge easily won the Presidential election and reflected popular sentiment against further American involvement in European affairs. They defeated James M. Cox and former Assistant Secretary of the Navy Franklin D. Roosevelt.

The next two decades saw the internationalism of the Wilson Administration and the large military that supported it disappear in the United States. The most visible evidence of the military came in 1932 in the midst of Herbert Hoover's presidency and the Great Depression. Veterans of World War I had assembled in Washington to demand payment of promised monetary bonuses for World War service. President Hoover dispersed their gathering with Regular Army troops. Hoover won the day, but in November he was routed at the polls by Franklin D. Roosevelt who would lead American armed forces for the next twelve and one-half years.

The worldwide Great Depression of the 1930s brought the use of armed forces back to the world. Allegiances of the World War changed. Italy and Japan, allies of Britain, France and America in World War I, strengthened their militaries and joined a remilitarized Germany under the leadership of Adolph Hitler. Japan occupied Manchuria and a considerable portion of China. Italy under Benito Mussolini conquered Ethiopia. By the start of 1940, Germany had reoccupied the Rhineland, joined in alliance with Austria, conquered Czechoslovakia and divided Poland with the Soviet Union.

In America, the Neutrality Act of 1939, enacted on November 4, 1939, reflected Congressional sentiment on war and international relations. Its goal was to "preserve the neutrality and the peace of the United States and to secure the safety of its citizens and their interests." It forbade the arming of American merchant vessels, restricted the use of American ports, and regulated commerce with nations engaged in armed conflicts. The Congressional hope appeared to be that Europe could avoid a renewal of the World War or that it would be fought on even terms and America could limit its role to the profitable supplying of needed imports and possible assistance as a neutral mediator.

Events of early 1940 changed those assumptions. In April, Germany conquered Denmark and most of Norway. Then, on May 10, Germany made clear that war in Europe would not be a repeat of World War I with its four years of trench warfare in Belgium and Northern France. German blitzkrieg led by tanks and fighter planes conquered Luxemburg, Belgium, and the Netherlands within days and overwhelmed France within a month. Great Britain, under new Prime Minister, Winston Churchill vowed to fight on after a heroic evacuation of British forces in France from Dunkirk. The Battle of Britain then matched the British and German air forces in the skies over England.

The United States Congress began to address a new world order that indicated an American Army the size of minor neutral European nations might not serve American interests. Legislation enacted from May through September addressed such matters as voluntary Army enlistments "in time of war or other national emergency"; appropriations for the Army and Navy; construction of naval vessels and aircraft including one million dollars for a facility at Pearl Harbor, Hawaii; assistance to governments of the American republics to increase their militaries; and funding for military construction. Chapter 689 enacted August 27, 1940, was designed to "strengthen the common defense and to authorize the President to order members and units of reserve components and retired personnel of the Regular Army into active military service." The President could call the soldiers "with or without their consent, to such extent and in such manner as he may deem necessary for the strengthening of the national defense." Such service, however, was limited to the Western Hemisphere and the Philippines.

The most challenging issue before Congress involved America's first peacetime draft. Even in the face of German success in Europe a substantial portion of Congress and the American public opposed involvement in a second war in Europe. The decision on a peacetime draft also advanced as Presidential and Congressional elections loomed in November 1940. Franklin Roosevelt became the first American President to seek a third term. Three crucial figures in the 1940 draft debate were Grenville Clark, George Marshall, and Wendell Willkie.

Clark was a Wall Street lawyer who had been a strong advocate if the pre-World War I Plattsburgh military training camps. Forrest Pogue's biography of George Marshall, Ordeal and Hope summarized Clark's role in 1940: "He buttonholed generals, congressmen, and like-minded associates, organized dinners, wrote letters to editors, recommended...the appointment to key positions of men friendly to his cause, and helped write legislation for presentation to Congress."

George Marshall was the Army Chief of Staff. In 1940, he faced strong streaks of "isolationism and the absence of militancy" in the War Department staff. Many of them had served in World War I and were convinced that American involvement had been a mistake. General Marshall was also a crucial advocate with Congress, many of whose members distrusted Franklin Roosevelt. Pogue observed that Marshall's "strength with Congress lay not in rehearsed lines or confidential asides but in the assurance he gave legislators that he was telling the truth as he knew it and that he served no party in his recommendations."

Wendell Willkie had been a surprise Republican Party nominee to oppose Roosevelt for the Presidency in 1940. He well could have opposed any Roosevelt actions that suggested greater involvement in European affairs or the growth of the military. Instead, he supported FDR's provision of destroyers for Great Britain and Congressional support of America's first peacetime draft. Harold Evans's The American Century observed: "[Willkie] put his convictions first. ... His generous support of both initiatives was one of the most courageous, selfless, and responsible stands in the history of American politics."

On September 16, 1940 Congress enacted Chapter 720. Its goal was: "To provide for the common defense by increasing the personnel of the armed forces of the United States and providing for its training." The Act declared "in a free society the obligations and privileges of military training and service should be shared generally in accordance with a fair and just system of selective compulsory military training and service." The Act applied to men between 21-and 36-years old with the President to determine the number of men needed. Service was for up to 12 months, but Congress could extend the 12-month period when "the national interest was imperiled." The President was authorized to create a Selective Service System. Further provisions of statute forbade "discrimination against any person on account of race or color" and authorized deferment from service for certain government officers, ministers of religion, essential industry workers, persons with dependents, college or university students until the end of the academic year, and persons "by reason of religious training and belief [who were] conscientiously opposed to participation in war in any form."

Violations of the Act could be punished by up to five years imprisonment or a fine of up to $10,000. Bounties and the provision of substitutes were forbidden. Service under the Act was limited to the Western Hemisphere and the Philippines.

In November, 1940 Franklin Roosevelt was elected to a third term as President although with a smaller majority than in 1932 or 1936. Roosevelt and General Marshall continued to build an American army. In Europe, Great Britain continued to be the sole opponent of Nazi Germany. The British Navy and Air Force prevented German landings of troops in Britain and forced German airplanes to pay a considerable price for their bombing attacks on British cities. In April 1941, German land offensives continued with the conquest of Yugoslavia and Greece. Then, in July, 1941, the major part of the German army invaded the Soviet Union. German forces swept across much of western Russia headed for Leningrad (former St. Petersburg) and Moscow. Winston Churchill made clear that his contempt for Soviet Communism took second place to an alliance with an opponent of Nazi Germany. An August meeting on ships off Canada between Churchill and Franklin Roosevelt also made clear Churchill's hope for an additional ally against Hitler.

In Washington, Congress addressed the future of the draft. Forrest Pogue summarized the political and military challenges. The "release of men and officers…meant the destruction of the battle-worthiness of nearly every American division." Non-renewal of the Act of 1940 meant "from 75 to 90 percent of the officers in the Regular Army units were reservists whose service was soon to end…. As for enlisted men, the outlook was no less grim. In all but two Regular Army divisions, the number of [draftees] ran from 25 to 50 per cent of the total strength. Hardest hit if the twelve-month period of service prevailed would be organizations on which Marshall was now depending for special support units such as engineers, heavy artillery, and anti-aircraft. The Chief of Staff faced the prospect of seeing National

Guard members, reserve officer, and trained selectees melt away within a few months."

The Service Extension Act of 1941 passed on August 18, 1941. Doris Kearns Goodwin, in No Ordinary Time, reported that the legislation passed the House by one vote. The single vote passage was secured by Speaker of the House Sam Rayburn waiting until votes reached a majority of one vote for the draft and then cutting off further changes of votes and announcing the measure had passed.

Congress declared "that the national interest is imperiled" and that the President could extend the 1940 Draft Act for 18 months and Congress might extend it for more than that. Further provisions authorized the President to order retired Regular Army members to active duty and to employ them "as he shall deem necessary in the interests of national defense." The Act further suspended any limitations on the numbers of men on active duty.

Debate over how the expanded military forces would be used continued for another three and one-half months. Then with stunning suddenness the need for the revived draft was answered. On December 7, 1941, Japanese naval and air forces attacked Pearl Harbor and Hickam Air Field in Hawaii with a heavy loss of ships, planes, and American servicemen. The next day Congress declared that a "state of war ... ha[d] thus been thrust upon the United States." The President was directed "to employ the entire naval and military forces [against Japan] and to bring the conflict to a successful termination ..." By December 11, Germany had declared war on the United States and Congress responded with declarations of war against Germany and Italy. On December 13, Congress removed "restrictions on the territorial use of units and members of the army of the United States," extending the periods of service of such personnel. On December 20, the Selective Service Act of 1940 was amended to cover "every male citizen ... and every other male person residing in the United States" between 18 and 65. They were to present themselves for registration. Every male between 18 and 45 was "liable for training and service in the naval or land forces of the United States."

Unlike World War I where significant American combat was limited to four months, American forces were involved in combat against Germany, Italy, and Japan from December 7, 1941 to September 2, 1945. Draftees were the considerable part of all American forces in those battles. Their service ranged from the superb to the dismal. Paul Fussell's The Boys' Crusade, The American Infantry in Northwest Europe 1944-45, recounts the service six months after D-Day in June 1944 of great units like the 1st Division and the 101st Airborne Division which "became lamentable caricatures of what they once were and resemble[d] nothing so much as the newest of the divisions, populated by the inadequately trained and the largely unwilling." Desertion, self-inflicted wounds, and a general avoidance of combat characterized a significant portion of the raw forces. In the Battle of the Bulge in December 1944, the 106th Division had 8000 troops surrender to the Germans with little resistance.

Harold Evans also put the American contribution in perspective. "The scale of the Russian effort is shown in historian John Ellis's calculation that the German Army and the SS spent 7,146 divisional combat months on the eastern front, but only 1,121 in Africa, Italy and northwestern Europe" against American and British troops.

Unlike World War I in which Germany was almost untouched by Allied and American forces until the Armistice of November 11, 1918, Russia from the east and the United States and Great Britain from the west unleashed ground and air forces on Germany up to the date of German surrender on May 8, 1945. Japan suffered serious air attacks on its territory and then was struck by the first (and so far, only) use of atomic weapons in combat with the attacks on Hiroshima and Nagasaki in August 1945. Clearly, a considerable occupation force would be needed in both countries before the wars could be truly thought to have ended. Paul Fussell reported General Eisenhower's plans for dealing with the 3500 members of the German General Staff. "[E]xtermination and liquidation are serious words, and Ike [was] using them literally and seriously. He means, kill them all. Issues like that are what the war was about, our desire to pretend it couldn't have been notwithstanding."

Congress on May 14, 1946 extended the Selective Service Act of 1940. It extended the duties of registration and liability for service for men from 20 to 30. A month later the Atomic Energy Act of 1946 addressed the "development and control of atomic energy." The Act began by noting: "The significance of the Atomic bomb for military purposes is evident." The remainder of the Act addressed peaceful uses of atomic power "subject to the paramount objective of assuring the common defense and security."

By 1947, Congress was prepared to end the draft. Chapter 26 of the Laws of the 80th Congress enacted on March 31, 1947, addressed the preservation of Selective Service records "following the termination of its functions on March 31, 1947." The liquidation of functions was to be completed by March 31, 1948.

One year later, the 80th Congress faced a very different world. Winston Churchill's warning in 1946 of an "iron curtain" falling across eastern Europe under the control of the Soviet Union was becoming real. In China, Mao Tse Tung's Communist Party was nearing a victory that would displace the Nationalist government of Chiang Kai Shek that had fought Japan as a member of the allies. Britain and France were seeing their colonies in Africa and Asia move towards independence leaving America as the significant liberal democracy in the world. The Cold War had begun and a strong American military was essential.

On June 24, 1948 Congress passed the Selective Service Act of 1948. Section 1 bluntly stated: "An adequate armed strength must be achieved and maintained to insure the security of this nation." To achieve this: "The obligations and privileges of serving in the armed forces and the reserve... should be shared generally, and in accordance with a system of selection which is fair and just, and which is consistent with the maintenance of an effective national economy." The following section authorized army strength of 837,000; navy and marine strength of 666,882; and air force strength of 502,000. Registration for the draft was required for men from 18 to 26 with a 21-month period of service. Further sections addressed the structure of the Selective Service System, selection procedures and deferments and exemptions including those for conscientious objectors. Section 20 made the legislation "effective immediately."

For a time in early 1949 it appeared that volunteers might be sufficient to allow a "draft holiday" until the Act's expiration in June 1950. In that month, however, Communist North Korea invaded South Korea and threatened to further expand Communist control around the world. Within a week, President Truman had declared a "police action" to stop the Communist expansion. The 81st Congress extended the Selective Service Act for one year and gave the President the power to order reserve units to active duty. In 1951 Congress enacted the Universal Military Training and Service Act which would induct over one and a half million Americans for Korean War service and another one and a half million for Cold War military service from 1954 to 1961.

Draftees and World War II veterans with a continuing service obligation were a major portion of the American forces that fought the Korean War. One of the most visible American "double veterans" was baseball legend Ted Williams who lost five years of an epic baseball career to serve his country in both wars. Republican Senator Warren Rudman reflected on his Korean War service: "I saw an unexpected theme emerge: The importance of my Korean War experience in my life and the bond I felt with other senators, such as [Republican] Bob Dole, [Democrat] Dan Inouye, and [Democrat] Bob Kerry, who had also known combat. If you have that experience, not much is left in life that will intimidate you...If as a young man, you have seen your friends die for their country, you are left with a sense of what is important in life and what is not."

The Korean War was fought from 1950 to 1953. Its initial stage saw the North Koreans occupy much of the South. The arrival of American forces then pushed the North Koreans back to the 38th parallel that marked the divide between the two Koreas and occupy much of the North. At that point, Communist Chinese forces entered the War and drove the American and South Korean forces back to the 38th parallel. The War then settled down to a stalemate and eventually to an armistice which preserved both Koreas and allowed America to exit from a war that appeared necessary, but hardly the success of the two World Wars.

The War assuredly did not end the threat of further tensions and conflict with Russia and Communist China. The draft remained an essential part of the American military for the rest of the 1950s and the early 1960s. Eminent military sociologist and draftee Charles Moskos reflects: "In my Princeton class of 1956, out of 750 males, well over 400 served. In the [Princeton class] of 2005—1,100 male and female—only 8 served."

James Fallows reflected in More Like Us (1989) that "[o]f all the men who reached age twenty-six in 1958, 79 percent had been in the military at some point." He further observed that "[t]wo powerful institutions encouraged the sense that most Americans were part of a single, broad, common culture. One was the public school system, and the other was the pre-Vietnam War draft. Both brought Americans of different classes into face-to-face contact with one another."

If Ted Williams symbolized the best of the Korean War generation, the late 1950s generation was well represented by singing idol Elvis Presley. At the height of his career, Presley was drafted and honorably served his two-year tour in Germany like many of his contemporaries. He later described his service as doing his duty and obeying orders. Presley's public image shifted from rebellious young entertainer to good citizen and soldier in the eyes of the American people, many of whom had a drafted son in the Army.

By the early 1960s, America faced its most serious military challenge in the jungles of South Vietnam. In 1954, France had lost a decade-long war to preserve its colony in Vietnam. Then Vietnam, like Korea, had divided into a Communist North and an autocratic, but western-leaning South challenged by a communist Viet Cong faction. Presidents Eisenhower and Kennedy cautiously supported the South Vietnamese government. Kennedy's assassination in November 1963 left President Lyndon Johnson with a war that was increasingly favoring North Vietnam and the Viet Cong. After winning an overwhelming victory in the 1964 election over strongly anti-Communist Republican Barry Goldwater, Johnson sharply increased the American commitment to the South Vietnamese government. The American presence rapidly shifted from a few thousand "advisers" to an American combat army that would total over half a million men in the late 1960s.

Faced with both the continuing Cold War against the Soviet Union in Europe and a recurrence of significant fighting in East Asia, American leadership faced the question of where to get more troops for full-time duty. One choice was to rely on the draft. The alternative was to mobilize reserve forces and the National Guard for potentially lengthy service outside the United States. The choice was the draft.

The perception of "shared sacrifice" disappeared with the continuation of the Vietnam War. A crucial factor was the coming of draft age of the large post-World War II generation. An expectation of military service was no longer a patriotic requisite for the young man who turned twenty in 1964. Writing in 1967 political scientists James Davis and Kenneth Dolbeare found that from Korea to Vietnam "military service had been required of only one quarter to one-third of the young men eligible for military service." They cite Defense Department statistics that of men reaching age 26 as of June 1964 "only 40 percent of the college graduates had served, compared to 60 percent of the college dropouts, 57 percent of high school graduates, and 50 percent [of non-high school graduates.]"

Writing in 1989 James Fallows reflected on draft avoidance by the upper classes of society. "[M]any former college boys began lamenting that they had not experienced the thrill of combat or racked up an admirable service record. In real life, Sylvester Stallone spent the war working at a girls' school in Switzerland; in fantasy life, he was Rambo. John Lehman, like Dan Quayle, spent the war in the National Guard, but as Ronald Reagan's first Secretary of the Navy he was usually photographed in a flight suit alongside a navy jet... millions of college boys who one way or another failed to pay the price had unintentionally prolonged the war." The consequence, as Vietnam combat veteran and future Army Chief of Staff Colin Powell said, was the burden of drafted service fell on members of the lower and lower-middle classes, many of them members of racial minority groups.

Eliot Cohen in Citizens and Soldiers, The Dilemmas of Military Service concluded that 30,000 draft eligible young men fled the country and as many as 500,000 "evaded the draft through various illegal means." College students were particularly prominent draft dodgers. Only 23 percent served in the armed forces and 12 percent served in Vietnam. Figures for high school graduates were 45 percent and 21 percent.

The Military Selective Service Act of 1967 attempted to justify exemptions from military service. But, by 1968 objections to the Vietnam War persuaded President Lyndon Johnson not to seek re-election. A popular form of protest of the War involved burning draft cards.

President Richard Nixon resisted calls for an immediate end to American participation in the War. However, he correctly calculated that a substantial element of opposition to the War involved the draft. He endorsed a return to selection of draftees by lottery for the first time since World War II. That limited draftees' exposure to actual induction to a single year. On December 1, 1969 the first lottery was held at Selective Service Headquarters in Washington. It covered all men born between January 1, 1944 and December 31, 1950. The first capsule drawn was for the date of September 14. All men with that birthday were assigned lottery number one. The lottery continued until all birthdates had been selected.

The lottery system continued until the last draft call on December 7, 1972. By early 1973 American forces were withdrawn from Vietnam and on January 27, 1973 the Department of Defense announced it was suspending the draft. In June, the Military Selective Service Act expired.

Writing in 1995, Washington Post columnist Jonathan Yardley reflected on his successful avoidance of the draft in 1962 for dubious physical shortcomings. He lamented that "today's young people" were deprived of his "experience of being scared to the quick by a force beyond my control" [the risk of involuntary military service]. Today's young people have "no Selective Service System...poised to reach out at whim and disrupt those lives as it pleases. As a consequence their sense of obligation and service to the national government is nonexistent, eliminated not merely by the end of the draft but also by a culture that elevates self over community."

Since 1973, attempts to either fully abolish or to restore Selective Service have engaged popular and Congressional attention. The limited Congressional actions have involved little more than requirements that young men should register for the draft. Non-registration became grounds for denial of federal student loans and for federal employment. For the last half century America has conducted its national defense with an All-Volunteer [military] Force.

Bibliography

Chambers II, John. *To Raise an Army: The Draft Comes to Modern America* (New York City: Free Press of Macmillan, 1987).

Eliot Chambers. *The Dilemmas of Military Service* (Ithaca, NY: Cornell University Press, 1985): 18–09, 165.

Davis, James and Kenneth Dolbeare. Selective Service: Present Impacts and Future Prospects. *Wisconsin Law Review*, Madison, Wisconsin (1967): 895, 908.

Evans, Harold. *The American Century*, (New York City: Knopf, 1998): 302, 320.

Fallows, James. *More Like Us* (New York City: Houghton Mifflin, 1989): 150–176.

Foote, Shelby. *The Civil War, A Narrative, Vol. II.* (New York City: Random House, 1963): 151, 635.

Fussell, Paul. *The Boys Crusade* (New York City: Modern Library, 2003): 129, 163.

Goodwin, Doris Kearns. *No Ordinary Time* (New York City: Simon and Schuster, 1994): 268.

Harries, Meirion and Susie Harries, *The Last Days of Innocence* (New York City: Random House, 1997): 461.

Mead, Gary. *The Doughboys* (New York City: Overlook Books, 2000): 416.

Millett, Allan. Papers on the Constitution, The Constitution and the Citizen-Soldier. (New York City: NYU Press, 1992): 96–98, 104–05.

Pogue, Forrest. *George C. Marshall: Ordeal and Hope, Vol. II* (New York City: Viking Press, 1996): 33, 56, 120–2, 146–47, 149.

Rudman, Warren. *Combat* (New York City: Random House, 1996): 274.

Strouse, Jean. *Morgan. Random House*, (New York City: 1999) 109

Yardley, Jonathan. The Island of My Discontent, *Washington Post* (October 23, 1995).

Section III

PERSONAL RECOLLECTIONS

Every draftee or "draft induced volunteer" over the 35-year period of American military conscription has a different story to tell of their interaction with the draft and military service. Tragically, for many, entry into wartime service was the last experience of their young years. For others more fortunate military service was an experience that shaped the rest of our lives. We offer eight accounts in our biographies that follow. We are all in our 70s and 80s with most of our lives behind us. Our military experiences help define the American military to the two generations of Americans that have grown up without even Jonathan Yardley's experience of brief exposure to mandatory military service.

Chapter A

EUGENE R. FIDELL

With a 1945 birthdate, it became apparent when I was in law school, or before, that I would likely have to perform military service. This was not something that I had given a great deal of thought to beforehand as military service had not loomed large in my family since my forebears came to the country from Russia and Russian Poland in the late nineteenth century. It is fascinating (to me, at least) to see how things unfolded.

It is a complicated story. On the one hand, my great-grandfather, Aaron Greenberg served in the Tsar's army. Oral tradition among my cousins has it that he was an Army barber. On other sides of the family tree, my paternal great-grandfather was said to have served in the brief Russo-Turkish War of 1878–79, while my maternal grandfather elected in the 1890s not to answer the Tsar's call. One of the few pieces of family memorabilia I possess is his draft notice. He fled, made it to New York, learned English in a hurry, and within a few years of immigrating graduated high enough in his class at the former Brooklyn College of Pharmacy to win a microscope as a prize. It's in my closet. Nicholas II also figures in my stepfamily; one of my stepsisters' proudest possessions is a photo of their dashing young grandfather in his Russian Army white tunic.

My father was born in 1909 and served briefly in the New York National Guard, including marching in Governor Franklin D. Roosevelt's inaugural parade. Regrettably, he never gave me any other details, and I imagine he was too old to be drafted in World War II. My maternal uncle, who trained as a dentist, served briefly in the Army in the 1940s, but again, details are few. He never discussed it. I never had the opportunity to meet my wife's father, but he was an Army doctor.

In my own generation, military service became a reality thanks to the draft. This was simply a fact of life for young men of my generation. Nevertheless, it was a new experience when my brother, also a lawyer, was commissioned in the Coast Guard, going on to serve for six years, that is, beyond his obligated service. He was assigned to legal duties in Honolulu and New York, earned an LL.M. in Taxation along the way at New York University, distinguished himself at the Naval Justice School, and was made a military judge before leaving active duty as a Lieutenant Commander. His time in uniform was personally and professionally rewarding and, not unimportantly, did not have much to do with the Vietnam War. His experience certainly influenced me.

In addition to my brother, it turned out that the stepfamily I acquired when my father remarried after my mother's death, included two military officers: one of my new brothers-in-law was a proud graduate of the U.S. Coast Guard Academy who went on to retire as a captain in the Reserve; the other had served as an Army junior officer in Germany.

In sum, from a childhood in which the military had played no role, by the time I graduated from law school, I was surrounded by family who had served or were currently serving. It never occurred to me to avoid the draft. The question was how to organize my time in uniform—and which uniform would it be?

The draft board was a little known but powerful fact of life for my cohort. In law school I had heard an amusing story from a friend from Los Angeles. According to his account, a law student who was the son of a well-known Hollywood figure went to his local board for a deferment. He met with the lady who ran the place, and when she learned what he wanted, she is reported to have said "I got Mr. [Bob] Hope' son, and I'll get you." This was not a good sign.

In my own case, I gave some thought to preempting the draft board by interrupting law school after my first year and trying for Navy OCS (Officer Candidate School). By that time, my brother was on active duty and service as such did not seem terrifying. In the end, I decided not to take a leave of absence because I was concerned that if I left school, I might not come back—not because of injury or death, but simply because my life might take some other direction, and I did want to be a lawyer. So I stayed in school.

I did, however, make some plans to find a path that didn't involve being drafted into the Army. To improve my chances of entering the Navy or the Coast Guard, I arranged to audit the navigation course at Harvard's NROTC Unit. They were very accommodating, and I spent a semester heading over to the ROTC building with my navigation textbook and gear rather than taking Business Planning or something practical like that. In the end, I did well in the course and the instructor provided me a nice letter that I was able to submit when I later applied for officer programs. As events unfolded, I wound up going to Coast Guard OCS, at Yorktown, Virginia, and had an easy time of it because I had already taken the hardest course in the curriculum. Not that I was particularly good performing "sight reductions" for celestial navigation, but I could plot a course fairly well, even though I never did serve on a cutter.

The draft remained in the picture, and the authorities were highly alert to thwart draft dodgers. Oddly, they had a practice of issuing draft notices even if a law student had taken every possible step to volunteer for the JAG Corps or some other officer program. The rule was that the JAG (Judge Advocate General) Corps could not enlist you until after you had been admitted to the bar, while for the draft board, it was full steam ahead following graduation. For my cohort of aspiring New York lawyers, everyone got a draft notice in the mail on the same day, which proved to be the day of the July 1968 bar examination. And so we all reported to the induction station on Whitehall St. the same day. Somehow the staff knew there were many law school graduates in the building. Fearful of demonstrations, the sergeant who briefed us helpfully explained that free speech didn't apply in that building. Think: *Alice's Restaurant*.

In the end, by filing an appeal to the State Director of the Selective Service System, I was able to defer my call-up date long enough to have a choice of Navy JAG and Coast Guard OCS, as well as get admitted to the bar. With a few months on my hands, I was fortunate enough to land a job at the International Bureau of Fiscal Documentation in Amsterdam through the intervention of one of my law professors. This was tremendously exciting because I had spent very little time abroad. The draft board had a different idea: at the time, if you had a draft call-up, which I did, you needed permission from them to leave the country, and if you left without permission, your call-up would be accelerated. So my dream job in Amsterdam vanished, thanks to Local Board No. 59. With time still on my hands, I landed a job at the Washington office of a mid-sized Wall Street law firm. Even this was linked to the draft, since the firm needed someone to back fill for an associate who was doing his military service for six months in the National Guard. (I returned to that firm after my military service, was generously given credit for my time on active duty, and became a partner on schedule with my peers who had not served.)

As between the Navy and the Coast Guard, I opted for the Coast Guard even though I had no guarantee of getting a legal billet because the commitment was a year shorter. I also liked the idea of being in the same branch as my brother. It was a small service, and a very small corps of "law specialists" as Coast Guard judge advocates were called at the time. All of the lawyers either knew or had heard of one another. Aside from OCS graduates and a few direct commission lawyers, the others had all gone to the same college—"the [Coast Guard] Academy." Many of them had studied law at The George Washington University, with one or two Harvard graduates thrown in.

Many years later, when I was teaching at Yale and wanted to be admitted to the Connecticut bar, I found myself rummaging around for my draft number, since the bar authorities insisted on that even though I was able to demonstrate that I had actually served for three years, seven months, and eight days from my DD214. I never did find my draft card, but I did notice that the needed information was right there on my discharge papers. This was good enough for the bar.

My active duty began inauspiciously, I was absent without official leave (AWOL). As it happened, there was a terrible storm the night before I was due to report to OCS in Yorktown, Virginia, and my bus was hours late. Happily, I had plenty of company, and no one made a big deal of it. OCS itself was arduous, but ultimately fun. In those days the Coast Guard was able to attract some serious talent, and there were quite a few lawyers and holders of master's degrees in my class. There were, of course, the usual ups and downs, such as demerits that could disentitle you to liberty. I remember one evening, when the demerits were read aloud in the mess hall, learning that I'd been "gigged" for doing unauthorized pushups in the passageway. I also remember that an ongoing issue was whether OCS candidates had illicit medications among their possessions in the barracks. There was a brisk trade in antihistamines, as Spring hit Tidewater Virginia and those of us who suffered from hay fever were desperate for relief. I suppose the Commandant was concerned that hay-fever sufferers would become useless out at sea (never mind the low pollen count on Ocean Station Bravo).

There were a few Jewish OCS candidates in my class, including one fellow who was trying to honor the laws relating to kosher food—no small challenge. Passover came during our time at Yorktown, and that presented a real problem for those of us who were not going to eat bread or leavened food for the whole holiday. A request was made through the chain of command for us to have matzoh at meals. The word came back from the chief petty officer in charge of the facility that there would be "no Jew food" in the dining hall.

On a somewhat related note, there came a time when a revival-ish singing group called "Up With People" came to OCS to put on a performance one Friday evening. We were all given a choice: either attend or remain in the barracks for field night (i.e., cleaning the decks and polishing the brass handles on the doors). Not surprisingly, everyone opted for attendance, myself included.

Come to find out, the show was clearly Christian oriented. A number of my platoon mates, knowing that I was pretty serious about my Jewishness, came over to apologize, correctly realizing that I must have found the performance off-putting since it was essentially compulsory. I decided to step out into the lobby of the training center theatre during the intermission, where I was approached by a Navy O-2, who was accompanying the touring group under Navy auspices. She made the mistake of asking me how I liked the show. I told her that in my opinion it was a violation of the First Amendment. I'm reasonably certain she had no idea what I was talking about.

A few people bilged out of my OCS class, including some who did so voluntarily. I thought this was despicable because they had gamed the system and taken a place that could have been filled by someone more committed. Still, time passed pleasantly enough that Spring in Tidewater, a mile down the road from the Yorktown battlefield and a few miles more from historic Williamsburg. My platoon officer remains a friend and I became dear friends with another platoon officer. He sadly died a few years ago. To this day, my best friend is someone I served with in Boston. I remain jealous that he got to go to sea; the closest I came was serving as the legal officer for the 1970 America's Cup Patrol Squadron. (The U.S. won that year, in four straight races.)

I thought I might get orders to a cutter, but the Commandant had other plans. I was assigned to the Marine Inspection Office in Long Beach, California, where I prosecuted merchant mariners who had misbehaved. This allowed me to practice administrative law before a hearing examiner and afforded me a chance to learn about the merchant marine. I also prosecuted a drug-related court-martial, even though I had not yet been to Naval Justice School and knew next to nothing about military justice. This was also right after the Military Justice Act of 1968 had taken effect, so no one knew much more than I did. It was my good fortune that the accused in that case, assigned to the U.S. Coast Guard Cutter (USCGC) *Minnetonka*, pleaded guilty.

After a few months, the Coast Guard decided it needed more lawyers because of the new law, which had expanded the right to counsel. As a result, OCS graduates with law degrees were offered the opportunity to enter the legal program, be promoted immediately, and possibly assigned to a different port. I promptly accepted and asked for and received orders back to Boston, where I had only recently spent three years studying law. On the way there I attended the Naval Justice School, where I actually did learn military justice (from some gifted instructors), then settled in, planning to spend the next three years in Beantown.

Duty in Boston was rewarding. The legal office was in the Kennedy Federal Building, near City Hall and Quincy Market, and I joined a group of smart and fun junior officers. We formed a Junior Officers' Benevolent Association and spent many lunch hours at the historic (and much lamented) Durgin-Park restaurant, various watering holes, and in the North End. The base was a 15-minute walk down Hanover Street. Friends from the First Naval District ("COMONE") were, well, friendly, although I don't think they took the Coast Guard too seriously. On the other hand, I did face occasional hostility in

Cambridge. Walking to Harvard Square in uniform one day, I remember a scruffy passerby asking: "How's the war going, killer?"

Everyone in our little office did military justice, either as counsel, or in the case of the district legal officer, as staff judge advocate to the District Commander, who was a rear admiral. In addition, I advised on tort and admiralty claims, the General Bridge Act of 1946 (which governs bridges over navigable waters) and served as a hearing officer for in-service conscientious objector cases. With the exception of one case where I concluded the applicant could serve in a non-combatant (I-A-O) status (a ruling Headquarters overturned, discharging the young man because it would have been too much trouble to find him a suitable billet), every case convinced me that the applicant's views were incompatible with military service of any kind.

The war troubled me and my contemporaries, both the reservists and the regulars. A key episode came when the U.S. conducted a bombing campaign in Cambodia, leading to demonstrations outside the federal building. Of course, we could not participate, but a number of us took the opportunity to terminate our participation in the savings bond allotment program on the theory that if the government had enough money to conduct the bombing campaign, it didn't need ours.

I also got involved in fisheries law, but this was by accident—I happened to be the only lawyer around when one of our cutters seized the fishing vessel *Conrad*, a West German trawler, a few hundred yards inside the then 12-mile contiguous fisheries zone off Cape Cod. I knew nothing about fisheries law and had only a couple of hours to bone up and work with the U.S. Attorney's Office. The case had a good outcome and led to my being transferred to the Maritime Law and Treaties Branch at Headquarters, which was responsible for overseeing all fisheries and drug enforcement at the time. At the same time, I continued to serve as counsel in courts-martial. One such case involved a mutiny aboard USCGC *Gallatin*, a high endurance curtter homeported in New York There were 10 defense counsel for the six Black enlisted men who were accused in this racially charged case. In the end, the charges were withdrawn from the general court-martial and disposed of through nonjudicial punishment (captain's mast).

On active duty I was involved in the high-profile Kudirka Incident, which involved a Lithuanian defector whom we allowed the Soviets to retrieve by force from the cutter *Vigilant*. It became an enormous scandal and led to congressional hearings, disciplinary action against the Admiral and the district's Chief of Staff, and reforms in how the Executive Branch coordinates in crisis situations. It was later the subject of a movie starring Alan Arkin, *Day of Shame*. Other memorable cases involved issues of hot pursuit of foreign fishing vessels, including one particularly tense incident with Soviet fishing vessels off Alaska.

In 1972, I left active duty, returning to the Washington law firm at which I had worked while waiting to enter the Coast Guard. My practice included environmental and nuclear regulatory work for electric utilities, but I continued my interest in two fields I had been concerned with in uniform: fisheries regulation and military justice. In my spare time I wrote extensively on maritime law enforcement. This led to appointment to a federal advisory committee concerned with tuna conservation and then to employment as a consultant in fisheries law for the UN Food and Agriculture Organization (FAO). For the FAO I undertook missions to Liberia, Sierra Leone, Dominica and the Cayman Islands.

My military service influenced my life even more heavily through military justice. I had not been impressed by the system when I was on active duty, and I had an intuition that it was a field in which I could make a contribution. I wrote extensively on the subject, and for 10 years I represented the ACLU as a friend of the court in court-martial appeals, including presenting oral argument in the Supreme Court in the landmark case of *Solorio v. United States*. This pro bono activity gave me an opportunity to pick cases, write briefs and argue appeals well before I would have had those opportunities at my law firm. It also led to a good deal of paying work in court-martial and other military matters, including Administrative Procedure Act and Tucker Act litigation in the federal courts. Eventually, at the firm I lateraled to in the early 1980s, I assembled a team of talented lawyers concentrating on military cases of every description.

In 1991, I co-founded the National Institute of Military Justice (NIMJ) with a few friends. NIMJ became a major activity, and I headed it for 20 years, eventually turning the reins over to my friend and former student Elizabeth L. Hillman, a brilliant Air Force veteran who has had a distinguished career as a law professor and then as President of Mills College in Oakland, California. Soon after, I was asked to become an adjunct lecturer at Yale Law School, an involvement that turned into a full-time job. I also became increasingly interested in comparative military justice, leading to active involvement with the International Society for Military Law and the Law of War. In 2014, I founded the Global Military Justice blog, which I continue to edit. To this day, I remain fully engaged in military justice, especially in its international and law reform aspects, and hope to continue teaching it for as long as possible.

I have also had the opportunity to make new law on several issues, including the long-running case of Sergeant Bowe Bergdahl, an Army soldier who had endured five years of brutal captivity at the hands of the Taliban. He pleaded guilty to a one-day desertion and misbehavior before the enemy (based on the same misconduct) in Afghanistan. The case turned out to raise a host of significant issues including whether a President's words and deeds can constitute unlawful command influence in violation of the Uniform Code of Military Justice. The U.S. Court of Appeals for the Armed Forces ruled that presidents can indeed be guilty of exerting unlawful command influence.

Because the matter was unfairly politicized from the beginning, many Americans have a seriously distorted understanding of what happened. Readers can get a sense of this by viewing the Bergdahl Defense Video Exhibit that was evidence in the case. It documents many of the outrageous things former President Trump said about this young man in the run-up to the 2016 election. Perhaps Americans will re-appraise the case now that our military presence in Afghanistan has ended.

None of this would have happened had I not served in the armed forces. For me, all of this has been as surprising as it is rewarding. Having interacted with the armed forces for most of my life, I have increasingly come to believe in conscription. The draft is democratizing and can serve as a needed check on adventurism by politicians. Military service is not for everyone, and is not, in my view, necessarily a credential for those who aspire to elective office. But for many people it can be an important and positive experience. And it is in the end a form of public service.

Mr. Fidell is a Senior Research Scholar in Law at Yale Law School, an Adjunct Professor of Law at NYU Law School, and of counsel at the Washington, D.C. firm Feldesman Tucker Leifer Fidell LLP.

Chapter B

TOM MACKIE

Family Background and Experience

Born in September 1946, I was one of the early "baby boomers" my father having returned home from duty in the Pacific theatre in late 1945. There was little family history, oral or written, or significant memories while growing up involving military experiences or service. My parents' generation served in World War II (WW II), as part of their duty and obligation with little fanfare or storytelling to their children.

Both my parents had left home in their late teens, met in a "neutral" location and at the end of WW II settled in the south side of Chicago, 500 miles from the nearest relative.

My father (Thomas W) was born and raised in Sault Ste. Marie, Michigan. My grandfather (Angus) was a butcher, as was his father, who was also born in the Soo. My grandmother, Adeline Matilda Shunk, was born in Ontario. Both their families were primarily farming families and had emigrated from Scotland to Canada via Prince Edward Island one or two generations prior. My grandmother had died before I was born, my grandfather soon after. There was the migrant attitude of moving to where there was work that became apparent in my father, as well as many of his offspring.

My father had one brother, Uncle Jim, who served in the Army in WW II in Europe. As far as I am aware, neither my father's father, nor earlier generations served in the military.

My father's sister, Kay, married another man from Sault Ste. Marie. They migrated to California at the start of the War where her husband Homer was initially stationed after enlistment in the Navy. She stayed there when he went to the Pacific, and they remained there when the war ended. They later became surrogate parents/grandparents when I returned from Vietnam and was stationed in California for 13 months.

My father graduated from the local Sault Ste. Marie High School in 1931 and found work in marine construction, going to work for a dredging company. By the late 1930s he had worked himself up to being captain of a hydraulic dredge working in the waterways near Hancock, Michigan in Michigan's Upper Peninsula.

My mother was born and raised in Concord, New Hampshire. Her mother's family (Roby/Jones) can be traced back to New Hampshire and Massachusetts in the late 1700s but with little detail other than names and dates. Her father's family (Ingersoll) arrived in America in the mid-1600s in Massachusetts.

Her father (Jonathan Ingersoll) attended Dartmouth College, but there is little detail (other than a set of Dartmouth dishes) as my mother's parents went through a very acrimonious divorce sometime in the 1930s. I met my grandfather once, sometime in the 1960s in Connecticut, but there was little linkage during my lifetime. I don't know whether or not he served in the military.

My mother was well educated for a woman at the time, graduating from Simmons College in Boston with a Bachelor of Science Degree in 1938 in a program, which was the early foundation of Physical Therapy in the United States. By the time she graduated, the depression and parents' divorce had minimized any family financial resources they might have had at the time. My mother had one sister and one brother. Her brother and I believe brother-in-law both served in the Navy in WW II.

After graduating from Simmons, my mother was faced with finding a job, in an economy not necessarily booming, especially for women. The story as she tells it, is that one of the few positions she could find was in a hospital in Hancock/Houghton, Michigan, 1,200 miles from Boston.

The family lore is that in 1939, my parents met in a breakfast café in Hancock and the rest, as they say, is history. In 1940 my father, his dredge and crew were being sent to a job site in Lake Charles, Louisiana. He proposed marriage and the deal was done. They traveled to Lake Charles where they were married in December 1940. My very staid grandmother (Marion) drove herself from Concord N.H. to witness the event and ensure the safety of her daughter.

In 1941, my father and the dredge were sent to a job site building a suitable port area in Trinidad, for the US Navy. Mother went along and they lived in Trinidad until late 1943.

While in Trinidad in late 1943 my father, his crew and dredge were all "drafted" into the US Navy, as part of the 301st Navy Construction Battalion (SeaBees). We were not aware of any specific military training that my father received, but as the Dredge captain he was made Chief Boatswain Mate/ Petty Officer. In 1944, he, the dredge and the crew were sent to Guam and then Okinawa for harbor clearing and construction following the invasions of the islands.

In late 1945, my father returned to the US, with dredge to follow. His unit was disbanded, and he returned to civilian life, immediately going back to work for the same dredging company (Great Lakes Dredge and Dock, Co.). He was sent to the South Chicago area where there was a significant amount of work for the company, given the vibrant steel mill, refinery and other industries based in the Chicago–Whiting–Gary area along the south end of Lake Michigan. My parents moved there, knowing no one other than through my father's work, and bought a small bungalow on the far southeast side of Chicago.

The area (locally known as the "East Side") became home for many first- and second-generation families, mostly European, dominated by Polish, Slovak, Serbian, Croatian and Italian. Minorities (people of color) generally had an unofficial red line they did not cross comprised of the Calumet River and Stony Island Avenue. The "Eastside" was our own little white ghetto.

I was born a little more than nine months after my father's return from the Pacific. I have an older sister who was born in 1944, after my father had left for the Pacific. Then after a gap of five years, my two brothers were born in 1951 and 1952.

I am a proud product of the Chicago Public School system (Jane Addams Elementary and George Washington High School). It was a positive time following the end of WW II, good local economy and a relatively growing and prosperous blue collar community.

Looking back, it seems that the parents in the neighborhood were putting all their prior experiences behind them and focusing on the future through family, work, church and community. The one lasting annual event that my mother participated in every year was the selling of poppies in memory of WW I on November 11.

I am not sure that my father really had a true "military experience." Rather he served as a dredge man (his trade) first, and a Chief Bosuns Mate second. There was little in his mind to discuss. However, he always did root for Navy when they played Notre Dame which seemed to be an annual affair.

Religion was important to my parents growing up, though neither of them brought any affiliation to any particular branch of Christianity with them. My first memories are with a local Protestant Church (East Side Bible) Then, about the time I was 10 years old, we joined the local United Methodist Church, with all four of us being baptized at the same time. By then we had begun attending church regularly, however, religion was rarely discussed with us outside that environment. It was through the church, however, that I got involved in scouting as the local troop was based in the United Methodist Church. Starting in the Cub Scouts, I went through the Boy Scouts and then Explorer Scouts.

High School and the Path Forward

In the early 1960s, there was little recognition or discussion of major world affairs. It was during Mayor Richard J. Daley's 20-year reign in Chicago. He was an Irish Catholic from the South Side of Chicago and well supported in our area. Politics centered around the city and local precincts, plus the election of John F. Kennedy, the first Catholic President.

Our parents never gave us strong direction as to career paths. Rather the stress was on hard work, respect for others, a sense of responsibility and independence. Having no relatives within a couple of days drive, we were a close family and remained so over the years, even when far apart geographically.

As a family, outside activities were focused on fishing, camping and cards (guess the last two prepared me somewhat for the military). My parents loved the outdoors. As a family, many of our early vacations were with a camper that my father had built, towed behind a station wagon that always overheated. We made two trips west, one to California and one to Montana. Campgrounds were relatively sparse and primitive at that time with AAA Triptik as our primary guide.

My summer jobs started at about the age of 15 or 16 (paper routes prior to that). The first was with a small Towing (Tugboat) company that a friend of my father owned. Then at 18 I was able to work summers; usually abbreviated stretches because of NROTC summer training, in the maintenance yard of the Dredging Company. There I was introduced to the 22 caliber rifle by some of the dock workers, shooting at the river rats in the early morning before starting work.

We were never told directly that we had to go to college. It just became part of the unwritten assumption as we were growing up. The family was not necessarily in a financial state that would make it happen, rather we seemed to have the belief and parental support that it could happen if we worked hard. My older sister (the smart one) received an academic scholarship for secondary math education to North Central College in Naperville, Illinois. She went on to become a Math Professor at Bradley University in Peoria and the author of math books, including a series of "Books for Dummies" (Algebra, Trigonometry, Calculus, Finite Math…).

Don, is about five years younger than me. After high school, not especially interested in college he considered working for the dredging company, but with the draft on the horizon he decided to enlist in the Navy. Turns out that the next year his draft number came in low, and he would probably have been drafted if not already in the service. After the service he spent the rest of his career in dredging and construction work.

My youngest brother, Doug, went to Wake Forest University on a full football scholarship (the athlete of the family), and then went to Law School. He became General Counsel for the Dredging Company with which my father spent his career. My father passed away in early 1972 while Don and I were still on active duty, and Doug was still in school. Doug eventually went on to become the CEO of the Dredging Company, working there until his retirement.

I guess my road to military service was, like some of the other events in my life, the result of circumstance and happenstance. It was not because of a focused desire for a military career or military mentality. The military services at that time were certainly held in good regard, at least in our area. There was little active awareness or discussion of what was starting to develop in Southeast Asia. Entering my senior year of high school (September 1963), I knew that I wanted to go into Engineering. Math and the sciences were my strong suit in high school. English and foreign languages were a challenge. History and social studies were interesting but not my main focus.

My early focus was the University of Illinois Chicago Circle Campus or Illinois Institute of Technology, both of which I could commute to from home. In looking at possible scholarship opportunities, one of the school counselors presented me with information on the Naval ROTC program, specifically the "regular" program where, if you qualified, the Navy paid all tuition, fees, books and $50 per month toward room and board (a significant portion of the cost at that time). Once in school, requirements were to complete eight (one per semester) three credit military courses at the NROTC Center, plus six weeks of active duty training each summer.

The Regular ROTC program is meant as a supplement to the Service Academies, to help fill the pipeline of regular, possibly military career-minded men. At the time, once commissioned with a Regular (versus Reserve) Commission, you had to serve a minimum of four years (versus two for the Reserve ROTC Program) with no "expiration" date. At the end of your obligation, you were then required to submit a formal letter of resignation of your commission for discharge.

My applying for the Program was supported by my parents and seen as a great opportunity for an education. The Navy seemed the logical choice given my father's background and my summer jobs which were always around or on the water.

The other "happenstance" was asking this good looking blond I knew in our class to go with me to a fall social event at the high school. She said she was already committed (or maybe just didn't want to go with me), so my second choice was a girl I barely knew whom I had met in the rehearsals for a school play. Cheryle Miklos, a junior, quickly became a close friend. Little did either of us know where it would lead us for the next almost 59 years (as of this writing).

The dominant political news at that time, in our Democratic Party dominated area, was the assassination of President Kennedy in November, 1963.

Around Christmas of 1963 I received notification of acceptance and was then given a list of 50 universities in the US at which the Regular NROTC Program was available. Not having given any thought to attending most of the schools on the list, I then had to quickly complete the application and acceptance process at the universities of my choice.

Deciding to stay within a reasonable travel distance of Chicago and going through the college catalogs, one of my teachers recommended that I look at the University of Wisconsin. With the NROTC Scholarship out of state tuition was not a concern. So along with the University of Illinois and a few other midwestern universities with good engineering departments, Wisconsin went on the list. When acceptances came in, the clock was ticking to decide and I selected University of Wisconsin without ever visiting the campus.

With the heavy load in the engineering curriculum, plus the additional three credit hours per semester in "Naval Science," it was expected to be a four-and-one-half to five-year course of study. In the end, I completed the program in four and one half years, graduating in January 1969 with a B.S. in Mechanical Engineering, B.S. in Naval Science and was commissioned as a Second Lieutenant in the Marine Corps on the day of Graduation.

University Life

My first year at Wisconsin I lived in a freshman dorm. With some dorm friends, I participated in fraternity rush week to see what it was all about. I am not sure what enticed me to join a fraternity. I had gone to a few houses during rush week with some fellow engineering students. I ended up joining Sigma Phi, a small and rather unique organization. It was through Sigma Phi that I met Mick McBee, who was later to be the best man at our wedding.

On the University of Wisconsin's campus, antiwar activity was steadily growing with the "foremost" event being the Dow Chemical protest in February 1967. It was after I graduated that a bomb was detonated in a University lab building, killing one researcher.

Early classes at the NROTC Unit (Orientation and Sea Power) focused on military, Navy and US history, followed up in the second year with Naval Weapons and personnel management. There were weekly drills and inspections, learning the military disciplines. We would be in uniform on campus at least once per week. I do not recall any serious or threatening issues with other students or protesters related to my being in the military during my entire tenure at school. There were, however, ample opportunities for debates and discussions of issues relating to the war and the draft, especially in my last few years, both on campus and within the fraternity.

Up to the time that I graduated, received my commission and completed further training prior to being sent to Vietnam, I never questioned whether or not I should continue in the Program. I always believed it was my duty and responsibility, not just because of the commitment made with the scholarship.

During the first summer's (1965) six-week training session I was stationed on a destroyer in the North Atlantic, based out of Newport, Rhode Island. The destroyer was the USS Basilone, named after a WW II Marine Medal of Honor winner, maybe a precursor of my future decision. Though I grew up with a father in marine construction and had summer jobs involved with dredges, tugboats, etc. in Chicago, Louisiana, and on the Mississippi River, I was not overjoyed with my time on the "tin can."

The second summer (1966) included three weeks of amphibious training with the Marine Corps in Little Creek, Virginia, and three weeks naval air orientation at the Naval Air Station in Corpus Christi, Texas. At the end of that summer's training, all cadets had an option to select the Marine Corps as a career path. The remaining two years of ROTC training and summer active duty training would be with the Marine Corps resulting in a commission as a second lieutenant in the Corps (versus Ensign in the Navy). It was August 1966 and I felt much more "comfortable" in the Marine Corps training and culture and I chose that option.

By then though the draft would not affect me personally it was certainly more in focus. Everyone would know someone, a friend or acquaintance that was potentially being impacted. Soon after the situation in Vietnam also came closer to home when my closest friend in high school was killed in action. He had stayed in Chicago to attend the University of Chicago. Then sometime in late 1966 dropped out of school and joined the Marine Corps. To this day I do not know for certain if he was a volunteer, a draft-induced enlistee or a draftee. He was killed in action in March 1967.

With the Marine Corps option in the NROTC program, the third summer's active duty training (1967) was a six-weeks Officer Candidate School formatted program at the Marine Corps Base in Quantico, Virginia.

In 1968, returning home to the Chicago area from training at Quantico, preparation was under way for the Democratic Convention to be held the last week in August. I remember the buildup and talk about the likelihood of protests and Mayor Daley's assurances that all was under control. I returned to campus for my last semester of school prior to the Convention and watched the Convention "activities" from afar. The protests and police actions that occurred there far outstripped anything going on in Madison at that time.

Over the years at Wisconsin, my relationship with Cheryle continued to grow. It was a bit of a commuter relationship, home on school breaks and before and after and summer training. Cheryle also made trips to Madison several times over those four-and-one-half years. Though we both knew of my obligation to the Marine Corps and the likelihood of my going to Viet Nam, in the fall of 1968 we became engaged. If there was concern on the part of our parents, it was not expressed to us. Cheryle's father, a turbine operator at the local power plant, was an Army WW II veteran, having served in the Pacific region. And, we were aware that her mother's first fiancée was killed in action in WW II.

The year 1969 began with my schedule pretty much dictated by the Marine Corps. Graduation and commission as a second lieutenant in January, then report to Officer Basic School in Quantico for assignment to a Basic School Class. Graduation and commissioning was on January 25, 1969. My parents and Cheryle made the trip to Madison for the ceremonies. I then packed my car and with just a short stop at home headed for Marine Corps Base (MCB), Quantico, Virginia.

Active Duty

Arriving in Quantico, I had a few weeks to wait for a new Basic School Company (class) to begin. I was assigned to H Company which was formed in early March. There were Training Companies that started every four to six weeks at that time, with newly commissioned officers, coming from various programs (Naval Academy, ROTC programs, platoon leader classes, some foreign cadets and other miscellaneous channels). The 21-week basic school curriculum was a mixture of classroom/lecture format balanced with field training applying the skills taught in the classroom where appropriate.

The major components of the training curriculum were:

1. Individual skills (rifle/pistol training, navigation, first aid/lifesaving, etc.)
2. Rifle squad leader skills. The rifle squad is the core unit of a Marine Corps infantry platoon.
3. Platoon leader skills.
4. Officer Skills (Leadership and Military Skills).

By the summer of 1969, there were several of the training staff who had experience in Vietnam so the training, though highly traditional, was also being adapted to the realities of warfare in Southeast Asia. Extra focus on guerilla warfare, ambushes (both setting them and avoiding them), booby traps, etc.

Sometime along the way, Cheryle and I decided to get married in the summer of 1969. We wanted to have the wedding prior to my overseas service, and as far as I know our parents were again supportive. There were undoubtedly some hormonal factors influencing the decision as well.

With the permission of the Basic School Command, we were able to schedule the wedding on the upcoming three-day July 4th weekend. I flew back to Chicago on Thursday evening with the wedding scheduled for Saturday, July 5th. Then on Sunday morning, the two of us flew back to Quantico, to our $90 per month un-airconditioned second floor "furnished" apartment.

On the Monday morning after the wedding, I headed out for two to three days of field training, leaving Cheryle alone and knowing no one. When I returned, her only request was for a TV (which we didn't own). We ended up with a $10/month, rent to own black and white TV from a pawn shop. We kept that TV for many years, with "Uncle Jack's Pawn Shop" etched in the rear casing with a solder gun.

Late July was selection time to determine our MOS . If you had serious career intentions within the Marine Corps, infantry was the optimal MOS path to take. Selection order was based upon class rank, and finishing in the top quartile, I selected artillery, closer to my engineering training and frankly a little less hazardous.

From Quantico I was assigned to the 12-weeks Army Artillery School in Fort Sill, Oklahoma with orders to report to the Western Pacific Command upon completion. We packed up everything we owned, which fit easily into our car. Having about three weeks before I had to report to Fort Sill, and not having had a honeymoon we took a road trip with a budget (room, food, gas, tolls, etc.) of $25.00 a day. Fortunately, we spent a few days staying with relatives along the way to help stretch our funds.

We then rented a three-month furnished duplex in Lawton, Oklahoma and training commenced in early September. There was a small number of Marines in our class, most of the class being Army Officers. Training again was a mix of classroom and field training, learning the skills of both being a Forward Observer, operating a variety of artillery pieces and Fire Direction skills. All this, prior to the advent of global positioning system (GPS) and computers, meant learning precise mapping skills utilizing slide rules, tables, compasses and protractors when calculating directions, elevations and powder loads for a variety of artillery pieces.

Artillery school finished in mid-December after which Cheryle and I drove back to Chicago. She had been accepted as a high school mathematics teacher in the Chicago Public School system and would be staying with her parents while I was gone. On December 17th, I flew to San Francisco to report in at the Naval Base on Treasure Island the following day.

The "highlight" of my last night in the US was having a few drinks alone at the bar in the hotel, while watching the entertainer Tiny Tim get married on the Johnny Carson show. The flight on December 18th was a TWA Charter Boeing 707 to Okinawa (my first time out of the US other than driving to

Canada) with refueling stops in Hawaii and Guam. When we arrived in Okinawa, I checked into temporary officer's quarters. I was part of a small group of Marine second lieutenants on the flight and we were told to "cool our heels" as most likely they would not be sending anyone "in country" until after the Christmas Holiday, however, we should check the bulletin board every day for updates.

And, in true military fashion, just a day or two later, my name was posted to report for transport to the 11th Marine Regiment HQ in Danang, Vietnam. I arrived in Danang on December 21st where I was to receive, a few days of briefings, orientation, and then further assignment.

The few details I remember of those first few days was learning the "rules of engagement" with emphasis on learning the typical dress and appearance of the civilians as compared to the Viet Cong and North Vietnamese Army (NVA) to ensure that we did not engage innocent civilians. Months later I recalled the "friend or foe" training when I had the opportunity to be in an observation tower with an Air Support forward observer on Hill 65 (Dai Loc). We watched an enemy support group coming east through the valley where they were unaware of being observed. They then disappeared, and soon a similar number of "civilians" emerged to continue heading east. They may have read the same briefing manual.

After a couple of days at the Regimental headquarter (HQ), I was transported by jeep to report to the first 175 mm Gun Battery on Hill 34, an hour or so WSW of Danang. Arriving there I was assigned as one of three Fire Direction Officers for the Battery. From the Command Center located in a bunker adjacent to the firing line, fire directions were given to the six guns in the Battery.

Photo: 175mm Gun on Fire Mission in Quang Nam province.

The 175-mm gun had a relatively short-lived career in the Marine Corps arsenal. They were self-propelled (tracked) and of a longer range than artillery usually associated with the Marine Corps. Their size and weight (over 30 tons) limited their mobility with much of the Vietnamese terrain, but the range was useful in supporting the far-reaching activity of the Marine Corps Reconnaissance Units, operating towards the Laotian border, as well as providing support to other various operations in the area. The guns fired a 150# projectile up to about 20 miles, with a fair size kill radius and, of course, unlike air support of that time, were available 24/7 and in any weather. A significant percentage of our fire mission activity was at night.

Our area of operation was primarily in Quang Nam Province which was the scene of significant action for the Marine Corps in the earlier days of the War (1965–68), but few named operations in 1969–70. The year 1968 saw the Tet Offensive, My Lai and President Johnson deciding not to run for reelection. Richard Nixon was then elected in November 1968 promising to end the war in Vietnam.

In the fall of 1969, when I was headed towards Vietnam, there began a nationwide series of the Moratorium to End the War protests. The War had become very unpopular. US strength in Vietnam peaked in early 1969 with slow drawdown beginning after that. Nixon's exit strategy was that of "Vietnamization," with decreasing US boots on the ground and increased bombing with a focus on hitting the infiltration routes along the Laos/Cambodian border. We were in a period of fewer major offensive operations. Most operations were short-lived offensive moves based upon intelligence information of an enemy build up in a particular geographic area.

Most of my first six months in country were spent on Hill 34. It is hard to recall the details of those first months. There was a daily routine of maintenance and training with many of the fire missions at night. The swabbing of the tubes and other required maintenance on a 175-mm gun was no small task.

There were occasional patrols checking the perimeter outside the encampment and a few runs into Danang and trips to the Northern Artillery Cantonment where three 175-mm guns were located. As we could be called on at any time for supporting fire, we always had some of our guns manned, and at night often loaded and set on pre-determined grid coordinates.

With that "closeness" we got to know each of the gun crews well. We had few significant issues with discipline during my tour and the officers and non-commissioned officer (NCO) staff were a good mix of new and experienced Marines.

The inherent dangers of what we did was brought home early in my time on Hill 34. Within a few weeks, we were on a night fire mission and there was an unusual explosion. Going out from the command bunker we found that one of the tubes (35-foot long barrel) had failed, shattering halfway up its length and spraying shrapnel to an extended distance. The 175-mm gun chassis is totally open to the rear where the gun crew all stationed. Fortunately, no one was injured. The luckiest individual was the powder man walking up with a four-foot long bag of propellant for the next round. One piece of hot shrapnel could have easily detonated the black powder primer or the propellant itself.

I do not recall us having regular access or at least listening to Armed Forces Radio, or any live broadcast as far as that goes. As it was well before the time of mobile phones, WiFi and the internet, news of the outside world came through on an intermittent basis. Mail delivery was good, but a long way from home. The latest "innovation" was to get a cassette tape from family recorded with personal messages.

While we did hear about the shooting at Kent State University in May 1970, there didn't seem to be any strong opinions among us one way or another. I don't believe that we were aware of the Apollo 13 crisis in April and when the book/movie came out years later, I had to ask "what happened?" It was all new to me.

Given the variables due to mail delivery and whims of the Marine Corps, Cheryle and I still managed to arrange and successfully execute meeting up on R&R. One week R&R was encouraged but not guaranteed. Around the first of July 1970 Cheryle, exhibiting her determination and sense of adventure traveled from Chicago to Sydney, Australia (like me, she had never traveled outside the US or Canada). At that time, I believe she had to fly Chicago to Los Angeles to Hawaii to Fiji Island to Sydney where she was waiting when I arrived. I was indeed fortunate to be able to stick with the dates we had planned many weeks prior, getting a jeep into Danang and flying an R&R transport flight from Danang to Darwin to Sydney. After a wonderful week together in Sydney and surrounding areas we headed on our separate ways.

Upon my return to the Battery HQ on Hill 34 I was given orders to take command of the Bravo Platoon which was comprised of three of the Battery's 175-mm guns and relocate to Hill 65 in the Dai Loc area near the foothills of the mountainous areas bordering Vietnam and Laos. Hill 65 was an established hilltop position selected for its difficult approaches from the surrounding fields and rice paddies. At the time there were already Marine infantry units based there. My Platoon as well as a Platoon of three 8-inch howitzers commanded by another Marine first lieutenant were moved there to provide expanded artillery coverage to operations being conducted in the area.

Photo: Bravo platoon moving from Hill 34 to Hill 65 in support of field operations in Dai Loc District, Quang Nam Province.

I had a very capable Gunnery Sergeant (Gunny Johnson) as second-in-command and a Platoon of about 30 Marines, which included three-gun crews of 8–10 men each, 3–4 Fire Direction Specialists/Radiomen and a corpsman. Primary Fire Direction control was conducted back at the Battery HQ on Hill 34.

The trip to Hill 65 was uneventful, the convoy consisting of the three self-propelled Guns, transport trucks and jeeps and an armored wrecker capable of retrieving one of the Guns in case of a breakdown. The route wound along dirt roads and fortified dikes. The self-propelled 175-mm guns were capable of close to 50 mph, though we never came close to that given the terrain and roads. The areas we traveled through had been through several years of war and occupation dating back to French colonial days. We quickly got settled in our new position on Hill 65, and immediately were put in action.

Most of our activity was in support of the ongoing small unit action aimed at suppressing any progress by the NVA of establishing any strength in the area, and at several of our fire missions were directed to the infiltration routes to the west and southwest of our location. Like when on Hill 34, days were spent in training, equipment maintenance, broken by brief intense moments of action.

Photo: Gunny Johnson training the crews on techniques of resighting the guns after a fire mission (prior to GPS)!

Then in early-/mid-September, we were directed to move the Platoon to another firebase position in another firebase position in An Hoa in support of other operations. At the completion of this assignment we were relocated back to Battery HQ area on Hill 34. Around that time orders were received for the battery, as well as other units in the Danang area to prepare to stand down for embarkation and redeployment back to the US.

We had little detail as to how this would proceed and as to who was going where. Sometime in early October we began to receive our individual orders. I was assigned with another lieutenant to supervise a temporary detachment that would bring the equipment of the 175mm Gun Battery back to the states, aboard the USS Juneau, LSD 10. The challenge was preparing the equipment to pass an agricultural inspection prior to embarkation in Danang for the port of Long Beach, California. This meant that months of mud, dirt and whatever accumulated in the undercarriage had to be meticulously removed from every nook and cranny. Around October 1, we stood down and moved the equipment to a staging area near the Danang Deepwater Port. Hand scrappers, wire brushes and water hoses were the primary tools. With the use of wreckers much of the equipment was put on their sides to ease access to the underbellies. There were some military mobile pressure washers available for use, and procuring them became a full-time job for our XO who would spend his time canvassing the area and bartering for time slots for their use. The inspections were not necessarily "white glove," but I believe part of the plan was to keep everyone busy with little time to anticipate or enjoy the opportunity to leave country, right up to the day of embarkation.

In total there were fewer than a dozen Marine junior officers, and 80–100 enlisted aboard with the responsibility of providing security and maintenance for the equipment while underway. The 175mm Gun Battery was moving pretty much intact, final destination being MCB Twentynine Palms, California.

My initial orders were a temporary assignment, with permanent orders to a billet yet to be determined. Somewhere around October 10 we embarked and departed Danang Harbor for what we were told would be a three-week transit to the United States, stopping briefly in Okinawa to offload supplies and equipment that was being left there. Our going away celebration was the last night in Danang and was capped off with a few incoming 122-mm rockets.

Two to three days later we docked in White Beach, Okinawa and were thoughtfully informed by one of the naval officers that we would be there for about eight hours and if we so desired, that we could go ashore to make some phone calls and do some shopping for duty-free items to take home or consume on the voyage. At this point in time (again...no mobile phone, internet, etc.), Cheryle had no knowledge of what was transpiring. Once in the Officers Club we decided to toast our departure at the Officer's Club Bar, which became quite a lengthy toast after which we made our calls, collect, home without regard to time or charges. It was weeks later when Cheryle's parents received their phone bill that we found out that it was a very expensive call ($125 in 1969 dollars), but well worth it, and which Cheryle and I paid.

The Navy crew on board was very accommodating, and we had very few issues on the trip home. It helped that it was a fairly new ship with good accommodations (relatively speaking). As the ship had accommodations for a much larger Marine contingent, there was plenty of space which helped minimize personal frictions. It was also monsoon season with some large rolling seas, which kept a certain percentage of our men in their bunks a good amount of time. In fact, we had one Marine lieutenant who rarely surfaced the entire trip.

The daily routine was typically breakfast and then to the equipment bays for formation, roll call, physical training and working on equipment. After lunch, there might be some training and often free time with the crew providing a movie, and/or activities which we left the NCOs and enlisted themselves to work out. After dinner the Marine officers usually gathered to play cards and enjoy our duty-free purchases. Later, there were always some pretty good mid-rats available in the Officers Mess. Quite frankly, most of the trip back was pretty much a blur, we consumed most of our duty-free purchases and we were treated well by the crew, who knew that we would have much rather have flown home than be with them...but so be it.

We arrived in Long Beach at the end of October for disembarkation and transportation to MCB, Twentynine Palms. Somewhere along the way I also had received my orders for my next assignment. After completion of my temporary assignment in assisting the relocation of the Battery to Twentynine Palms, I was to report as Officer in Charge of the Marine Security Detachment stationed at the Marine Air Station in Yuma, Arizona.

Cheryle, our car and all our belongings arrived at Twentynine Palms within a week, driving from Chicago with the help of her mother, my mother and my sister. As soon as we were able, Cheryle and I drove to Yuma to check out the assignment, and decided that as remote as Twentynine Palms was, Yuma was even more so. In addition, Twentynine Palms was primarily an artillery center, my MOS. I still had two years left on my obligation and was certainly more at home in that environment.

Upon return from our trip to Yuma, I met with my Battalion Commander, and he recommended that I contact my career monitor at HQMC. I made my case that as a 0802 (artillery) officer, Twentynine Palms was a much more suitable assignment. I was almost immediately given a change in orders to allow me to remain there.

Duty at Twentynine Palms consisted of a fair amount of training, much of it out in the desert impact ranges and occasional trips to Camp Pendleton for larger field exercises. I was also screened and granted a higher security clearance for assignment as the Battalion "nuclear weapons officer." A little scary when you think about it, but we had 155-mm nuclear artillery shells (fraction of a kiloton) designed to be used in a conventional war situation against a mass of enemy troops. While in Twentynine Palms, I also participated in a project developed at the Aberdeen Proving Grounds to be able to fire the 155-mm shell out of a 175-mm gun to get a greater separation between our units and the enemy; with the idea of getting the nuclear round out over 30 miles from friendly lines.

The Officers Club on Friday night was the place to be, especially for married couples, often followed by gathering at someone's home after for BBQs, etc. Las Vegas, at only one stop sign and two turns in 200 miles away across the desert was an easy last-minute destination as well.

Twentynine Palms, was a military oriented town and that first year back from Vietnam, I do not recall any first-hand issues with anti- war or anti-military sentiments, rather just the opposite. Our favorite day trip would be to Palm Springs (about an hour drive). In February 1971, Marines from the Base were invited to be honor guards at the Bob Hope Desert Classic Golf Tournament. Palm Springs in general was very hospitable to us when there. But our favorite weekend getaway was the Ojai Valley where my Aunt and Uncle still lived, never having left the area after moving there during WW II.

In August 1971, our first child Amy was born in the Base Dispensary (no hospital at the time in Twentynine Palms), about 10 months after my return from Vietnam. Like father, like son! Late in 1971, I was notified of an opening at the Marine Corps Recruiting Station in Chicago for the Assistant OIC. Based in the Chicago Loop on LaSalle Street, the Office had responsibility for 25–30 Recruiting Stations in Northern Illinois (as far south as Peoria) and NW Indiana (Gary, Whiting and Hammond). Going back to our hometown and families with a new granddaughter made this opportunity very attractive. I was given the assignment to start early January. The move turned out to be very fortuitous, as at the time my father was suffering from what turned out to be terminal cancer. He passed away in February 1972, soon after our move back. We were all fortunate that he had the opportunity to meet his first grandchild and we had the opportunity to spend some quality time with him in those last few months.

Moving back to Chicago and being out and about as part of my assignment certainly brought me into a different atmosphere with respect to people's attitudes towards Vietnam and veterans.

In moving back, we rented a second floor flat in an older house in La Grange, Illinois, a near western suburb of Chicago. The apartment was within walking distance of the commuter train into downtown, so I did not have to drive in and Cheryle would have the car. Riding the train in uniform on a regular basis quickly made me aware of a certain discomfort and unease at that time of many people with the military. I don't recall getting any of the "welcome homes" and "thanks for your service" comments common today, and riding the train was a bit lonely. It was more like being shunned or wearing a Scarlet V on your chest.

Each of our 25–30 recruiting locations typically had 2 NCO grade Marines. At the Main Office was the CO (a major), me (AIOC), a Sergeant Major and four to five administrative types. The recruiters in the field were starting to run into more resistance to their physical presence recruiting at the schools, or career day presentations that were more common in earlier years. I was involved in a number of school system visits to try to address the resistance. We had very few "ugly" episodes, just less cooperation. At the same time, the Marine Corps was grappling with the upcoming ending of the Draft. The number of draftees put into the Marine Corps was not significant at that time, but we did depend upon the "draft-induced" effect. We had monthly recruiting quotas to meet and the Marine Corps selling points were the prestige, selectivity, and brotherhood of the Corps. With the draft scheduled to end in June 1973, all the Services were working on plans to address the change. The Marine Corps had a contract with J Walter Thompson (which I believe continues today), and that summer I was sent, with other Recruiting

Office Officers from around the Country, to a training and briefing on the upcoming recruiting campaign in anticipation of the end of the Draft.

The sobering news that summer was finding out that one of the young Marine Officers who was part of our circle in Twentynine Palms, was killed in Vietnam. When in Twentynine Palms, he was concerned that he would miss out on a tour in Vietnam as the Marine Corps presence was being reduced. He was sent to WestPac about the time we moved to Chicago and was killed in April 1972 in the northern border area in Quang Tri province.

Though our officers were not responsible for casualty notifications to families, we were assigned as a liaison to families of the Marines listed as Missing in Action. We had the responsibility to maintain regular contact with the families on a regular basis, plus be there for them if any questions or issues arose. I had four families in the greater Chicago area that I dealt with. The one that still brings back bittersweet memories was the older Polish immigrant couple whose son had gone missing when his platoon was on patrol along the coast up north. He and some buddies, while on an extended patrol, had taken a pause for a swim in the ocean. It was believed that he probably was caught in a rip tide and the body was never found, but he was still listed as MIA at the time. Sometime in the summer of 1972 his mother passed away and I attended the funeral, in my dress blues representing the Marine Corps. As I entered the funeral home, the already distraught father saw me and initially thought that I was his son. Very tough visit!

Then at Christmas we were given direction to deliver flowers to all the families of the MIAs. Last minute, and knowing the father, I decided that flowers were not appropriate for him. It was early evening and I stopped and bought a fifth of whiskey which he and I managed to drink a good portion of while sitting at his kitchen table.

The other interesting aside was when I was visited by a Marine Officer who worked out of the MIA Office in Washington, D.C. He was en route from Korea to Washington with briefcases containing the recently discovered partial remains of two Marine MIAs from the Korean War. The search never ends.

In 1972, after a little more than three years of active duty, I was promoted to Captain. I was again counseled on a possible career path going forward, but had already made my decision to resign my commission when my obligation was fulfilled. In the fall of 1972, I gave my "90-day notice" submitting a formal letter of resignation to HQMC resigning my Commission as a regular officer. I enjoyed my duty as a "field" Marine in khakis. But, by this time, I had realized that I was not meant to be a "Dress Blue" spit and polish career Marine.

During my time on active duty, the level of experience, maturity and knowledge gained cannot be matched, and I have the utmost respect for those who make the Marine Corps their career and fulfill all aspects of what it takes to be a total Marine (khaki and dress blue) but it was not meant to be my career choice. With the reductions of staff levels in Vietnam, I did not anticipate an issue and the resignation was readily accepted, though I was still on the hook as an inactive Reserve Officer for two more years.

My focus was now on getting some employment lined up for when discharged. While I had the BSME and BSNS degrees, the technical skills as an Artillery Officer were not necessarily heavily sought out in the civilian market. However, the leadership experience and gain in maturity of that same four years were definitely an asset in terms of my marketability.

Post-Active Duty Life

In late 1972, there was not a strong labor market. One immediate option that was offered was from the Dredging Company with which my father had spent his career. Their Corporate Offices were in Chicago so that was one of my first visits. I met up with old friends of my father for lunch and was offered a job before I left. While I greatly appreciated having that opportunity readily available, I wanted time to test the waters and see what else was out there.

At the time there was a job placement firm (Lendman Associates) that found a niche market successfully focusing on the large number of junior military officers being released after their two to four years of service. The "Lendman Weekends" were a regular event on the east and west coast of the US where large military bases were located. Fortunately, there was a Lendman Weekend scheduled in Chicago for October 1972. The weekend consisted of having about 20 companies (mostly large Fortune 500 types, with a few smaller regional firms) each making a presentation on their company and job opportunities to a group of about 100 officers/ former officers with interviews then scheduled over the next few days.

After setting up interviews with four of five companies whose names I was familiar with, I filled my interview "dance card" with a company I had never heard of, Parker Hannifin Corporation, an industrial motion control company based in Cleveland, Ohio. Their Operation's Manager, who was part of the interview team, was a University of Wisconsin Mechanical Engineering graduate, so the interview went well, and they asked that I come to Cleveland for a second interview. As they say, the rest is history as I spent my entire career with Parker Hannifin, retiring in 2005 as a Group Operating President, Corporate Vice President. The Company continues today as a very successful worldwide diversified manufacturing company in the field of motion control technologies.

As I look back at the first four years of civilian life, I am amazed at what we accomplished. What was the influence of our family, our military discipline and experience in our success in pulling it off? Parker Hannifin was a large proponent of further education at all levels. For me it meant that they encouraged my obtaining an MBA. Of course, it had to be on my own time. Their commitment was financial support. In addition, I was able to draw on the GI Bill. For the next four years I took two three credit evening courses per semester, fall and spring, and was awarded my MBA by Case Western Reserve University in June 1977. At the same time, Cheryle and I continued with our "family plan," as well. Tom was born in May 1974 and Tim in March 1977. I was still working full time, so twice a year as the semester was coming to an end with exams and papers due, Cheryle would pack up the one to three kids and go to her parents for a week or so in Chicago so that I would not be distracted.

In 1977, I had my had my first opportunity to explore involvement with veterans organizations when we moved from Cleveland Heights, Ohio to Mentor, Ohio. It was not only a larger house for the growing family, but also closer to a new assignment with Parker. One of our new neighbors was former Navy and active in the local American Legion. Finding out about my background, Cheryle and I were invited to a social event at the local American Legion Post. I found that I was by far one of the younger attendees. At dinner when introduced to a lady whose husband had recently passed away, I was told firmly that her husband had fought in WW I, and that had been "a real war!" All I could think about was that Vietnam was pretty real to me and my contemporaries, to the friends that I lost and their families, and to the 58,000 plus others killed in Vietnam. Possibly I overreacted, but between that comment and meeting no one of my era, I never pursued the opportunity to join.

However, a few years later a group of veterans in the factory where I was Division Manager were involved in forming a new Vietnam Veterans VFW Post. I agreed to join (and am a lifetime VFW member today), but with family and work priorities and a certain unease as the Division Manager sitting around having too many beers with "the troops," I never got too involved. To this day, I have not had the inclination to or felt the need to actively participate in a veterans organization. However, I totally support the role they play in helping and advocating for those whom have served in the armed forces.

I am not sure what influenced Cheryle's and my attitude towards our mobility over our life, be it our military experience, parents, family culture, genetics or more likely a combination of all of the above, but we made several relocations over and after my career. While the Marines dictated our mobility at the beginning of our marriage, Cheryle and I found that we would be willing to move anywhere within reason including internationally, for the right opportunity both for the experience a well as the career. Other friends and family could not understand why we would make a "move," especially as our family was growing, but our attitude was always "why wouldn't we."

One tradition of the Marine Corps that has continued for Cheryle and me in recent years is the celebration of Marine Corps Birthday. By tradition, the Marine Corps recognizes the birthday of the Corps every November 10th. The Birthday is recognized not only in active and reserve Marine units, but also at many veterans organizations where there is an active Marine contingent. We attended several of the Birthday Balls held by Reserve Units where my nephew was assigned in Florida. These provided the opportunity to meet many of today's Marines, many of whom have had the multiple deployment experience as my nephew.

The other lasting aspect of having first signed on with the Military in 1964 is the physical training and discipline, or maybe as my wife sometimes calls it, the addiction. While I participated in sports in high school, I cannot attest to being a great athlete or being imbued with an inherent desire to train, train and train. However, since selecting the Marine Corps option in 1966, the habit of training two to three times a week has continued throughout my life. With my worldwide travels throughout my career, I would always find a gym to work out in or an area to go for a jog. I have run outdoors in many countries around the world, including participating in a "Hash House Harriers" run in the jungles of Singapore with a few work colleagues, one of whom served with the Navy Small Boats in Vietnam. I was not in shape for that. Then when my knees began to bother me about 10–12 years ago, I switched to bike riding which continues to this day.

I have often been pulled back to thinking about the military and military service. When my sons were of military age there was no draft and no driving geopolitical need for such, so there was little discussion of military service. Tom (oldest son) was focused on Civil Engineering, attended Ohio State University, graduated and had a successful career in that field living in Dayton, Ohio. When Tim (youngest son) was having a few issues with college life in his second year at East Carolina University, I suggested that he pull out of school and consider the military. Whatever the motivation, his third year was a real turnaround and he successfully graduated with a degree in construction management.

The closer link has been through my nephew Jim. He, according to my sister, had a somewhat rebellious youth and after high school enlisted in the Marine Corps. Jim was still in his initial enlistment when he participated in the invasion of Iraq. He subsequently (after marrying a Florida girl) stayed in the Marine Corps Reserves, based with a Reserve unit in West Palm

Beach, Florida. Jim has subsequently been activated for additional tours to Afghanistan and a year in the Country of Georgia providing training and support to the Georgian military. His last six-month tour became a year because of COVID issues not allowing his unit to return.

His experience, and that of other reservists certainly raises the question of the role of the US Reserve organizations. If the Reserve units are meant to supplement the regular armed forces as needed in time of crisis or war, have we been ignoring the fact that our Regular Forces are understaffed and underfunded for the realities of the world we live in. And does this allow our politicians to continue to fly under the radar in terms of manning, budget as well as real life and death decisions regarding our military and their deployment.

Chapter C

MICK McBEE

I grew up in a small town (4,200 people) in post-WWII Appalachia, and I remember that there was universal respect for military service. Most fathers served in the military and virtually every family was somehow impacted by the War. The War was a shared experience. As a youngster in the early 1950s, I did not sense there was any distinction among persons who volunteered, were drafted or did not serve at all. Furthermore, there was great respect for President Eisenhower, who had been the Supreme Allied Commander.

Although the Vietnam War created divisions within the country as to the support of the War, the military and the draft, most of that was not apparent in our small town of mostly blue collar and farm workers. Most draft age men expected to serve upon graduation from high school except for the small percentage, 10 percent, who would attend college. My perspective on the draft was limited to observation of others as nothing beyond my registration was expected other than a college deferment. Then before graduation from high school a Naval Reserve Officers Training Corps (NROTC) scholarship was awarded to me. In fact, I naively thought the draft card was related to draft beer. For, along with a driver's license, it was the ticket to be able to purchase six percent beer at 18 years.

Ancestral and Immediate Family Military Experiences

As far as I know, no ancestors of mine served in the military prior to my parents except an ancestor of my paternal grandmother who fought in the Revolutionary War qualifying her for the Daughters of the American Revolution (DAR). My paternal ancestors were farmers who were early settlers in West Virginia. My maternal grandparents emigrated from Italy as children. An apprentice watchmaker, my father joined the Army in December 1941, gave up a stateside clerk's job on a command staff to go to OCS (Officer Candidate School). He served in combat in Italy earning the French Croix de Guerre for leading his company in the rescue of French troops being overrun. My mother was an Army nurse and they met when he was hospitalized after being wounded. They married in Bari, Italy and I was my mother's ticket home early as they did not want pregnant nurses on active duty. After father returned from overseas, three sisters were added to the family. Also, all four of my father's and mother's two brothers each served in WW II. Other than a second cousin, I am the only family member to serve since WW II.

Interestingly, my wife's parents also met and married while serving in the Navy in WW II. Her father and maternal uncle were at Pearl Harbor on December 7, 1941 although they did not know each other at the time.

Although exposed to all these people who served in WW II, none of them ever discussed their wartime experiences. However, mother's favorite TV show was MASH, because it reminded her of the antics and humor she experienced in a similar field hospital. Without any mention of his actions, the only comment that I recall from my father was at 94-years old when he affirmed the statements in a TV documentary as to the ineptitude of French forces during the battle of Monte Cassino.

Military service also impacts families with a sense of service along with that of the service member. My wife was raised as a Navy brat as her father spent 30 years in the Navy. With the regular reassignments, the travel, changing schools frequently and ease of making new friends with other children with diverse similar experiences creates a social maturity that most of us do not develop until years later.

Early Experiences

Growing up across the street from a grade school playground, the neighborhood gathering place, offered the opportunity to play pick up athletic activities and neighborhood tactical games such as hide and seek, kick the can and cowboys and Indians most of the days when not in school. In a small town, there was opportunity to actively participate in as much organized team sports as one desired.

In high school, without having to be a top athlete, I was able to participate in the whole range of athletic teams: football, basketball, baseball, track and golf. Of greatest impact was playing football under a coach who was an intense ex-WW II marine and who instilled a sense that one could perform beyond your own expectations, as well as, developing teamwork and responsibility to each other in defined roles. That led to great success—35 wins and only five losses in four years. These lessons and experiences carried over to military service and many other life activities.

Few of us participated in cub and boy scouts and my participation was not particularly distinguished. However, the 10-day adventure hiking in the New Mexico mountains at Philmont Boy Scout Ranch at age 16 was a significant maturing event in life for getting to know oneself and developing self-reliance and leadership.

Father was not a hunter but, in high school, I regularly went hunting as sort of a mascot with three adults from the community who were models of good outdoor and gun practices.

As editor of our high school newspaper, I was given almost complete independence by the faculty adviser. This provided valuable experiences as a leader to get the best out of a volunteer staff. Problem solving, planning and organization skills were also developed to meet deadlines. organization and planning to meet deadlines.

As co-founder of a high school science club I shared responsibility for conducting a yearly science fair with recognition and qualification to advance to broader competitions. Participation in Boys' State provided insight into the political operations of local and state government.

Other valuable experiences during grade and high school were working in the family jewelry store in many roles, including bookkeeper, and having newspaper routes for eight years through graduation from high school.

Intending to attend Case School of Applied Science (later merged with Western Reserve University) to study engineering and play football, my plans changed upon receiving an NROTC scholarship to the University of Wisconsin. I became the first in the family to attend college. My father had been the first in the family to graduate from high school having to leave the family farm to live with his grandmother in town.

Selective Service System and College ROTC

Although I had no experience with Selective Service while on the NROTC scholarship, later having a number three in the birthdate draft lottery would have led to some form of military service upon graduation. However, I was aware that most male high school classmates served in the military. Many classmates volunteered to avoid the draft as only four other males from my class of 100 (approximately one-half girls) expected deferment by going to college.

College enrollment was only a deferment, not an exemption, from the draft. The looming draft surely led to robust voluntary non-scholarship enrollment in ROTC for the Army, Navy and Air Force.

The NROTC program provided a full scholarship, books and a small monthly stipend and three six-weeks summer training experiences for me: (1) as an enlisted man aboard a Navy destroyer; (2) split between amphibious warfare and beach landing training and actual piloting experience in aviation indoctrination all while in a basic training type of discipline and physical fitness regimen under Marine drill sergeants and (3) indoctrination as a junior officer aboard a conventional diesel powered submarine.

Membership in the NROTC program provided a sense of belonging in a small group rather than swimming alone in a very large university many miles from home. Extracurricular activities included helping to organize the annual military ball and acting as part of the color guard for university athletic activities. As a senior I served as the executive office of the ROTC command responsible for organization of the military ball and parade.

While I was not the most dedicated student, college life offered an opportunity for a wide variety of non-academic rewarding experiences. These included part time jobs as a student assistant to the tool and die maker responsible for operating the mechanical engineering department laboratories and constructing faculty projects; administrative duties in the financial aid office during registrations; as a residence house fellow and as a bartender, a very educational experience in human nature.

Membership in the Sigma Phi fraternity and living in the fraternity house for four years was the most life-shaping experience of the college years. Sigma Phi was not the typical animal house of fraternity. It placed an emphasis on academics and our home was a historical landmark Louis Sullivan home in a residential neighborhood across the street from the University president and on the opposite side of campus from Greek row. As part of a core leadership group, we learned much as we resurrected the chapter from very low membership to a robust and academically successful group.

While serving on the student senate I was a political moderate with very vocal voices on both ends of the political spectrum who claimed to be representative of the student body. In the Student Senate, I authored and passed a bill to conduct a survey on the Vietnam War. With the expertise of the campus Survey Research Department, a survey was conducted as part of the Spring 1968 student elections. The results were extremely surprising. The responses from the five choices were plotted on a bell curve with a nearly vertical peak. This showed that a very small minority had strong opinions on either end of the spectrum. The vast majority had no firm opinion one way or the other on the Vietnam War.

Finding that the engineering curriculum interfered with my extracurricular activities because it was too time consuming, I transferred to the business school midway through my third year. This necessitated permission from the Navy for an extra year without the scholarship. Luckily, I received a Student Activity Grant generated from campus parking fines. That allowed me to take a three-month motorcycle trip to Europe with a fraternity brother rather than needing a summer job. This was a particularly broadening experience for someone from a rural small town in Appalachia. Especially rewarding was crewing for a month on an eighteenth-century Dutch fishing vessel called a botter that hosted a variety of international students, mostly women, through the Dutch Student Agency.

Back to the Navy, the opportunity to take field trips during semester breaks to Naval Aviation bases and actual piloting experience during the second summer inspired my desire to become a pilot. Participation in the Flight Indoctrination Program (FIP) during my fourth year provided civilian flight training leading to a private pilot's license without any obligation to the Navy.

This confirmed my decision to apply for flight training. The FIP was implemented to self-identify persons who would probably go into flight training but who did not actually like flying. Identification before going to flight training and then quitting or washing out saved the Navy from great expense and disruption of the career of the young officer.

Active Duty Military Career

After graduation and commissioning, I was assigned to administrative duties with the flight training command before flight training. During that time, I met my wife Pat at a party in New Orleans. Over the next 11 months, flight training was completed and we were married. While awaiting further training we were assigned to recruiting duty in New Orleans, my wife's home town, during which we celebrated the birth of our daughter and Mardi Gras.

After three months training in anti-submarine tactics and in the helicopter I would fly, I joined the squadron on an aircraft carrier for the remaining six months of a cruise in the Mediterranean Sea.

As a strange coincidence, I was involved in four incidents with Soviet forces. Curiously, one night while flying a routine plane guard pattern off the starboard side of the carrier the ever present electronically equipped Soviet fishing trawler fired flares in our direction. No apparent reason was ever ascertained.

Second, while in a hover with dipping sonar in the water, the Soviet trawler charged us to force us out of the hover. We were much closer to the carrier than we would ordinarily operate in order to calibrate the directional aspect of the sonar equipment. It was surmised that we were perceived as a threat to detect a Soviet submarine underneath the aircraft carrier. Flippantly, we teased the jet pilots that, if they were launched in war, they would have to plan to land somewhere else as the carrier would be sunk by the shadowing sub.

Later, out of curiosity, we independently set out to try to detect the sub. Although its presence was suspected, it apparently had not previously been confirmed. We were part of the first trial to add helicopter and fixed wing squadrons on an attack carrier. The carrier previously would have been escorted only by surface anti-submarine ships which could not detect a submarine masked by the carrier. Because of our ability to vary the depth of the sonar transducer we were able to detect a sub. To the disbelief of the intelligence officers, we were actually able to confirm the presence of the sub with a graphic printout from a new piece of equipment that we were evaluating among other new electronics on the newest H-3 helicopters.

Fourth, one morning while transiting back to the US from the Mediterranean we found ourselves in the midst of a group of Soviet warships headed to Cuba. Two helicopters were launched to observe them. Coincidentally, they did the same. More bold than us, the Soviet helicopter was hovering very close to the carrier and taking pictures. We were recalled to chase it away. Never before considering a helicopter dogfight, we had to improvise when they would not leave. We carried no weapons, but as a larger and heavier helicopter our downwash would make their helicopter uncontrollable if we hovered overhead. When we approached slowly as though we might hover above the Soviet helicopter, they headed for home.

The following year after preparing for another cruise to the Mediterranean, we were sent all the way around from the East Coast on an emergency deployment to the Tonkin Gulf after the bombing of Haiphong Harbor. Although we were only to be there for a short time until replaced by a West Coast Carrier, we kept being extended, eventually not coming home until after eleven months. In transit, all of our antisubmarine electronics were removed to provide greater capacity for cargo and passenger carrying utility missions as the Tonkin Gulf was too shallow for subs. In the end, all of that equipment was ruined because of the humid environment in which it was stored aboard the ship and the electronic cables in the aircraft were damaged by the cargo we were carrying. After returning home, what were the newest H-3 helicopters had to be replaced.

That time off of Vietnam involved heavy flying hours taxing the maintenance of the helicopters because that model was only deployed on the East coast of the US. That stretched and delayed the logistic supply chain of replacement parts. That presented quite a challenge of leadership and resourcefulness that was met with significant success and valuable lessons for future application.

As an aside, during that period of the Vietnam War in 1972–73, the air war, if you could call it that, changed substantially. There were no longer any enemy aircraft in the air, thus, no real mission for fighters. To accumulate points for air medals, the F-4 fighters, not really meant to be bombers, were loaded with bombs for little more than target practice on low value targets. After failing to take out assigned higher value targets like a bridge, a single

A-6 bomber would be sent in a couple of days later to knock it out. In essence, large amounts of munitions were being dropped at great expense with no significant tactical or strategic benefits.

Also of significance, during that cruise, was involvement in two accident investigations. One was when a pilot was involved when an engine exploded on the deck of the aircraft carrier. The other followed a non-fatal loss of a helicopter investigating a light on an emergency buoy that was thrown overboard on New Year's Eve. It was an apparent prank because no one was missing when the emergency muster was taken. I was a member of the accident investigation team and was assigned as the recorder of the proceedings and drafter of the final report.

During my last year in the squadron, I served as the Quality Assurance Officer and chief maintenance test pilot. I was tasked, in addition to day-to-day operations, with inspecting, testing and accepting the new replacement aircraft from the manufacturer. Then we deployed to test a new anti-submarine aircraft carrier escort force concept with the added capabilities of our new helicopters.

These helicopters were newly equipped with radar, passive sonobuoy deployment and monitoring capability and magnetic anomaly detection equipment (MAD). These gave rise to very significant changes in capabilities and tactics. Previously, we primarily resolved searches for submarines using active or pinging sonar. Submarines could hear at a greater distance than they could be detected and even when they were close enough for detection, they could speed away faster than their location could be resolved sufficient to attack them.

In contrast, the passive buoys only listen without alerting the submarine of our presence. They give only the direction of the noise made by a submarine enabling triangularization from multiple buoys. Then we could fly over the plotted course and precisely detect the submarine with the MAD gear sufficiently precise to attack with a torpedo. In fact, my crew was given credit for three kills during this exercise. This was in great contrast to many previous exercises during which I have no recollection of any helicopter crew ever sufficiently resolving a contact to make a simulated attack let alone being credited with a kill.

By this time, Pat and I had decided to get out of the Navy and go to law school. In the interim, we opted to accept an assignment to Tulane University as an Associate Professor of Naval Science. This allowed us to return to Pat's hometown, New Orleans for the birth of our second child. The next two years were spent teaching organizational behavior and leadership to senior ROTC midshipmen. For proficiency flying, I qualified to fly multi-engine aircraft. Unfortunately, Tulane Law School did not accept part time students. Thus,

I studied for an MBA in accounting planning to become a Certified Public Accountant (CPA) if law school did not work out.

Post-Active Duty Military Connections

Because we decided that New Orleans was not a good place to practice law or educate our children, we submitted applications to various law schools around the country. We selected Arizona State University Law School and we moved to Tempe, Arizona.

During law school I served in the Navy Ready Reserve (prepared for quick deployment like the National Guard) for three years. I flew twelve weekend days most months plus two-day drill on weekends providing comfortable financial support for a family of four. I was being paid for two days for every day that I flew. As a result, I was being paid generally for 26 days per month as a Lieutenant Commander (O4). After being admitted to the bar, I ended my naval service notwithstanding promotion to Commander (O5). A challenge as a new lawyer was adjusting to support my family with less income than I earned as a law student.

In the last decade, approximately every two years, we have attended reunions of the squadron that made the 11-month emergency deployment to the Gulf of Tonkin. Most attendees served as enlisted men under threat of the draft. They were all high-quality servicemen, served with distinction and went on to successful careers in military and/or civilian life. They were in contrast with the limited experience of the immediate post-draft Navy volunteers. As Assistant Maintenance Officer, I was responsible for getting personnel into technical schools to maintain the necessary level of qualified technicians. It became more difficult to get people with academic aptitude high enough to get into the necessary advanced schools. I left the squadron before it was apparent whether there was any effect on operational readiness.

Military Service and Civilian Career

During my three years in law school, my military aviation experience qualified me for a law clerkship with an attorney who practiced aviation law. More significant was a part-time job with an aviation and vehicular crashworthiness technical expert who invented and manufactured crashworthy fuel systems for military aircraft and race cars. Also, I was permitted to attend the Survival Investigator's Training Course he conducted for, among others, all National Transportation Safety Board (NTSB) accident investigators. This, along with assignment to summarize every crashworthy fuel system integrity patent application, provided a background for the area of specialization in my legal practice.

After law school I worked as an associate attorney almost exclusively on aviation crash litigation. Ten years of flying in the Navy was of significant benefit especially on helicopter crashes. Understandably helicopters are much more complex than fixed wing aircraft and few attorneys had experience as a helicopter pilot. My boss used that to market our services to referring attorneys and it gave me the opportunity to gain much experience.

In particular, I had the opportunity to coordinate a multiparty case involving the crash of a helicopter in the North Sea during a North Atlantic Treaty Organization (NATO) exercise. Another party was represented by one of the best trial lawyers in the country who was just returning to practice after a heart attack. Therefore, I benefitted tremendously from his tutelage as he asked me to take the lead and carry the bulk of the load in taking depositions. He had a devilish wry sense of humor and took great joy in practicing law. His counsel, emphasizing the need to enjoy the practice of trial law in the face of competitive pressures we face, served me well for the remainder of my career.

After five years, I had the opportunity to start my own practice with two significant cases and a line of credit from the banker of a colleague who had great success after going on her own two years earlier. Like her, my focus was on defective product liability litigation. Furthermore, from my military experience and lessons learned from observing good and counterproductive practices, I was confident that I could form and motivate a committed team.

Over time the practice narrowed to vehicular crashworthiness. Crashworthiness focuses on the ability to survive or mitigate injuries in aircraft or vehicular crashes involving seatbelts, seats, doors, safe crash energy dissipation or redirection of forces away from occupants, structures that preserve sufficient safe occupant space and the prevention of post-crash fuel fed fires. As opportunities fortuitously came along, my practice narrowed largely to post-collision fire cases.

Blessed with a high-quality staff we often coordinated multiparty and multidistrict cases with other attorneys. In particular, the last few years of my practice largely involved a collaboration nationwide on similar post-collision fire cases to break through corporate secrecy and stonewalling of a vehicle defect resulting in over 300 deaths. The truth of the field experience was even hidden from the design engineer who was responsible for making design changes to mitigate serious injuries and deaths.

After fifteen years of my own small law firm, financial security was achieved allowing me to close my office and exit the roller coaster of high-pressure practice of complex litigation on contingent fees requiring substantial personal investment in most cases.

Clearly my military service led to the part time law school job that was the foundation of my law career Also, success would have been much more difficult without the lessons learned from my military experience.

Qualities developed and honed by military service were essential to success in complex highly contentious litigation against many of the largest and most litigation savvy corporations. Among them, leadership qualities and organizational abilities were most significant. As with most significant endeavors, few accomplish much without the support of a committed team. Although military discipline is an essential structure for military activities, teamwork and the sense of common purpose, are necessary for success. Over-domineering top–down leadership and ambitious self-serving leaders are too common in the military. However, having the good fortune to see the contrast in leadership styles was beneficial to me.

The second commanding officer under whom I served was a shining example of how to get buy-in and outstanding performance from subordinates in demanding high-pressure circumstances. It was always clear that he understood and was looking out for the circumstances of everyone in the squadron.

One example was a somewhat unique policy. After weeks at sea operating 12 hours on and 12 hours off, no one was permitted to go on liberty upon reaching port until everyone was ready to go ashore. This meant that, until the lowest level members of the squadron who were responsible for handling the aircraft had serviced and washed all the aircraft were finished, no one went ashore. As you might guess, rather than being left behind while most other went ashore, they had a lot of help completing their work. This created a sense of teamwork and common purpose that were the foundation for success as the squadron won all possible unit awards during his command.

The test pilot training and experience helped develop attention to detail to focus on setting priorities over distractions under pressure that are important to trial practice in developing and trying lawsuits in complex cases. Also, important traits honed in flying are detailed planning and time management.

Non-flying experiences as quality assurance officer, chief maintenance tests pilot and aircraft accident investigator were valuable lessons in safety and quality control practice to understand root causes in design and manufacturing defect failures lawsuits.

As quality assurance officer, all test pilot complaints and maintenance write offs were reviewed and notes were kept on the idiosyncrasies of each of the eight helicopters. Quality assurance senior enlisted men in each of the maintenance disciplines (airframe, power plants, electrical and electronic) inspected all critical maintenance on the aircraft, as well as investigating maintenance errors. All inspection failures and errors were investigated to determine root causes. Whenever there were significant errors or lessons of educational value to others, unsatisfactory report (UR) messages had to be sent to all operators of similar helicopters. While broadcasting your shortcomings to the world of peers, it was important for URs to professionally reflect frank, thorough, and accurate analysis for the benefit of others. Also, test flights had to be flown before aircraft were returned to service after critical maintenance, or to help the inspectors diagnose the causes of recurrent problems.

Technical and human factor experiences that were valuable in the evaluation of product failures, vehicular crashes and resulting injuries were the crux of my law practice.

After 15 years sufficient financial security allowed me to close my office. Free from financial pressure, the next 21 years were devoted to volunteer social justice activity and a varied pro bono law practice (characterized loosely as poverty law). I took inactive status as a member of my Bar Association.

This freedom afforded the opportunity to expand horizons and understanding of a much broader cross section of humanity than previous life experiences had provided.

Volunteering at a free legal clinic and as a volunteer pro bono mediator for a nonprofit low-cost mediation service, provided exposure to an incredible variety of legal predicaments people confront without the financial means to otherwise experience a semblance of justice from our legal system. Also, legal matters that were too involved for non-profits to handle were accepted on a pro bono or minimum fee basis. This was an eye opener as to how unscrupulous people prey on people of little means who are virtually helpless. This quixotic endeavor was often very rewarding like the big brother called upon to level the playing field to confront the bully.

Other social justice activities included co-founding and managing a free medical clinic; a charter member of an organization providing financial assistance to the needy primarily in the form of rent assistance, utilities and food; prison ministry; co-founder of a parish social justice ministry; parish representative for the formation of an area interfaith advocacy organization; and organizing member of the local chapter of an international social justice solidarity organization.

In addition to the realization of the need for a free medical clinic, two other activities highlighted the scandalous shortcomings of the health care system in Texas. As a member of a health care committee of the interfaith organization, research on healthcare economics was enlightening. Advocacy before the Texas Legislature was only modestly successful as the legislature deferred to the national proposal being advanced by the Clinton administration.

Another activity was service as chairman of the Comprehensive Assistance Committee (CAP) formed to administer an annual grant. The program is designed to help families deal with overwhelming circumstances whether they be short or long term. In addition to social workers, other medical, financial and legal professionals from the parish community conduct evaluations and formulate plans for financial and counsel assistance. As it has turned out, more than 80 of the 93 cases to date have been precipitated by the economic fallout of a family member's medical condition for which there was no safety not even, in some instances, where there was health insurance.

Other Observations

From personal experience and observations, I strongly believe that some form of compulsory national service would be helpful to young men and women and, in turn, the country as a whole. It could be military, other government service, service with religious or other forms of non-governmental organizations. It would be important that such service would not be seen as a penalty, like community alternative criminal sentencing, but as an opportunity to be involved in a potentially diverse team working together beyond only self-interest.

Personally, the structure and near-term certainty of the NROTC scholarship program and the payback commitment of military service provided the opportunity to mature and become grounded through growth in understanding of self, others and my place in the world before setting into a career path. This is in contrast to observations of peers and other young people who struggled or bounced around as they tried to find their place in the world.

Several observations explain the significant benefit of youth service. This includes, not only the young people in the military, but young people involved in AmeriCorps, Teach for America, Peace Corps and Mormon missionary opportunities.

Living near a large Mormon community for three years provided frequent opportunities to visit with young door-to-door missionaries. Representing some Mormon clients gave me the impression that their coming-of-age endeavors provided grounding and maturity that served them well, before embarking on life's path beyond the evangelical mission.

Multiple AmeriCorps volunteers were observed as full-time staff for the local Habitat for Humanity chapter planning, organizing and supporting the volunteer built weekend. They seemed to be given a lot of responsibility and competently and enthusiastically provided a valuable service significantly extending the application of funding for the benefit of the community while providing the volunteers with meaningful experience.

Similarly, over 22 years as a volunteer at a large multifaceted charitable social justice organization (food pantry, housing first homes to formerly homeless, job training, after school and summer feeding programs for students, computer skill training for adults, transitional housing and training to young adults aging out of foster care, legal clinic, food service training operating a café, medical clinic and support services by social workers) AmeriCorps volunteers provided valuable service to augment the full time staff and volunteers. To see the benefit of their service to the needy provided a great sense of accomplishment and dignity to these young adults.

Also, a German exchange student found it rewarding to satisfy his compulsory service as a nursing home attendant while resolving his decision to go to medical school. These forms of service, in addition to the benefits to the participants, benefit otherwise underserved people often in ways not otherwise feasible economically or because of shortage of staff.

These forms of selfless service can be eye openers to the situations faced by others and help develop a sense of service and shared commitment for the common good developing self-confidence and appreciation of the human dignity of those not as fortunate as they. If such experiences were more universal, the broad cross section of the population would have enlightening experiences outside their normal narrow lane of life experience and comfort zone. This would help develop a greater sense of selflessness and shared experience committed to the general benefit to the country and the common good.

Without the draft, the all-volunteer military seemed to become less diverse and less representative of a cross section of the country's population as well as the previously mentioned lower academic aptitude. Furthermore, a few unfairly bear the burden of service in combat making serial repeat deployments, some for much of a 20-year career.

In contrast to a nearly universal sense of shared purpose and experience in the post-WW II era, and, to a lesser extent, the post-Vietnam era, there is far less understanding of the role and nature of military service. Notwithstanding the divisiveness of the Vietnam War, I have a sense we are more divided as a country with less sense of common experience than even during the Vietnam War.

The common shared experiences of the era of our parents going through the great depression, New Deal, including work programs, and WW II gave rise to a robust middle class and a somewhat egalitarian sense of well-being for our generation.

By contrast the 2020–21 Covid-19 pandemic and resulting economic downturn seem to be driving divisiveness and inequality rather than shared experience and common purpose. In between, the Vietnam War, 1980s and 1990s savings and loan crisis and the 2008 housing crisis did not seem to bring the country together either.

In temporary contrast, the experience of September 11, 2001 was somewhat unifying. However, I was very surprised at the reaction of my soft spoken, gentlemanly and largely apolitical father in his 90s concerning the flag waving patriotism adopted by some at the time. Seemingly out of character, he was offended by drivers of pickups and cars waving flags to demonstrate patriotism in contrast to he and his brothers who served in combat and never saw the need to publicly demonstrate their patriotism but did so quietly by their actions. He felt it was empty symbolism by people that he did not think were willing to make sacrifices for others.

It seems that to some degree, there is an all too pervasive sense that the economy is a zero-sum game where an advantage to one has been offset by the loss of another. The experience of working as teammates in public service for the benefit of other can help demonstrated how win-win situations can benefit others without loss to oneself.

There is also a sense that the military is far less representative of the country's population than it was when I served in the decade from 1969 to 1979. In fact, over roughly 50 years, I know of only one child of an acquaintance who has served in the military. He had been the senior patrol leader in our Boy Scout troop and retired after a military career as a green beret. Many, if not most, of the boys encountered during six years as assistant scoutmaster attained eagle scout rank. Yet, I do not recall any serving in the military. It is a shame that the country and the armed forces completely missed such an ideal quality resource.

One other former eagle scout and his wife served in Teach for America after graduating from college before going to graduate school. They regarded serving in a poor community in contrast to their upbringing in an affluent community, as an eye opening and rewarding experience. I am sure their students benefitted richly as well.

Chapter D
ARNE SALVESEN

Cliff Westlund was an unusual high school teacher. He encouraged you to think for yourself. As a sophomore in Mr. Westland's English class at Wausau (Wisconsin) Senior High in 1953/1954 this was a new experience for me. For example, when Mr. Westland asked each of us to select a favorite poem and recite it to music for the class each student had to make decisions.

Similarly, when he assigned class members to write a story of their lives 10 years into the future each of us had to think for ourselves. This exercise brought me face-to-face with the reality that over the next 10 years I would certainly be subject to the draft. I had an obligation to serve my county in the military. How would I do this? I hardly knew anyone who had served in the military. My father, an immigrant from Norway, where he performed his six-month long Norwegian service obligation in a chemistry lab, knew absolutely nothing about the US military. So he could not provide an example or even offer valuable advice. I would have to think for myself.

I had heard of Wausau high schoolers receiving congressional appointments to a military academy. One of my best friends, taking lessons to earn a pilot's license, told me that his father was already working on getting him an appointment to the newly founded Air Force Academy (which he subsequently received). But the military academies held little attraction for me.

The University of Wisconsin in Madison is where I wanted to study. I wanted to be a Badger. At college I would be deferred from the draft for the duration of my studies. Then, as a college graduate, perhaps I would be qualified to become an officer. This appeared to me to be a more attractive alternative than being drafted for two-year's active duty or enlisting in the reserves with a six-month active duty and a very long commitment in the reserves.

So, I started to research in the school library how one could become a military officer without graduating from one of the academies. This is where I learned about the ROTC. Little did I know then at age 16 that this knowledge would provide the pathway for my entire life.

High school was a breeze for me. In my class of 450 students, I ranked academically with the top 10 students, lettered in football, excelled on the debate team and was elected class president. During my senior year in 1955/1956, I learned about the NROTC (Naval Reserve Officers Training Corps) program which was almost like a university scholarship. It offered free tuition, cost of books, $50/month, and a regular commission in the USN fully equivalent to that awarded to graduates of Annapolis. Recipients were required to pass four years of naval science instruction, attend three training exercises during summer vacations and assume a naval service obligation of three years. There was an NROTC program at the University of Wisconsin in Madison.

When I told my parents that I wanted to apply for acceptance in the Regular NROTC program they were initially opposed to the idea. They were not opposed to the military as such. They had often seen me in my Boy Scout uniform and knew that I was comfortable in a disciplined environment. I had earned the Eagle Scout award and become a Boy Scout camp leader. What worried them was the three-year active duty commitment. But as I assured them that I viewed three-year's duty as an officer to be preferable to two years as a draftee they dropped their resistance.

It was a very hot day in the spring of 1956 when I boarded a bus with a half dozen or so of Wausau High classmates for examination and interviews at a naval recruiting center in Minneapolis. There we joined a large group of applicants from other high schools in Wisconsin and Minnesota. We were required to strip to the waist and line up in single file to have a blood sample drawn. An officer suggested we sit down if we felt faint. I was near the front of the line watching the corpsman jab the boy just ahead of me and fill his syringe with the boy's blood. That view, in the heat of the room, suddenly got to me. I fainted dead away. I soon awoke lying on a cot with my blood being drawn. One corpsman was laughing and telling another, "There are 50 admirals in the other room now sitting on the floor."

Despite this personal fiasco on my first experience of having blood drawn, I must have made a good impression on the senior naval officers who conducted the interviews. For within a few weeks, I was advised that I had been awarded an NROTC scholarship and had been accepted in the Regular NROTC program at the University of Wisconsin starting in September 1956. I was the only student from Wausau High School awarded an NROTC scholarship that year.

At the University of Wisconsin in Madison I studied mechanical engineering with an emphasis on heat-power. Naval Sciences courses were in addition. These were three-credit courses, meeting for three hours/week. Freshman year (4th class midshipman year) the course was History of Sea Power. Sophomore year (3rd class midshipmen year) the subject was marine engineering and gunners. Junior year (2nd class midshipman year) we studied navigation. Senior year (1st class midshipman year) course was leadership. Also, all midshipman attended a two-hour long drill session every Thursday afternoon in full uniform. Four years of these drill sessions (conducted with rifles) insured that all 1st class midshipmen could not only march themselves but also command a marching group.

All Regular NROTC midshipmen were also required to participate in three summer training sessions, two aboard ship and one with Marine Corps/Naval Aviation instruction. The sessions lasted six weeks.

During the summer of 1957, I was introduced to shipboard life as a 4th class midshipman with six weeks aboard the heavy cruiser USS Albany (CA-123). We sailed from Norfolk, VA through the Panama Canal, over the equator, to reach Valparaiso, the seaport for Santiago, Chile.

Life aboard ship was very much like the life of an enlisted sailor, with the 24-hour day divided into watches, manual labor duties, food served cafeteria style, sleeping in three-high bunks and supervision provided by 1st class midshipmen. The main deck of the Albany was made of hard wood. Each day we 4th class middies would sweep, wash down and "holy stone" this wooden deck from bow to stern. This was done in exactly the same manner as that aboard a ship of the line in the days of Admiral Nelson, 160 years before.

My GQ battle station was in the number 2 powder handling room where bags of gun powder were positioned to fire the number 2 battery of the ship's eight-inch guns. This room also housed the fire control computer for this gun battery, a huge machine of mechanical cams, gears, knobs and dials into which variables such as range, ship's speed, and wind speed were entered to control the position and control of these massive guns.

I grew up in Wisconsin. But as my parents were Norwegian I had spent two summers in Norway, a country quite different from the USA. I could speak and understand Norwegian. But even my limited liberty ashore in Chile—dressed in uniform—revealed a brand new world: different language, strange food, dinner starting at 8:00 p.m., kids on the street instead of in school, unusual police uniforms and strangers wanting to meet and befriend us.

My 3rd class midshipman training during the summer of 1958 consisted of three-weeks Marine Corps instruction at Little Creek, VA followed by three-weeks Naval Aviation training at Corpus Christi, TX. In a mock amphibious landing exercise, I managed to impress our Marine Corps instructor with my aggressiveness in surmounting a barbed-wire barrier from which I still have a scar on my leg. Despite earning this personal badge of honor I decided then that I could never be happy as a Marine Corps officer.

In Corpus Christi all midshipmen were given a taste of flying with a training hop in the back seat of a jet trainer. I still remember the pilot asking me over the intercom as we taxied down the runway what university I attended. When I told him he burst out into song with "On Wisconsin, On Wisconsin ..." Then, as we lifted off the ground, he asked if I'd like to experience some aerobatics. As soon as I said "Sure" he headed straight up, leveled out and dipped the left wing down and turned the jet trainer and my horizon by 90 degrees. That move alone caused great discomfort. The barrel-rolls that followed made me extremely nauseous. We finally landed and I recovered enough to clean out the vomit in my cockpit. I knew then that I would never again fly in a small aircraft to say nothing of becoming a naval aviator.

In the summer of 1959, I received orders for my final summer training as a 1st class midshipman to report aboard the radar destroyer USS Hanson (DDR-832) based in San Diego, CA. On the Hanson I joined a handful of 1st class middies who directed a larger group of 4th class middies for six-weeks cruising along the coast of California. Right off the bat I made friends with another 1st class midshipman, John Watts, from the University of Texas. The two of us acted as leaders of the entire complement of midshipmen aboard the Hanson.

One day we were all treated to a short cruise in the Pacific aboard the USS Tilefish, a diesel-powered submarine. The Tilefish performed a diving operation to demonstrate submarine tactics to the midshipmen aboard. I was impressed with the professionalism and teamwork of the officers and men of the Tilefish. All of them had volunteered for this special type of naval service. But I noted that this sort of service largely involved secret underwater operations.

Each 1st class midshipman aboard the USS Hanson was invited for diner several times in the ship's wardroom. There we experienced first-hand the informal living environment of commissioned officers. For the first time in our budding naval careers, we were being served by mess boys. Our table was covered by a cloth; food arrived in individual portions; and coffee was served in a cup with a saucer. The world of officers was different from the world of enlisted sailors. It was the world of gentlemen.

Earning a BS in mechanical engineering together with a BS in naval science required 4 ½ to 5 years of undergraduate study. With the permission of the Navy, I stayed for 5 years so that I could also take some liberal arts courses. During the fifth year in Madison (1960/1961) I learned about the Naval Nuclear Power Program designed for recently commissioned officers. It sounded right down my alley because my ME concentration was in heat-power and I had even taken a course in nuclear power generation. Shortly after completing a written application for the Program, I received orders to report for personal interviews at the Bureau of Ships Nuclear Power Division in Washington, D.C. This was the naval division famously headed by Vice Admiral Hyman Rickover.

So I flew from Madison to Washington for personal interviews with Admiral Rickover and his staff. It was a Saturday when most people had the day off. But not Admiral Rickover and his group at NR (Naval Reactors). After some preliminary interviews with staff officers, I was escorted into the Admiral's office. He was seated behind his desk while an aide to his right took notes. The Admiral asked me if I was engaged. When I said no, he made some comment about the lack of initiative by the coeds in Madison. Then he asked if I had a hobby. When I said reading was my hobby, he gave a dismissive look and asked what I liked to read. I promptly replied that I liked reading eighteenth-century British literature. Apparently satisfied, the Admiral then dismissed me.

Later I heard from one of the other 20 or so midshipmen applying for the Program that a midshipmen from Yale had told the Admiral that his hobby was mountain climbing. The Admiral then instructed this midshipman to obtain a Polaroid camera from one of his staff officers and arrange to have his photo taken at the top of Monkey Mountain. This midshipman discovered that the mountain in question was located at the Washington, D.C. Zoo. He traveled to the zoo, managed to climb the mountain, had a photo of himself taken, returned with the photo to the Naval office, and subsequently learned that meeting this challenge from the Admiral earned him an acceptance in the Naval Nuclear Power Program.

A week or two after I returned from my trip to Washington, I received notice that I also was accepted into the Naval Nuclear Power Program. There was one condition: extending my active duty obligation by a year in light of my undertaking 12 months of nuclear power training. I agreed to this extension of my active duty obligation from three years to four years. I promptly received orders to proceed as soon as I graduated (and was commissioned as an Ensign in the USN) to the US Naval Shipyard at Mare Island, CA.

I drove to Mare Island from my home in Wausau, Wisconsin in June 1961 and checked into the Bachelor Officers' Quarters (BOQ). This first phase of nuclear power training was a bit disappointing because it was really only an extension of what I had been doing for five years: receiving classroom instruction in college-level subjects such as physics, chemistry, math and marine engineering. I did OK finishing academically in the top 25 percent in our class of 48 officers. Not bad for not studying very much (and having a girlfriend living in nearby San Francisco).

It was at Mare Island that I first met Naval Academy graduates. I got along well with them. Many of them envied officers commissioned through NROTC because Academy grads had only BS Naval Science degrees while NROTC grads had degrees known outside of the military. Ensigns who were

Academy grads (sometimes known as "Ring-knockers" as most wore large Academy class rings) usually felt destined to make a career in the navy.

The sixties were a time when the US Navy built a great number of nuclear subs, both attack class and Polaris class. So there was a correspondingly high demand for submarine officers who were nuclear trained. In 1961 several nuclear subs were being built at Mare Island. One day our class got an opportunity to visit a submarine under construction in the shipyard. These submarines were huge, four or five times larger than diesel subs like the USS Tilefish in which I had experienced an underwater dive as a 1st class Midshipman. It was easy to stand fully upright in a nuclear sub. They were even outfitted with a wardroom and comfortable showers. Student officers were actively encouraged to commit to submarine service. However, I continued to prefer duty in a surface ship, even if that meant accepting a billet in a destroyer or another type of non-nuclear ship.

The classroom portion of nuclear power training ended in December 1961. The next step would be training on a prototype reactor plant onshore. These prototypes were full-sized reactor operating plants exactly the same as those built aboard nuclear-powered ships. The Navy had two prototype plants: Westinghouse-design A1W located in southern Idaho or General Electric (GE) design D1G located in upstate New York. Both prototype reactor plants were of the pressurized water coolant concept but entirely different design. A1W is the naval designation of a reactor plant used on a carrier and designed by Westinghouse. D1G is a naval designation for a reactor plant used on a destroyer/frigate and designed by General Motors.

Most Mare Island students were assigned to the Idaho Westinghouse A1W prototype for the PWC reactor plants used aboard all nuclear-powered submarines and the newly-built nuclear carrier USS Enterprise. PWC stands for pressurized water reactor which is a type of nuclear reactor design. However, I and a couple of other fellow students received orders to report to the New York GE D1G prototype for the PWC newly designed reactor plant to be used aboard the nuclear frigate USS Bainbridge then under construction.

I lived in a small apartment in Saratoga Springs, commuting to the reactor plant. The D1G prototype was new, the entire facility rebuilt from the remains of the GE liquid sodium prototype. Training consisted of learning how the D1G plant operated and demonstrating this knowledge in being able to perform every single operation whether it be mechanical (e.g., starting a pump), electrical (locating an open circuit breaker), electronic (monitoring the height of the control rods) or supervisory (directing the emergency shutdown of the reactor). Satisfactory completion of the training would take six months. But because the facility often was not operating the process for me was almost 10 months. During my time at D1G I became good friends with another officer, Naval Academy grad Hugh Duncan.

A classmate from Nuclear Power school at Mare Island, John Grafton, completed his training at the A1W prototype in Idaho Falls. Thereafter he took submarine basic training and reported for duty aboard the nuclear-powered attack submarine USS Thresher (SSN-593). On April 10, 1963 the Thresher sank while performing deep diving tests after undergoing a shipyard overhaul. All 129 naval and shipyard personnel aboard, including newly arrived Lt(jg) John Grafton lost their lives.

In October 1962, after completing all requirements at the D1G prototype, I received orders to report to an operating ship. I had hoped to be assigned to the USS Bainbridge, then nearing commissioning at Bethlehem Shipyard in Quincy, MA. But I feared that I would be sent to billet with a non-nuclear ship. To my surprise I was directed to report to the USS Enterprise (CVA (N) 65) the first and only nuclear-powered aircraft carrier home ported in Norfolk, VA. CVAN is the naval designation for an attack carrier which is nuclear powered. I was thrilled. The Enterprise had eight Westinghouse PWC reactor plants operating four main engines. I would be putting my nuclear power training to use with the Navy's finest fighting ship powered by the world's latest nuclear power installation.

Reaching the Enterprise turned out to be no simple matter. Why? Thanks to the Cuban Missile Crisis the Enterprise and its air group were directed to leave Norfolk for the Caribbean Sea in support of a possible amphibious landing in Cuba. I was lucky to secure transport from a fleet oiler out of Norfolk to the south. From the tanker I was high-lined to the aircraft carrier USS Essex from which a few days later I was flown to land aboard the Enterprise. Fortunately, President Kennedy and Chairman Khrushchev managed to secure an agreement for the peaceful removal of the missiles in Cuba (and American missiles in Turkey) so that the navy could dissolve the Cuban blockade and the Enterprise could return to Norfolk. This was the beginning of my adventure aboard the USS Enterprise which was to last two years and eight months. My friend from D1G Hugh Duncan was also posted for duty aboard the Enterprise.

As I joined the Enterprise in October 1962 it was the world's largest warship. The ship's company numbered 3,000 men of which 150 were officers. The air group with its 100 aircraft added another 1,800 men including 250 officers (mostly pilots). So deployed for action at sea, the Enterprise was a small city of 4,800 men (including 400 officers).

I was assigned to the Reactor Department, Reactor Mechanical (RM) Division and, very fortunately, shared a stateroom with LCDR Floyd "Hoss" Miller, a senior officer in the Reactor Department.

Hoss was an outstanding officer and a terrific role model for me as a very junior, inexperienced officer. We quickly became friends and remained so long after I had left the Navy. Hoss had an exceptional career in the Navy, later serving as Captain of the nuclear-powered frigate USS California during the Viet Nam War, becoming Real Admiral, leading a battle group in the Pacific, and wrapping up his career in the Navy as head of all recruitment for the Navy.

The Enterprise left Norfolk on February 6, 1963 for a seven-month deployment with the Sixth Fleet in the Mediterranean. Entering the Med and relieving the USS Forrestal (CVA 59) we assumed our duties as leader and flagship for the battle group. Our routine was typically one week at sea followed by one week in port. On this cruise Enterprise made port calls on Cannes, Athens, Palermo, Naples, Corfu, Taranto, Rhodes, Beirut, Genoa, and Barcelona. The Admiral seemed to like Cannes because we made a total of four week-long visits to this lovely city during the deployment.

The old recruiting slogan, "Join the Navy and See the World" certainly applied for me. How fortunate I was to have declined service in a submarine as most of my duty would have been spend below the surface of the sea.

I was appointed Reactor Station Officer for the Number 4 propulsion plant for which I took responsibility for necessary maintenance and repair. Repairs were almost always conducted while the ship was in port. Officers in the Reactor Department enjoyed only limited shore liberty when the Enterprise was in port. While the ship was under way, I worked diligently on leaning everything there was to know about how the four different propulsion plants on the Enterprise worked. Since my prototype operating experience was with the GE-designed D1G reactor plant design I had a lot to learn about the Westinghouse-designed A2W reactor plants on the Enterprise. I finally became certified as Propulsion Plant Officer in May 1963 thus able to assume total watch responsibility of an operating propulsion plant. I felt great. A2W is the naval designation for the reactor plants on the USS Enterprise. There were eight of them on the Enterprise.

During the ship's first visit to Cannes, I happened to meet a nice French girl. I decided to take some shore leave to meet with her when the ship visited Genoa. I took an Italian train from Genoa to Ventimiglia, a town on the border where I would disembark, pass through customs and proceed aboard a French train to Cannes. At that train station I met Karin Hoffmann, a very attractive German girl who, studying French at the University of Nice, was returning to Nice from a visit to her home in Germany. We hit it off right from the start. So I arranged to visit her in Nice. Thereafter she agreed to visit Cannes and join me for dinner aboard the Enterprise.

Photo: Karin Hoffmann with USS Enterprise in background at anchor in bay of Cannes.

This chance encounter at an Italian train station was the beginning of a long relationship, sustained largely through correspondence by letters between Karin and me, ending in our wedding conducted in the Black Forest in September, 1966.

At the end of August the Enterprise was relieved of its duties in the Sixth Fleet by the USS Independence (CV 62) and returned to Norfolk, its home port. For the next five months the priority of the Reactor Department was to conduct major repairs. My role was in directing the removal and replacement of several reactor coolant pumps. Much of the work was conducted by highly skilled personnel from the Newport News shipyard with whom I developed a very friendly and effective working relationship.

My personal performance with coolant pump replacements was excellent and was acknowledged as such by senior Reactor Department officers. As a consequence I and fellow officer Henry Baily were selected to head an important and complex repair operation, to plug a leaking tube in the 2B3 steam generator. The 2B3 was one of 32 steam generators in the Enterprise's four propulsion plants.

Photo: Arne Salvesen on Flight Deck of USS Enterprise with Island in background.

This leak was starting to cause radioactive material to transfer from the primary coolant system to the secondary steam system where it could contaminate the entire propulsion plant. Newport News devised a new procedure to plug the tube while this reactor plant was shut down in port in Norfolk. The procedure, never before conducted in a navy nuclear power plant, was carried out by two crews of navy personnel working 12-hour shifts and directed by Henry and me. Working in an environment with significant danger of radiation exposure and potential release of contaminated material we plugged the tube in two weeks with only allowable radiation exposure to our men and with no material contamination. Later in May, Henry and I were each awarded an official navy commendation for our achievement with the leaking steam generator tube.

On February 8, 1964 the Enterprise embarked from Pier 12 at the Norfolk naval station bound for service again with the Sixth Fleet in the Mediterranean Sea. We operated much as we did the previous year with weeklong visits to Istanbul, Cannes (twice), Naples, Genova, Palermo, Taranto, Barcelona and Palma.

Photo: Commendation Awarded to Arne Salvesen by Commander Smith, Reactor Officer aboard USS Enterprise in Mallorca, Spain.
Source: Official U.S. NAVY Photograph.

I had volunteered to remain with the ship in Norfolk over the Christmas and New Year's holiday so that I could receive shore leave for a week while the Enterprise was in the Med. I wanted to visit Karin, then living at her home in the Black Forest. After this visit with her in Germany, and meeting her parents, I felt our long-distance relationship was becoming ever more meaningful. The Enterprise concluded this Med deployment with an historical cruise together with two other nuclear-powered ships, the USS Long Beach and the USS Bainbridge. Dubbed "Operation Sea Orbit" this first ever, around the world cruise with three nuclear-powered ships started in the Med on July 31, 1964 and ended in Norfolk on October 3, 1964. Along the way port calls were made in Karachi, Sydney and Rio de Janeiro.

Early in this deployment I had been promoted to the status of Engineer Officer of the Watch (EOOW), the ship's top operating engineer qualification. This officer has overall responsibility to the ship's captain for operation of all reactors, propulsion plants, and all auxiliary equipment. It was my luck to be the EOOW the night before Enterprise was scheduled to weigh anchor and depart from the bay of Rio de Janeiro on our way to Norfolk. While moored, the ship's propulsion plants, steam catapults, and most auxiliaries were not operating. Six reactors were shut down. Only two reactors were operating to power two turbine generators to meet the "hotel load." I worked all night to ensure that the 4 Propulsion Plant Watch Officers got eight reactors, four propulsion plants, eight turbine generators and four steam catapults, plus other auxiliary equipment all started. It was with relief and a great sense of accomplishment when at 0800 hours I could turn the watch over to my relieving EOOW and the Reactor Officer with the announcement that the ship's propulsion plant was "Ready to Answer All Bells from the Captain."

At the conclusion of Operation Sea Orbit the Enterprise headed to the massive dry dock at Newport News shipyard for refueling and major overhaul. I continued on board as Reactor Station Officer for Number 4 Propulsion Plant, newly promoted from Lieutenant Junior Grade to full Lieutenant. My job was to act as coordinator between the ship's company and shipyard personnel to complete all work to refuel and overhaul my plans. Then I started work on newly refueled reactors and under the close watch of a Naval Reactors representative performed a detailed operation test for the plant. Here in the shipyard I kept my plant consistently on schedule so that we completed refueling, overhaul and testing. This was completed just as I concluded my Navy active duty obligation in June 1965, four years since it began with my commissioning in Madison, Wisconsin.

I left Enterprise, took a short trip home to Wausau, and then flew off to Germany in order to visit Karin at her home in the Black Forest. That summer we got engaged. I took a few months' vacation with her in Europe and studied the German language at the University of Freiburg, before flying back to the USA in search of a job in engineering.

Job interviews followed before I accepted a project engineering position with Zimpro, a builder of waste treatment plants. Zimpro was based in my home town Wausau, Wisconsin. Six months later Karin and I were married in Germany. We rented an apartment for five months in Wausau before traveling back to Germany to supervise the startup of a new Zimpro waste treatment plant. I was selected as project engineer for this plant because, since meeting Karin, I had learned to speak and understand German. Additionally, Zimpro asked me to represent the company with its sales in Germany and the Netherlands.

On the way to Germany, we stopped in Boston to visit with John and Martha Watts. John was my best friend when we were both First Class Midshipmen aboard the USS Hansen out of San Diego. John was then studying for an MBA at Harvard Business School. During that two-day visit John invited me to accompany him to a class at Harvard for a day. This was a very pleasant experience for me and I started to think about getting an MBA myself.

During the following year in Germany, I discovered that I had much more work satisfaction in my sales assignments than in my engineering tasks. This realization reinforced my interest in obtaining an MBA to help change my profession from engineering to management. While we were still in Germany, I took the graduate business examination and applied for study towards an MBA at Harvard and at Stanford. I was accepted at both. I selected Harvard, gave notice to Zimpro and applied for education assistance under the GI Bill.

Funds from the GI Bill, together with a loan from my father and income earned by Karin working as a biochemistry assistant at Brandeis University, financed my MBA. My shipmate John Watts was kind enough to recommend me to the consulting company Arthur D. Little for employment during the summer between my first and second years at Hirsch Bedner Associates (HBA).

Upon graduation with an MBA in 1970, I was recruited by the CO of Mark Controls Corporation, Gary MacDougal, to be his assistant for corporate development. Gary had also been in the Regular NROTC program and served for three years on a destroyer in the Navy before earning an MBA at Harvard.

I worked for Mark Controls for the next 20 years, mostly in general management positions. The sale of Mark Controls led me to employment over the next six years with a few other large companies including Rockwell International and Heidelberg Druckmaschinen. In 1996, Karin and I purchased our own business, Tronex Technology, Inc. This was a small manufacturer of precision hand tools used in the manufacture of electronics, medical devices and jewelry. The company was located in Northern California. The Company's sales and earnings greatly increased until, after 23 years, we sold the business in 2019 to a much larger company and retired.

The eight years I spent in national service with the US Navy, four years as a Midshipman and four years as a Commissioned Naval Officer on active duty, were exceptionally important and rewarding for me personally. The training and work environment in the nuclear Navy were demanding. They demanded my best performance. Meeting the requirements in this exacting environment gave me the confidence that I could do the same in other challenging work situations.

My wife and I have now been married for 55 years. We met in Ventimiglia, Italy thanks to the US Navy. Without that happenstance meeting while I was serving my country with the Sixth Fleet my life would have turned out completely different.

The men I met during my naval service have had a major influence in the shaping of my character. Many became personal friends and remained so for years following my days of active duty. One of these Navy friends even had a great influence on my career-changing decision to secure an MBA. And this life-altering learning experience was financed for me, in part, by the GI Bill.

Also, the Navy helped to increase my international perspective on life inherited from my Norwegian immigrant parents.

I am proud of my professional achievements serving in the Reactor Department deployed aboard the USS Enterprise and in the Newport News Shipyard for refueling and overhaul. I have served my country well in a role limited to very few exceptionally qualified, and highly trained, young service officers.

On balance I believe that I personally benefitted far more from my service in the Navy than I paid for in terms of years of duty to the Navy and alternate paths of life. I owe a great debt of gratitude to my country and the US Navy for providing me the opportunity to serve in the capacity I did.

Chapter E

LEIF SALVESEN

SELECTIVE SERVICE SYSTEM — REGISTRATION CERTIFICATE (Duplicate)

- First Name: Leif
- Middle Name: Richter
- Last Name: Salvesen
- Selective Service No.: 47 38 40 552
- Date of Birth: 2 Nov. 1940
- Color Eyes: Blue
- Color Hair: Brown
- Height: 5 ft. 8 in.
- Weight: 155
- Other obvious physical characteristics: None
- Was duly registered on the 3rd day of Nov. 1958

Marathon Co. Local Bd. 38
Selective Service System
504-1/2 First Street
Wausau, Wis. 54401

(LOCAL BOARD STAMP)

The law requires you to have this certificate in your personal possession at all times and to surrender it upon entering active duty in the Armed Forces.

The law requires you to notify your local board in writing within 10 days after it occurs, (1) of every change in your address, physical condition and occupational (including student), marital, family, dependency and military status, and (2) of any other fact which might change your classification.

Any person who alters, forges, knowingly destroys, knowingly mutilates or in any manner changes this certificate or who, for the purpose of false identification or representation, as in his possession a certificate of another or who delivers his certificate to another to be used for such purpose, may be fined not to exceed $10,000 or imprisoned for not more than 5 years, or both.

Your Selective Service Number, shown on the reverse side, should appear on all communications with your local board. Sign this form immediately upon receipt.

FOR INFORMATION AND ADVICE, GO TO ANY LOCAL BOARD

It was a cool November day in 1947 and I had just turned seven-years old. It was the first time in my life I felt out-of-touch. What was I to do now, I wondered? To this day I can still picture myself in Crooks' drive-way playing basketball with my neighborhood pals, some of my age, others older and bigger. It was the first time in over six months that I had seen my friends, but it felt so odd. I could understand what they were saying but they couldn't understand me.

My mother, older brother and I had just gotten back from a six-months stay in Norway. In my eagerness to play with Norwegian boys of my age, who of course couldn't speak English (I bet they could today), I had to learn to speak Norwegian, and in so doing, I had forgotten my English. We hadn't intended to stay that long in Norway but passenger ship availability was quite uncertain in those times right after WW II. So here I was speechless with my old friends. Fortunately, it didn't take very long for all my spoken English to return and I was back to being a regular kid once again. (Note: if this country is interested in teaching foreign language skills—this is another example why instruction should begin at an early age.)

Yes, it was but a small piece in the puzzle of one's life that you put together as the years and decades pass. But, it was significant in that it was the first time I felt alone facing a problem on my own. Up to then, I, as most other boys and girls, relied on their mothers and fathers to look out for us. The first "fright" remained with me. The second time I felt such a foreboding was when after finishing graduate school my draft status changed from "student deferment" (2S) to "available, fit for general military service" (1A).

Ah—But Let Me Begin at the Beginning

I was born on November 2, 1940, in Wausau, Wisconsin. I was the second son, my brother, Arne, having been born two and one-half years before me. Our parents were both born in Norway; my father in Bergen, my mother in Oslo. My father, a chemist, was educated at The Norwegian University of Science and Technology in Trondheim. He came to Wausau in 1927 to work in the chemical research laboratory of a paper mill in Rothschild, Wisconsin. On a ship back to visit his family in Norway, he met my mother who had been visiting her relatives in Minnesota and Illinois. She thought she'd seen America for the first and last time. But that was not to be, they married in 1932 and lived the rest of their lives happily in Wausau, with many trips back to Norway visiting family and friends.

Norway was occupied by the Germans from April 9, 1940 until May 8, 1945. I was only four plus years old when WW II ended but my parents told me how strenuous it was for them worrying about both their parents, a brother and two sisters plus other family members. They received mail from them, mail which had been opened and stamped on the outside that it had been read by the Germans. So the letters from and to them in Norway had to be cautiously written so as not to be obviously critical of Germany nor of the German occupation of Norway. Fortunately, all my parents' family members lived through the occupation. I could not imagine growing up without my mother and father. Most everyone feels he/she had the "best parents in the world." I know that I felt that way back then and have thought that way throughout my life. I was fortunate to have a mother and father who loved me, cared for me and were always interested in me, and later, our family's fate. Hardly a day goes by that I don't think about them. I found my wife's parents equally loving and caring. I was/am truly—"Leif the Lucky."

I graduated from Wausau High School in 1959, entered the University of Wisconsin in Madison that fall, and graduated in January 1964 with a BA in Economics. While there I joined Sigma Phi fraternity (where I met Don Zillman). My brother Arne had joined three years prior. I lived in a dormitory my freshman year, in the fraternity house the next three years, and my last semester in a rented house with three others. The Sigma Phi house is no ordinary "frat house," but is quite unique in that it was designed by Louis Sullivan, Frank Lloyd Wright's mentor in 1909 and it's been a fraternity house since 1914. It was designated a National Historic Landmark in 1976.

My father had a six-month obligation to serve in the Norwegian army which he did in the mid-1920s. I had no older relatives in the United States who may or may not have served in the military. Thus, I had no real familiarity or knowledge about the military until I got to the University of Wisconsin. At that time there was an obligation for males to take Army ROTC classes in their first two years at school. It was an introduction, but it didn't leave me with any lasting impression. The classes included military history and strategies, and rifle and hand-gun shooting practice. Either the Army didn't exert any high-level pressure for us to stay on after the mandatory four semesters or they did and it failed to register with me.

There was an event in the spring semester of my sophomore year that I vividly recall. John F. Kennedy had been elected president in November 1960. In an attempt to overthrow Fidel Castro's regime in Cuba, President Kennedy okayed a small group of Cubans who had fled when Castro overthrew the US-supported Batista government. This "Bay of Pigs" episode was an utter failure. In its failure, Castro gained further support in Cuba and with many Central and South American countries.

That summer of 1961 I went to the University of Oslo's International Summer School in Oslo, Norway. It was a great chance to interact with a wide range of young people from all over the world; many from countries that had recently or were currently undergoing internal or external strife. It made me realize that I was slowly but surely moving from being a carefree kid to young adulthood. Going on at about the same time was the Berlin Crisis (June–November). Soviet-controlled East Germany had begun constructing a wall surrounding the City of Berlin in an attempt to stem the tide of East Germans fleeing Communist East Germany for the West. Between 1949 and 1961 more than 2.6 million East Germans, out of a population of 17.6 million had escaped to the West. Fearing this provocative act might lead to armed conflict the Wisconsin National Guard's 32nd Infantry Division (the famed Red Arrow Division) was called up. Some Wisconsin friends that I knew were part of that call-up That makes military service personal and gets your attention. Fortunately, it did not lead to conflict for the 32nd Division, but it put the world and its potential for havoc in a more threatening perspective that could well involve me in the coming years.

Just shortly before graduation from the University of Wisconsin another Sigma Phi brother, Joe Swanson, told me about a graduate school in Glendale, Arizona that I might be interested in. Turned out, I was interested and in February 1964 I began at the American Institute for Foreign Trade (known as Thunderbird School of Global Management and now part of Arizona State University's MBA program). The two months prior to graduating from Thunderbird I signed up for job interviews. I quickly found out that companies were very hesitant to talk with anyone who would have a military obligation upon graduating. I graduated with a Bachelor of Foreign Trade in January 1965. I was single at the time and as far as I knew there was no physical reason that would cause me to be exempted from being drafted.

So, now I'm back to that second time I was faced with a life decision that only I could deal with. My draft status went from 2S to 1A or, in other words, I became subject to the draft. I returned to my parents' home in Wausau. I wasn't there but a few weeks when my new 1A draft card arrived. Within the month, I received notice to report to the Milwaukee YMCA for my draft physical. I and a full busload of potential service inductees arrived in Milwaukee one day, were examined, and returned back to Wausau the next day. I shall never forget that bus ride. All but a handful of us were 18 or 19 years old, recent high school graduates. I was 24. It was a quiet three-hour bus ride. I've often thought back on those young men on that bus, wondering if those that did enter the service and saw duty in Vietnam, returned home safely. Just recently I checked a list of young men who died in Vietnam, listed by city, state, age and years served. It seems there was one young man on the list who could have been on that bus.

I don't recall if I found out there in Milwaukee or soon after that I had passed the physical. I had heard talk about the Coast Guard having a program of six-month active service with a six-year reserve obligation as being a good way to "get around being drafted" by the Army, I did look into it, but it was filled up at the time. I also inquired about the Wisconsin National Guard, but it wasn't taking new applicants either.

There was no other way around it. I found myself facing a military obligation that I had to deal with. I thought I would rather serve as an officer than as an enlisted man and as my older brother had gone through the Navy ROTC program, I thought, I'd see what the Navy had to offer. I took the test to apply to Navy Officer's Candidate School (established in 1951) and passed and was accepted. My dad drove me out to Newport, Rhode Island, and dropped me off on May 15, 1965 on the parade grounds where I was told to fall in and start marching. We took courses in military history, leadership, seamanship, navigation, military law, engineering, naval warfare and damage control. Most of us passed, but there were some who didn't. They were re-assigned to another base and served out their obligation as enlisted sailors.

Photo: Ensign Leif Salvesen in our Navy house on the base of the Naval Oceanographic Facility in Pacific Beach, WA in 1966.

After four months of schooling, I was deemed an officer and a gentleman, and in Navy terms, a freshly minted Ensign in September 1965. About half-way through we were asked to list our preferences for duty assignment. I had listed three different ship types: (LSD (Landing ship dock), destroyers and cruisers). The Navy, in its wisdom, instead assigned me to shore duty. After two weeks of communications school in Newport and six weeks of oceanographic schooling in Key West, Florida, I flew to my duty station at the Naval Oceanographic Facility in Pacific Beach, Washington. I served there for a 17-month stay and then was transferred to a similar Oceanographic Facility in Pt. Sur, California and served another seventeen months and my 40-month active duty requirement was completed.

My Time at Naval Oceanographic Facilities

Five months after I was commissioned, on February 12, 1966, I married the woman of my dreams, Nora Deeley. We had met at a beer supper at my fraternity in October 1960 and we had dated on and off ever since.

Let me now describe exactly what sort of duty I had at those two Naval Oceanographic Facilities.

The Oceanographic Naval Facilities in Pacific Beach, Washington and Point Sur, California were small, about 120 enlisted men and 12 officers and were in scarcely populated communities along the Pacific Ocean. Pacific Beach, Washington is 28 miles northwest of Aberdeen. I was warmly welcomed by Ensign Paul Hundt, who was assigned to be my 'sponsor' as he too, was from Wisconsin. Paul and I became life-long friends, he had a very successful financial consulting business and was the driving force in building a Catholic School in Milwaukee. Sadly Paul died December 30, 2021. His son, Peter, told me his Navy experience had a strong influence on his father's life.

Point Sur is 22 miles south of Carmel, California. There were also Naval Facilities along the Pacific Coast in Adak, Alaska, Coos Bay, Oregon, and Centerville and St. Nicolas Island, California.

I look back on my stay in the Navy with affection, satisfaction and appreciation. I mainly served as a watch officer with ever-rotating six-hour shifts. At Point Sur I also served as the Administration and Personnel Officer as well as Welfare and Recreation Officer. I enjoyed working with the officers and men (very few women in the Navy then). Many of the younger men had never been out of their hometowns until they entered the service. Also many, me included, had very little contract with men of different races. So for most of us it served as a real eye-opener. Prior to the Navy, while I had been to Norway five times, I hadn't seen much of the United States beyond Wisconsin.

However, those trips to Norway did make me aware of the different attitudes, customs, viewpoints and traditions that people carry with them.

Now, let me tell you a little about what the mission was of those thirty Oceanographic Naval Facilities that were scattered up and down the east and west coast of the United States.

The Sound Surveillance System (SOSUS) was a passive sonar system developed by the United States Navy to track Soviet submarines. The cover story on the shore stations, identified only as a Naval Facility (NAVFAC), was that it was doing oceanographic research. Those of us who worked in tracking Soviet subs needed to have a top-secret clearance. The first facilities were built in 1958, all were decommissioned by 1991.

This was during a period when the Cold War was hot with rhetoric and bluster. The Naval Facilities mission was to track Soviet submarines. We had to assume the submarines carried nuclear weapons which could be directed at the United States. This was at a time the weapons had far less range than they do now. So submarines near our coasts potentially presented a real danger to the country.

The NAVFAC watch floor had banks of displays using electrostatic paper. These were examined by the personnel trained (sonar men) to identify submarine signature. Submarines, ours and the Soviets, had their own identifiable signatures, their own DNA if you will. The diesel engines gave off a much more distinctive signature and were easier to detect than did their nuclear subs. The ocean can be a busy place, so the watch officer and the sonar men had to uncover any Soviet sub's signature and then track it against the many, many commercial ships out there. When two or more arrays held a target the bearings from each array gave an estimated target position by triangulation. The system could provide information on the presence of the submarine and an approximate location for air or surface antisubmarine warfare assets to localize the target.

In February 1968, at Naval Facilities West Coast Headquarters in Treasure Island in San Francisco, I was awarded "Expert Oceanographic Analyst" by the Commander Oceanographic System Pacific for exhibiting the highest standards of professional performance and achievement.

At the end of the Cold War, the Navy decided to allow this system to be used by scientists with suitable security clearances, in what was called "dual use." SOSUS is now used to study hydrothermal vents and pinpoint underwater volcanic eruptions. The system is also used to study to vocalizations of whales.

What with Russia's invasion of Ukraine on February 24, 2022, I can only hope the United States has in place a system that can identify foreign submarines near our shores even more accurately than we were able to do at the Naval Oceanographic Facilities 50-years ago.

Some Thoughts on My Active Duty Life in the Navy

We particularly enjoyed our last seventeen months at the Naval Facility at Point Sur, California. The fact was it was in one of the most beautiful parts of this or any country had a lot to do with it. I also met a fellow officer, Bob Dude, who would be a life-long friend (also an Expert Oceanographic Analyst). Sadly, he died in August 2020. But the main reason for our love of Point Sur was that on early Sunday morning, August 27, 1967, our daughter Britt, was born in our 1960 Ford Falcon on US Highway One between Big Sur and Carmel, two weeks early. As best we could figure, she arrived just north of the Bixby Bridge.

As I mentioned, I enjoyed my stay in the Navy to the degree that I looked into extending my tour of duty. I had been commissioned as a line officer, as are future officers at OCS and line officers usually find themselves at sea. Considering I had been shore-based for my first three years, I knew I would spend a substantial part of the next 10 years, or so, at sea. That being the case, I looked into applying for Supply School because there officers spend most of their time shore based. They weren't taking any applications from line officers at the time, so, somewhat regretfully, I said goodbye to my active duty service in the Navy in September 1968.

What were the positives of my brief military service? We all learn how to give and take orders in life. Most times, it's more of the latter than the former. But in the service and as an officer or as a high-rated enlisted person you get more of an opportunity to have a balance of giving and taking of orders. Military service generally offers these leadership and followership opportunities at a much earlier age than one would in civilian life. I feel the friends made while on active duty in the military can be more meaningful and longer-lasting than those made while in one's early days on the "outside." I guess there are a lot of reasons for that affection for one another in the military; you're generally all working away from home, you're all working in uniform, you're all from "all over" in this country making it likely for people to reach out to meet and greet one another. Then there's the fact that most are serving when they're young, carefree, full of life so they have all those reasons to stay connected to their pals, so later in life they can talk about their adventures (and mis-adventures) when they were young looking and young at heart.

Had I not signed on with the Navy OCS program what would I have done? Fleeing the country for Canada was not ever considered. I'm sure I would have been drafted; the choice then being whether to be drafted into the Army for a shorter stint or sign-on for a longer stint with the Navy as an enlisted man. Those being the alternatives, I'm glad I went to Navy OCS.

I was under the impression that my being an officer in the military would have afforded me a leg-up on applying for a job on the "outside." I didn't really feel my experience in the military was positively evaluated back then—I'm not sure if it was the ill-feeling many had about the Vietnam War or not. I am not really sure it is any different today except for those who plan a career in politics, so when they get out (as quickly as they can) they can then brag about putting their life on the line for their country. For enlisted men and women, I fear it's maybe worse, with companies fearing they might be taking on a potential or real PTSD employee. Back in the late 1940s, African Americans were more fully integrated in military life than they were in civilian life. I wish I could say the same for women in the military. The number of women in the military have increased many fold since my days, but, sadly, they still are faced with ever-increasing incidents of sexual harassment.

My Life after Active Duty

After my discharge, I first worked as a pharmaceutical detail man (read salesman) for Eli Lilly & Co. for two-and-one-half years in Kansas City, MissourI. I thought that might lead to employment in Lilly's international marketing division. It didn't and I didn't like the drug business or calling on doctors so I sought employment elsewhere. While in Kansas City, I served two years in the Navy reserves, achieving the rank of lieutenant. I was a gunnery officer. We met one evening a month and I took two two-week cruises to the West Coast. The weekly meetings were loosely run and little concrete training was accomplished. I met and established a number of good friends, but I'm glad my gunnery knowledge was never severely tested. With the draft being discontinued in 1973, those who signed up for the National Guard have as good a chance of serving in an overseas war (Afghanistan and Iraq) as those on active duty. Now that to me, doesn't seem rational or smart.

The definitive highlight of our Kansas City time was the arrival of our son, Stenn, on September 17, 1969, in a hospital.

Back in the job hunt I got lucky fairly quickly. It seemed Wrangler Jeans (VFC Corp) was looking to fill a sales position in their Chicago Merchandise Mart location. I got on well with the sales manager and was hired. As far as I can recall I was asked little about my military experience. We four picked up stakes and moved to Wheeling, Illinois. After a brief nine-month stay there, by chance a sales opening occurred in Wisconsin. We lived for four years in Greendale and eight years in Port Washington while I traveled around the state. In 1984 an opportunity arose in Texas and I was asked if I was interested. I said I was but wanted to ask my wife first. Upon hearing about it she stated, "when do we leave?" I worked and thrived for the Red Kap Division of VFC from 1984 until I retired in 2004, after 33 years with the company.

Nora enjoyed working at the University of Texas–Dallas Library for 13 years before she retired in 2000.

In retirement, we've enjoyed life, our children, other family members and friends. We've traveled to many parts of this country and the world, taken classes at the local community college, and recently on-line visit art museums, gone to plays, operas, exercised, read and stayed in touch with those we love and like and stay up-to-date with current events.

Some Reflections

A good deal of the above did not have to do with military service. But it serves as a background to who I am and what I think. There's a world of difference between how military service was looked at 60 years ago and how it's looked at today. Today the military can't be praised long and loudly enough. As an institution it has the highest approval level of any organization in or out of government. Why? Could it be that the Pentagon manages their ever-increasing budget so well? No, not really. To quote Fareed Zakaria in his Washington Post column of March 18, 2021:

"The Pentagon operates in a realm apart from any other government agency. It spends money on a scale that it almost unimaginable—and the waste is, too. Every government agency is required to audit its accounts, but for decades, the Pentagon simply flouted this law. In 2018, it finally obeyed, paying $400 million for 1,200 auditors to examines its books, yet it still could not get a clean bill of health. As writer Matt Taibbi noted in a brilliant 2019 expose of Pentagon accounting, the auditors 'were unable to pass the Pentagon or flunk it. They could only offer no opinion, explaining the military's empire of hundreds of acronymic accounting silos was too illogical to penetrate.' The Defense Department has failed to pass two more audits since then."

Why is it that the military is so poorly organized that no one can get a handle on how to fix it, yet it has such high public approval? Also, why is it that today when we see men and women in uniform we're encouraged to thank them for their service? I've long felt it was to help assuage the general public's guilt for not having served themselves. Deep down most people feel everyone has an obligation to serve and protect the country they live in. For all sorts of reasons they choose not to, thus giving the military a pass on how they're run and fawning over the men and women in uniform telling them how wonderful it is they serve makes non-veterans somehow feel they are doing their part.

I think America should institute a national service obligation for all men and women between 18 and 26 years to serve in the military or some other national service program. What better way to bring Americans together than to serve together. Recent statistics show that 91 percent of whites hang out with other whites, 83 percent of blacks with other blacks and 63 percent of Latinos with other Latinos (PBS NewsHour February 25, 2021), so this country still has difficulty assimilating. Serving together at an early age would provide a different structure which would tend to lead to a more blended society.

I asked myself if I were to magically move back in time and found myself finishing graduate school but without having to face a military draft, what would I have done. Would I have enlisted or sought out Officer Candidate School? I think the answer would have been—NO. I would have taken the easy way out and dodged serving our country.

But would that have been the wise decision—I think not. Many times in life you have to make difficult decisions, the easy ones are not always the right ones. I'm glad I served and I would wager the vast majority of veterans who have served feel the same way. By reinstating the draft, along with offering national service programs, you multiply that number of glad and proud Americans.

When talking about anything that's "hard to do," one has only to look to President John F. Kennedy's speech given at Rice University in Houston, Texas on September 12, 1962 about going to the moon. Could anyone then have imagined anything harder to do than going to the moon? But, on July 20, 1969 this country accomplished the impossible by landing on the moon and ahead of schedule.

"We choose to go to the Moon....We choose to go the Moon in this decade and do the other things, not because they are easy, but because they are hard; because that goal will serve to organize and measure the best of our energies and skills, because that challenge is one that we are willing to accept, one we are unwilling to postpone, and one we intend to win, and the others, too."

Let Me Conclude with the Following

Wayne Terwilliger died on February 3, 2021, in Fort Worth, Texas. He was 95 years old. He played for nine years in the major leagues, including years with Jackie Robinson and those famous Brooklyn Dodger teams in the early 1950s. He went on to manage and coach in the minor and major leagues for another 53 years. All of his accomplishments in the national pastime came after he served in the Marines in the Pacific theatre in WW II, including at Iwo Jima and he said that "nothing in his sixty two years in baseball was more important than two years in the military."

Rest in Peace, Twig.
    And I rest my case.
    Very respectfully
    Leif R. Salvesen

Chapter F

PAUL STRIEBY

Photo: The photo of the C-130 is from the National Vigilance Park at Fort Meade, Maryland and is a tribute to the C-130 that was shot down over the Soviet Armenia in 1958. It is in remembrance of the lives lost in the incident. The names of the backend crew members were on a plaque that hung over the door of our mission briefing room at our unit at Rhein-Main Air Base, Germany. As our crews departed for a mission, the plaque was a constant reminder that our mission was serious and potentially deadly.

Photo: Picture of the RC-135 RIVET JOINT aircraft is a stock photo from the web that shows the type of aircraft I flew on for many of the later years of my career. It is a major Reconnaissance and Intelligence collector, and a much modified airframe. The one in the picture is one I actually flew on multiple missions.

My family had little military background, although there is a remote genealogy link to George Armstrong Custer. My Dad was in a war-essential business during WW II. Dad's education was in Organic Chemistry, and he was pretty much self-taught in Statistics and Quality Control. He told me that at one time during the War his Quality Control expertise was on-call for some war industries. One instance he talked about was visiting ammunition plants, to help institute methods to improve the consistency of production and to detecting faulty ammunition, so it wouldn't be delivered to the military. In his off time, he assisted the local NRA rifle club's mission to make sure that every WW II draftee from the area was rifle trained before they departed to military training.

Growing up in Appleton, Wisconsin, I led a much-sheltered life. Appleton was one of those towns with unwritten laws against outsiders, particularly black and brown folks. Even when the Globetrotters played in town, they were not welcome to stay there overnight. I am happy to report that things have finally changed today. When the Green Bay Packers have a home game, the visiting team stays at a hotel in downtown Appleton.

When I arrived at the University of Wisconsin and joined our fraternity, I was on the bad-boy list with the fraternity cook, Flo, a very sharp-tongued black woman. If I remember correctly when I was first introduced to her, she ran me out of her kitchen with the words, "Get that white boy from Selma out of my kitchen." I think that some of my most important learning came from my relationship with Flo. We worked together daily when I was the house manager and we grew to trust each other.

My oldest brother, did a three-year tour in the US Navy as a bandsman, serving on the Admiral's band on the USS Missouri before it was taken out of service.

How did it happen that I went into the military? Simple answer is that I changed major in college, dropping out for half a semester to keep from failing my Applied Math and Engineering Physics program. Before I could enroll in the next semester in a new major (Psychology), I received a classification update form from my local draft board as I had just turned 21 years. The draft board did not reinstate my 2A (student) deferment. I was enrolled in a summer session when I got my draft notice. Phone contact with the draft board said I was safe through summer session, but would be called in the fall, so not to enroll.

I had no in-person contact with my Draft Board as I had no relationship with any of the board members and I was in Madison, the board in Appleton. All my communication with the board was via mail or phone.

I had gotten married the September before and married folks were exempted from the draft, but President Johnson changed the rule the week before we got married so that only married folks with children were draft exempt. That change put me back as draft eligible, so there was lots of evening activity in hopes that my then wife, June, would quickly become pregnant. It took longer than we figured.

I left the University of Wisconsin without graduating, due to my shift of major, lack of application to study and self-distraction. Along the way I had several not fun interviews with the Dean of Men (Don Zillman's father), and was asked not to come back for a while.

Not wanting to go into the Army, I signed up in a delayed enlistment program in the Air Force. My recruiter told me to ignore the draft notice I had received. I was sworn in the Air Force Reserve in November and reported for Boot Camp the following February. Coincidentally, June got pregnant as best we could tell the evening I returned from swearing into the AF Reserve with a commitment for follow-on active duty.

Boot Camp at Lackland Air Force Base in 1966, near San Antonio, Texas was a struggle in some ways. I was not in the best of physical condition, but soon I was keeping up with the middle of the pack in all the physical aspects, and excelling in academics. I underwent lots of testing to find out just what the Air Force thought I was qualified to do for them. Several of the tests had me scoring well about the average recruit, and I was interviewed to be a Chapel Assistant in the Chaplains Office. I was also tested on the ability to learn languages. Having taken Spanish in high school and German at University of Wisconsin, taking the Defense Language Aptitude Test (adopted from the Modern Language Aptitude Test) wasn't really difficult. Having enlisted in the "General Field," I was immediately selected for the Language Field. Meeting the needs of the Air Force, I was sent to the Army Language School in Monterey, California to learn Albanian. Yes, I had to get an Atlas to see just what and where Albania is. (Answer; on the east side of the Adriatic Sea across Italy on the west side.) No bigger than New Jersey, Albanian has a fairly unique language with a complex grammar, second only to Latin according to our instructors. After a 47-week course all seven of us in the class graduated with level-3 proficiency in reading, writing and aural comprehension.

Our first daughter was born at nearly Fort Ord (now long closed) during the time we were there. I was numbed when I was presented with the hospital bill when we took our daughter home. It was all of $3.15…$1.05/day for rations for my wife in the hospital. Fortunately, I had $25 in my pocket which is what my Air Force recruiter had told me a military hospital would charge for a birth.

Those of you who have studied a foreign language in high school or even college have no idea of what happens at the Defense Language School. It is no picnic, 6-hours/day in the classroom with roughly six or seven students per class with rotating native instructors. Then at night, one has to learn by heart the next day's lessons. Rinse, repeat for 47 weeks. It is hard, and lots of students wash out, but a graduate can have close to native language understanding. It is simply intense. However, I will add that if one doesn't use the language for a long time, it fades. I can still understand some of my various languages, but I could not read a newspaper, or ask for directions in any of them now. However, it can come back to haunt you even after you retire from active duty. In the early days of the Balkan conflict in what was Yugoslavia, I was working as a defense contractor, and got a phone call from my former Operations Officer from Mildenhall air base. He told me he was about to recommend calling me back to active duty because of my expertise in Albanian. At that time, I had passed over 30 years from my initial enlistment date and I pointed out to the good major that if he wanted to recall me past my 30-year time-line, he would be required to obtain the President's signature. I said if they really needed me, I would be more than happy to serve and to draw up a contract to use me as a civilian contractor. Never heard back from him…

Further technical training in the classified specifics of becoming a cryptologic linguist followed at Goodfellow AFB in Texas. Also, in connection with the requirements for my flying assignments to come, I attended altitude chamber training and AF aircrew survival schools. I was assigned to Rhein-Main Air Base in Germany where I stayed for five years with frequent flights to and from Athens, Greece over those years. Operating radios and tape recorders in-flight, one of my jobs on the plane was to serve as the analyst taking inputs from all the operators on board and reporting via secure communication any timely information to various ground sites along our flight route. Needless to say, I am still under oath not to say much about a lot of my career.

While on this assignment, another daughter was welcomed into our family. This necessitated a move to an unfurnished apartment and money that we didn't have was needed to buy furniture. That meant that I decided to take advantage of a re-enlistment bonus, so we could make that move. So, at this point I was at least considering a 20-year minimum career in the service. Not much later, I was selected for promotion to E-5 (Staff Sergeant).

In 1973, when the Air Force no longer had a need for airborne Albanian linguists, I got orders to attend the East Coast branch of the Army Language School, Anacostia Naval Annex, in Washington, D.C. to learn Vietnamese.

In 1974, after Vietnamese Language School on the way to my next assignment, I attended Jungle Survivor School in the Philippines and then on to a remote base in Thailand (Nakhon Phanom Royal Thai Air Force Base) where I served as a senior analyst during the latter part of the Vietnam War. I was not flying on this tour but worked with many flying units supporting them with intelligence. During the time I there, my unit provided support to the US evacuation from Phnom Penh, Laos, the evacuation of Saigon (where we produced hot and timely intelligence that went directly to President Ford) and the recovery of the crew of the USS Mayaguez.

In 1975, I flew back to the States, picked up my family in Wisconsin and drove across the US to California to catch a flight across the Pacific to Okinawa. I was once again back on flying status and flew long (18 hours) RC-135 (RIVET JOINT) missions in the Gulf of Tonkin again as the mission analyst and communicator. I had not been there long when the national interest was drawing away from the Vietnam conflict and the word came out that the missions would cease. After a six-week period of wondering what would happen to all my fellow Vietnamese linguists, a decision was made that we would still fly, but at a reduced number of missions per month. Daughter number three was born in the US Navy Hospital in Okinawa. I was promoted to Technical Sergeant (E-6) and continued to function as a shift commander when I wasn't flying. When the 30-months ended, it was time for a new assignment.

In 1978, once again, I got lucky and was sent to the Army Language School (now known as the Defense Language Institute) in Monterey, CA, this time to learn Czechoslovakian. Forty-seven weeks later I was on my way to Hahn Air Base in Germany. I served as shift commander and had a crew of approximately 15 to take care of. During that short tour, I was promoted to Master Sergeant (E-7) and hit that level of my career to be sent to the NCO Academy at Kapaun Air Station in Germany. After graduating from the Academy, I was asked to accept an assignment as an instructor there. Three years later I was selected to Senior Master Sergeant (E-8) and asked to become the Commandant of an NCO Leadership School at RAF Upwood, England. Both of these assignments brought me training in classroom instruction and curriculum development. I enjoyed teaching and helping my students get through the courses. I also attended the US Air Force Senior NCO Academy at Gunter AFS in Alabama during this time.

At the end of this tour, there were few options for my next assignment. I had my choice of going to Fort Benning as an Air Force liaison with the Army, or I could attend advanced Vietnamese Language training. I chose neither and went in 1985 to my first assignment in the United States as superintendent of the Cryptological Language Technical Training School at Goodfellow Air Force Base, San Angelo, TX. While there, we were attempting to modernize our military language training. We wanted to move to computerized training and had to harness lots of technology to transition from the methods I had been through in the 1960s to a much more modern methodology that we struggled with my entire time there.

I was selected for promotion to Chief Master Sergeant (E-9) and reassigned in 1988 to RAF Mildenhall, England as the Superintendent of Operations of a RC-135 RIVET JOINT flying unit. Best assignment of my career, even thought it was during some really challenging times in the first Gulf War with needing to manage some 350 flying operators being at home and away in the desert. My unit was perhaps in the middle of the supply channel to our operators in the desert. Many people and supplies came in to RAF Mildenhall and we would arrange to get them onto tanker aircraft that were constantly shuttling to and from Saudi Arabia. I would often be tasked to buy items locally and get them to our folks in the desert. What you need to know is that in normal peacetime, RAF Mildenhall was locked down between 2100 and 0600 hours, and if we were to land after 2100 hours the local member of Parliament would receive a multitude of calls from local residents complaining about the noise. Post Desert Storm, I was at a social function when the local member of Parliament walked up to me and we chatted for a while. I told him it must have been real hell for him with the airfield in function 24/7. He replied that all our neighbors understood what was going on and he received absolutely no calls about the noise. Our unit was on a 24-hour duty, and our commander designated that I would work the 1700–0600 hours shift as acting commander.

RAF Mildenhall was an extremely busy place with planes (mainly tanker aircraft) going to and from Saudi Arabia. One night I needed to get a small pallet of special equipment to our folks in the desert and knew which tanker was going to be accepting the pallet. Fifteen minutes before that plane was due to land, I called Base Operations and asked which parking spot on the ramp it would be in. The answer; "it will be in the empty slot, but I won't know what spot will be empty in 15 minutes, call me back when it lands and I might know then."

My unit's budget (which I managed) went from normal to the highest in my command. Many of my personnel were constantly rotating in and out of the theatre. They were flying many more flight hours than the Air Force permits in peacetime. There were constant waivers to process, endless family separations for my folks and helping the families of the deployed folks however we could. We made certain that every separated family had a contact in the unit to go to when help was needed. The result of that was we burned out the majority of the Arab linguists in the Air Force and their families. Many left the Air Force when they could. In the middle of all this, our unit in Athens needed to close and all those assigned there assimilated into our squadron in England. I had to go to Athens, close down the operation, move what equipment we needed, get rid of all the furniture and fixtures and turn the building over to the Greek Air Force after ensuring there was absolutely no classified information left behind. End of an era, as I was one of the people who would fly back and forth from Germany to what was then our detachment in Athens in its early years.

Returning to the States in 1991, my last assignment was at Fort Meade, Maryland, as project/program manager for several national Joint Chiefs of Staff level programs. I retired from active duty in 1993 after 26 years of service.

If I had to say what the biggest value I gained from my service was, it would be the experience in being an effective leader. The fact that for almost all of my career I had a fairly high-level security clearance made the transition to civilian life wide-open. The clearance was almost an instant ticket to finding a job in fields where I could make continuing contributions to national security.

I continued using what I had learned on active duty as a contractor, doing what I loved best in my Air Force career, doing Intelligence analysis. I was involved in lots of interesting stuff including helping develop an advanced concept program demonstrating that it was possible to control drone aircraft via Satellite communications. Oh, where that has affected things, I can only imagine. I spent several years working at NSA improving the flow of intelligence to the warfighters. In 2000, my final career move took me to Dayton, Ohio, where I worked in sensitive analysis at the US Air Force National Air and Space Intelligence Agency, right up to age 72.

Thinking back, if the draft hadn't impacted my decision to enter the Air Force, I would probably not have done military service as I had already interviewed and been offered a position as a personnel manager for Kimberley Clark in Upper Michigan. However, the draft basically forced my choice. I would have missed many of the experiences that made me who I am now.

Part way through my military career, I put all my military education together with some college computer courses I took along the way with my UW credits and applied to the University of the State of New York Regents program and was awarded a BS degree (with some 215 credits). Finally.

I really think that a reinstatement of the military draft or a national service commitment could help what I see as a lack of backbone in many of our youth these days. The relationships we had with citizens of the countries we lived in opened our eyes to their circumstances and helped form our world sense. Note that while I served in Thailand, our military involvement was drawing down and my units were not awarded time towards the Vietnam Service Medal. Likewise, during the Gulf War, I only flew over Saudi Arabia one time and landed in-country. I was not present during the actual hostilities.

My military service was driven by a number of factors. However, my three daughters grew up in a life that included lots of relocations, losing and then making new friends. All three have grown up to be what I consider great citizens with a healthy appreciation for other countries. Only rarely have we seen anti-American sentiments and we had great relationships with the neighbors we had in local villages and towns.

Overall, Military Service meant much in my life. The relationships with fellow airmen of all races, creeds and beliefs certainly was a major part of what I learned….and am comfortable with.

Chapter G

JOHN TEWHEY

Over two million troops served the Union in the Civil War, five million US troops were in uniform during World War I, over sixteen million served during WW II, six million during the Korean conflict and over nine million during the Vietnam era. I was never in a foxhole. I never looked down the barrel of a gun in wartime. I was never the target of a wartime bayonet, bullet, or bomb. But I gave four years (five percent) of my life to serve my country during my formative years and I am proud to be among the more than 40 million men and women who have served and have the honor of being a US Military veteran.

I don't wear an American flag pin. I don't belong to the American Legion or the Veterans of Foreign Wars. I have never attended a military reunion. I seldom attend a Memorial Day or Veteran's Day parade or observance. But I am inwardly proud to have served. It is a personal and private sense of pride. Sixty years after being discharged, I retain an organized file of military awards, ribbons, documents, photos and souvenirs from my Air Force years, realizing that they are of value to no one but me and may eventually be tossed when my memorabilia and possessions are sorted one day.

My wife and two oldest daughters sacrificed during my military service by my frequent absences in Europe, South America and the Vietnam war zone while I served as a geodetic survey officer and while I served a 13-month tour in Korea as a fuels management officer. I am proud to have served, but I also benefitted greatly for having served. I was 10 years into my civilian career when I assumed as much management responsibility, liability and risk potential as I was given as a young Air Force lieutenant and captain in my mid-twenties. A substantial reward for having served honorably for four years was the opportunity to utilize a generous GI Bill of Rights support to pursue three years of post-graduate education at Brown University in Providence, Rhode Island. That led to my attaining a PhD in my chosen field of geochemistry. The advance degree allowed me to have a rewarding career as a science researcher and the owner of a successful science-based business. Thank you, Uncle Sam.

If I had not been an ROTC (Reserve Officers Training Corps) participant or had not been subjected to the Vietnam era draft, that is, if I had not served in the military, I would have likely still pursued post-graduate education through the doctorate level. But it would have been a long, tough slog without GI Bill support. Instead of completing the PhD curriculum at Brown in three years, it would have likely taken five or six years due to the necessity to combined work and study to support my family.

If I had not served in the military, the young scientist who showed up for work at the University of California Lawrence Livermore Laboratory in 1974 would have been somewhat of a highly educated bumpkin. I grew up in a small town in central Maine and went to a Maine college 70 miles from home. Prior to being commissioned a 2nd Lieutenant in the Air Force, I'd never been in an airplane, never been in a job that involved management of personnel, never traveled far from Maine and never had been live-tested in a way that exposed my strengths and weaknesses.

Being in the Air Force stretched me mentally, physically and emotionally from the day I reported for duty at F.E. Warren Air Base in Wyoming. At Warren, I travelled the world with a small squad of men and established precise and secure monitoring stations for geodetic satellites that relied on nanosecond timing coordination among sites. When something went awry, and it frequently did, it was my responsibility to fix the problem with the help of my team. When I was put in charge of aircraft fuel storage and distribution at McGuire, then Kunsan, then Homestead Air Bases without any prior training or experience, it was my responsibility that the fuel was always contained in storage tanks and trucks and that the utmost safe practices were maintained.

At each site, I made great effort to assure that I knew the troops and staff, that they knew me, and we both knew how to manage and operate the storage and distribution systems. In the course of my four years of service, I learned about myself and the vast array of peoples of all ranks, skills and backgrounds that I worked with. I learned and progressed by being curious and proactive and, as a result, I experienced tremendous personal growth and confidence that have served me well. Post service, as a new scientist at Lawrence Livermore Laboratory in 1974, I became a group leader within two years of arrival, and a major project leader within four years. After joining the Maine-based E.C. Jordan Engineering firm in 1981, I became a group leader upon arrival and was a division leader responsible for 70 people within four years. I doubt that would have been possible without my Air Force experience. Upon leaving the Jordan firm in 1987, I built an environmental consulting firm that endured for nearly 30 years. I retired at age 71 in 2014.

With this lifetime background, let me offer a study of my upbringing and my military career. When I was growing up in Lewiston, Maine, I lived near my maternal grandparents and visited them often. My grandmother, Clara Legendre Tewhey, kept a photo of her and her three sons on the dining room buffet. The photo was taken on her back lawn in the Spring of 1946 and her sons are in a military uniform. The three had recently been discharged from military service in WW II and, by chance, they had arrived home on the same day. A proud and thankful mother kept that photo on her buffet her whole life, and it has been passed on to me.

My father, William Tewhey, served in the Navy on USS LST 515 (Landing Ship Tank) in the Europe–Africa–Middle East Theatre and his ship was active on the beaches of Normandy in June 1944. My Uncle John was a Marine and served in the Pacific Theatre, Uncle Richard was in the Army and served in Europe. From a very early age, I appreciated the significance of the homecoming photo. My dad and uncles were good citizens, family men, athletes and lived close by. They were good role models for me and my brothers. And out of respect for a wonderful woman, I have a daughter and a granddaughter named after my grandmother, Clara.

I grew up during the Korean War, the Cold War and when I entered Colby College in the Fall of 1961, the Vietnam War was escalating. One reason that I chose to attend a small, liberal arts college in Waterville, Maine was the presence of a long-standing US Air Force ROTC unit on the campus.

There were many advantages to joining ROTC. I was motivated to eventually serve in the military, preferably the Air Force; I could eliminate concerns of the pending draft call; military history courses in my junior and senior years; and I received a modest monthly stipend when, at the end of my sophomore year, I committed to receive an Air Force commission upon graduation. In a busy college schedule that included a work–study program as part of a Colby scholarship, a double chemistry-geology major, and a four-year participation in varsity football, ROTC was not a significant burden.

I was selected to be a member of the honorary Arnold Air Society in my senior year and I emerged with a favorable rating from the mandatory month-long Officer Training Corps at Dow Air Force base in Maine in the summer before my senior year. During that session, I closely observed the half-dozen cadets in my flight who came from military schools and measured myself against their actions and progress.

I was commissioned as a 2nd Lieutenant in the US Air Force during Colby graduation week in the Spring of 1965. I was also married during that week to Gloria Nolin of Lewiston, Maine. I applied for and received a two-year deferment from active duty to attend graduate school in the field of geochemistry at the University of South Carolina in Columbia, South Carolina. At the completion of my MS in geochemistry in the summer of 1967, the Vietnam War called and I was denied a further education deferment to pursue a PhD in geochemistry. I received orders to report for duty in September 1967 to the 1381 Geodetic Survey Squadron at Francis W. Warren Air Base in Cheyenne, Wyoming.

I didn't realize it going in, but the four years spent as a junior Air Force officer were about to offer me an extended period of growth experiences that would strongly influence the direction of my post-service life. In the following bullet points, I will briefly describe the ever-changing opportunities and challenges offered to me in my duty assignments.

My First Air Force Assignment

The 1381 Geodetic Survey Squadron was responsible for setting up regional survey grids based on satellite/star imagery that relied on nano-second time synchronization among widely separated stations. The purpose of the survey grids was to assure aim and target accuracy of ICBMs located in silos throughout the western United states.

Once set up, I had the responsibility to "hitchhike" across the globe on military aircraft carrying a 150-pound atomic clock to synchronize system timing. I spent sufficient temporary duty in Southeast Asia to be awarded the Vietnam Service Medal in 1968. Remembered challenges included: (1) While in northern England on a timing assignment, having to rush the clock to the Royal Greenwich Observatory near London to get it resynched when the batteries prematurely failed, (2) As a newbie 2nd Lieutenant being asked by the Squadron Commander in Wyoming to "hitchhike" on military aircraft to Tan Son Nhut air base in Vietnam to set up and facilitate a meeting of the Squadron Commander and in-country interested parties the following week.

I learned much during my time at Warren AFB—the work week was never 40 hours, not 50, nor 60 hours. While traveling and setting up stations, I listened, learned and realized that I had the overall responsibility of the tasks at hand, but not the know-how. I worked to gain the respect of the people I worked with by being interested and supportive, while working hard to think, plan and provide a well-coordinated travel and work environment.

My Second Air Force Assignment

After spending 18 months in Wyoming, the Air Force experienced a shortage of Fuel Supply Officers and I received unexpected orders to report to McGuire Air Base in New Jersey to assume the role of Fuel Supply Officer and oversee a 70-person fuel storage and aircraft refueling operation. Why me? The Air Force's thinking was geologist=earth=source of petroleum=a match. McGuire was a Military Airlift Command (MAC) facility occupied principally by large transport aircraft.

My initial assignment at Warren AB involved technical management. The assignment at McGuire involved people and logistics management with a huge component of safety in fuel storage and handling. I overlapped with the outgoing fuels officer for a few months and spent copious amounts of time getting to know the storage and dispensing systems, the airmen workers, and especially, the senior NCOs. There was no way that I was going to be able to learn all the ins-and-outs of fuels management, so I concentrated on getting to know the 70 men in my charge and the safe handling of fuel.

There are two types of fuel on an air base, aviation fuel for prop planes and jet fuel, and never should they meet. When they do, there is usually a plane crash. There were no plane crashes on my watch at McGuire. Chief Master Sergeant Leone, a 30-year veteran in fuels management was my teacher and guide during my year on the base. I met with him each and every morning and conferred with him many times during the day. It was clear why he was an E-9, a smart and straight-forward truth teller who taught me more than any Fuels Management class could have possibly delivered. What I learned in my year at McGuire prepared me for my next assignment.

My Third Air Force Assignment

In the Fall of 1969, I received orders to be the Fuels Management Officer at Kunsan Air Base, Korea. I started my 13-month assignment at Kunsan AB on December 17, 1969 and departed for home on January 17, 1971. I spent two cold, white Christmases in Korea. There was a buildup of Air Force resources in Korea in the late 1960s in response to the aftermath of the USS Pueblo capture and crises of January 1968. An F-4 Fighter Squadron was stationed at Kunsan AG and I was responsible for 35 airmen and NCOs who operated and supported the fuel storage and distribution systems.

Every day that I was at Kunsan AB, I quietly thanked CMSgt Leone of McGuire for his year of patient monitoring of a novice and untrained Fuels Officer. Something I noticed in examining records of the fuel management personnel at McGuire and at Kunsan was that the annual written evaluation forms of the enlisted men, especially in the lower ranks, were bland, rote and not descriptive of the obvious differences in the job performance of individuals. I made it a point to get to know the people I was responsible for, especially in Kunsan where people were away from home and vulnerable to off-base temptations. I interviewed each person in my unit several times during my 13-month tour and practiced management by walking around. In doing so, I was able to provide specific examples of performance in the many evaluations that I wrote. I tried to clearly differentiate among the mediocre, the good and the great.

During my tour at Kunsan, I had the unenviable and frightening experience of overseeing the cleanup of a 30,000-gallon spill of aviation fuel. Korean contractors were doing repairs of a storage tank and a weld burst resulted in the spill of fuel into a diked area surrounding the tank. Storage bladders were brought out of storage and the fuel was pumped from the dike into the bladders, but not before the fuel leaked through the dikes onto surrounding farm land. The farmers began trying to recover fuel for their personal use and my job became one of isolating the spill from our curious neighbors and assuring the safety of the recovery operations. Fifty hours after the spill occurrence, the site was cleaned up, all reports had been filed, and I returned to my quarters. Whew! I received the Air Force Commendation Medal for my job performance at Kunsan AB and I was promoted to Captain while in Korea.

My Fourth Air Force Assignment

While at Kunsan in December, 1970, I received orders to become the Fuels Management Officer at Homestead AFB in south Florida. There had been a crisis at the base due to a recent air crash in the Everglades of an Air Force prop plane that had been refueled with JP-4 (jet fuel). Upon arrival I was asked to administer a thorough evaluation of the fuel storage and distribution systems to assure compliance with Air Force requirements. The assignment was advantageous to me because I had a mandate to explore, question, discuss, meet and report on all aspects of the fuel management operation.

The system was actually in pretty good shape. In the middle of the night, a hapless airman had force-fit a JP-4 refueling muzzle onto a prop plane fill tank and held it in place while the tank filled. Thankfully, there were no major injuries in the crash, although several EMT responders received snake bites during the rescue operations.

An interesting result of my reporting of the inspection and my nomination of several fuels personnel for awards was that the Fighter Wing Commander asked me to be his ghost writer for awards and recognitions. That led to discussions of my plans subsequent to the conclusion of my four-year tour of duty. To make a long story short, I was urged to become a career Air Force officer and was offered the opportunity to be an instructor in the Chemistry/Geology department at the Air Force Academy in Colorado Springs, Colorado, coupled with the opportunity to pursue a PhD in the field of Geochemistry. At the time of those discussions, I had already applied for and been accepted into the PhD program at Brown University in Rhode Island, supported by a fellowship and the all-important GI Bill. I chose the latter route. I received the Air Force Commendation Medal for my job performance at Homestead Air Force Base.

I emerged from four years of active duty in the US Air Force a better and smarter man than the young man who walked in the door as a 2nd Lieutenant four years earlier.

Life has been very good to me. I was married to a wonderful woman for 53 years and we raised three daughters who have made their way in life and have given us six healthy, energetic and curious grandchildren. My Air Force experience was shared with my wife from beginning to end and it was enriching for both of us in every way. The photo of my father and his two brothers returning alive and well from WW II was a simple and effective motivator to serve my country and that, in turn, served me well.

It has been clear to me since my service days and thereafter, that Army, Navy and Air Force ROTC units at small and large colleges have been of great benefit to the participants and to the military. I strongly believe that the services benefit from a healthy mix of officers from service academies and ROTC units. While on active duty, I observed that the matriculants of the service academy stood a little straighter, adhered to tradition and comprised a justifiably proud cadre who are more prone to become career officers. The officers coming out of ROTC units tended to be more Colombo-like in character and polish. They hadn't been well-versed in military tradition and tended to be left-leaning, which fostered a more open dialogue with the NCOs and troops. My relationships with the NCOs in my charge were somewhat casual and always productive and positive. I learned from them, and I never detected a hint of disrespect from any of them. All of the ROTC cadets who chose a military career from my era at liberal arts Colby College attained the rank of Colonel (O-6), and one attained the grade of Major General (O-8). The sample is small, but it reflects their value to the services.

There have been great changes in the attitude and participation in military service in the 50 years that have passed since my military service. I know few people who are currently serving in the military and I have detected little interest in serving among millennials or Gen Zs. There are few ROTC units in Maine colleges at present, and there are no units at the three prestigious liberal arts colleges (Bates, Bowdoin and Colby) that hosted ROTCs in the 1960s. The military is diminished by their absence. My sense is that the bulk of the young people entering the military today intend to be career service persons. That trend likely represents a cost-efficiency for the DOD.

None of my three daughters ever showed interest in participating in the military. I have little say or sway in the life pathways chosen by my grandchildren, but if a grandson or granddaughter expressed interest in joining the military, I would share with him or her my highly favorable opinion of military service. I support the concept of public service opportunities for young men and women, whether it be military, Peace Corps work, teaching in underserved systems or focused internships. I am aware of an American–Israeli family in my neighborhood who have sent their 20-year old son back to Israel to spend two years in the Israeli Army. I admire that gesture and know that the young man will benefit from that experience. My support is derived strictly from my positive personal experience. There have been no internal or external negative aspects of my military experience, before, during or after my term of service.

Chapter H

DONALD ZILLMAN

I start with family memories that date back to the Civil War. Three generations of Beneckes and Zillmans had seen some form of military service before I needed to address my own military service in 1966–69. In 1861, Louis Benecke was a recent immigrant from Germany to Missouri when the Civil War began. Louis joined the Union Army and fought the Battle of Shiloh, was captured by Confederate forces, released after six months and continued service for the Union cause. That background set the stage for a lifetime of law practice and government leadership in his home town of Brunswick, Missouri.

His daughter Luci married Christian Zillman. Christian had attended the United States Naval Academy at Annapolis for two years but then withdrawn for further civilian education leading to a law degree and a career in law practice in Chicago. Christian was too old for the WW I draft. Our WW I family veteran was my grandmother's second husband, William Mack. Uncle Bill served in General John J. Pershing's American Expeditionary Force.

Christian and Luci's oldest son, Theodore (after Teddy Roosevelt) was born in 1905. He was 12-years old when America entered WW I. He was certainly old enough to appreciate the American involvement in the War and the fact thar he might someday face military service. Before then, however, he had graduated from the University of Wisconsin, joined the family law practice, suffered through the Great Depression and in 1936 married my mother, Helen.

On Pearl Harbor Day, December 7, 1941, Dad was 36 and Mom was 28. Congress had reinstated the draft in Fall 1940 after the German blitzkrieg had conquered France in little more than a month. Young American males who had survived the Great Depression now faced participation in war against two of the world's major military powers.

Dad's age left him out of the first draft calls and discouraged him from immediately volunteering. Within two years, however, it was clear that the draft would need to reach men in their late 30s or older. Dad was inducted into the United States Army and underwent basic training with boys and young men half a generation younger than he was at Fort Benning, Georgia. Dad's athletic skills saw him through basic training. He then opted for Officer Candidate School. Various assignments around the United States followed. Helen was able to join him at some, but not all, of these duty stations.

Ted's prior experiences then kicked in. The University of Wisconsin needed an "over age for grade" lieutenant to assist with the multiple connections between the campus and the military. Ted's credentials fit the bill and he and Helen were shortly headed for Madison. They would stay there for the rest of their lives.

One of the items on their "to do" list was children. In August 1943, they decided to start a family, a decision for which I have been ever grateful. That month found America heavily engaged on both Atlantic and Pacific fronts in WW II. The Allies had achieved their first major success in North Africa some months earlier. They would shortly invade Italy. In the Pacific, a bloody slog to capture Guadalcanal had continued a year of progress in the war against Japan. Winston Churchill had spoken of such successes as being "if not the beginning of the end, at least the end of the beginning." However, a military junior officer, even one with Ted's comfortable Madison berth, could hardly have predicted the next years of his life.

My birthday in May 1944 brought a letter of congratulation to Ted and Helen from a colleague at an earlier military post. Three weeks later, that officer would die on D-Day in Normandy. The loss of much blood and treasure would continue, but within my first year of life Churchill's prediction moved from the "beginning of the end" to the end as Hitler committed suicide in his Berlin bunker and Germany surrendered. In August 1945, two atomic bombs obliterated Hiroshima and Nagasaki and brought an end to the war with Japan.

The Zillmans' life stabilized in Madison. Ted was discharged from active duty. He continued his work at the University in a civilian position helping the University to adjust to that remarkable federal law, the Serviceman's Readjustment Act of 1944, better known as the GI Bill of Rights. A major piece of the statute was federal financial support for discharged servicemen and women who wanted to attend college.

One crucial issue facing the Congress was whether the only veterans eligible for GI Bill financial aid were those who had their college programs interrupted by entry into the service. Supporters of that position, with its obvious budgetary implications, argued that a veteran who had no expectation of ever attending college before entry into the military should not be eligible for the GI Bill. They were backed by the testimony of prestigious college presidents who argued those soldiers would be hopelessly unqualified for college. Congress disagreed and the GI Bill was offered to both the soldier–student eager to get back to college and those whose wartime aspirations were to survive the War and get back to their prior job on the farm or the factory. American higher education changed forever.

One small indicator of the change was the end of the long-standing campus traditions of sophomores hazing, often violently, incoming freshmen. The sudden, massive arrival of GI Bill freshmen on hundreds of campuses changed the dynamic. Sophomores who were too young or had otherwise avoided military service attempted to lord it over mature GI Bill freshmen who had stormed the D-Day beaches or flown bomber raids over Tokyo. The results were predictable.

Dad threw himself into the work of his alma mater and eventually advanced to the post of Dean of Men, the senior student affairs officer on campus. Helen gave birth to son Richard in May 1946, set up a home near campus, and threw herself into campus activities. Ted continued as a reserve officer in the Army and returned to uniformed service for a few weeks each summer at Camp McCoy, 50 miles from Madison.

That was our major contact with Dad's military service. Like most of his generation, he rarely shared "war stories" with his sons. Likewise, he did not join the American Legion or other veterans' organizations. We never asked why, but we suspected he had ample veteran friends in the University and Madison communities and that his spare time was limited. It was clear that he admired those who had served and that he had ample chances to reminisce with fellow veterans when he wanted.

Dad also didn't hunt or target shoot. Gardening and fishing were his outdoor activities. He had inherited father Christian's primitive summer camp in northern Wisconsin, five hours north of Madison. The camp was a wonderful experience for his young boys with fishing, swimming and other outdoor enjoyment only steps from the camp's front door. Helen was a good sport but did bear the burden of a camp that lacked electricity, where water was drawn from a pump and heat and cooking fuel were drawn from the ample wood that we would harvest on the property.

One of Dad's clear ties to the military was his passion for the American Civil War, likely prompted by the Benecke family experiences. Ted's organizational skills helped to create a Civil War Round Table in Madison as the centennial of the War approached. This men's dinner club could draw on the professional talents of the University's prestigious History Department and other experts on the "late unpleasantness." I was thrilled to attend a few of the meetings in my mid-teens. Dick and I were even more thrilled when dad (and sometimes mom) packed up the car and began touring Civil War battlefields from Virginia to Tennessee. That passion for American history has lasted a lifetime.

My elementary schooling took place at Shorewood Hills School, less than half a mile from home. This was the 1950s and post-War America at its idyllic best. Dwight Eisenhower was the low-key, but quietly successful President who led and typified the era of "America on top of the world." In an era of military tensions, Eisenhower was the ideal President and commander-in-chief. As one congressman remarked: "Who am I to tell Ike Eisenhower what a commander-in-chief is supposed to do?" Eisenhower helped to settle the Korean War and then refused to push America into war in southeast Asia to help preserve French colonial rule. He handled the Cold War with the Soviet Union in a fashion that prevented a Hot War from breaking out between the prominent two nations possessing nuclear weapons.

My exposure to military matters during this time was limited. School did provide occasional "preparation for nuclear war" with class exercises that directed students to "duck and cover" under their desks in case nuclear war took place. Our excellent principal treated these as routine matters rather than an opportunity to terrorize the students. We took her quiet suggestions that these exercises were futile in case of real nuclear war, but that real war was unlikely and should not define our lives.

The Cold War with Russia did come closer to home in my eighth-grade year with the Soviet launch of Sputnik which placed a man in space. There was a genuine fear that Soviet science, with its military implications, had moved ahead of American science. President Eisenhower encouraged Americans not to overrate the Soviet achievement, but he did encourage a race into space with the Russians.

Dad and mom encouraged Dick and me to try a number of activities. One involved the use of guns. I had several hunting trips for small game with Dad and friends. I don't recall any successful shooting on my part but I understood the attraction for others. The Shorewood Hills Police Hall basement offered a shooting range. My success with targets was no better than with birds and small animals. The same could be said about two years of piano lessons and Little League baseball. I moved on to other activities.

I attended high school at Wisconsin High School, sponsored by the University of Wisconsin's Department of Education to aid in training aspiring teachers. The school's close connection to the "Wisconsin Idea" vigorously encouraged the pursuit of truth and a delight in learning. At the high school level this translated to a faculty who valued free and open discussion, respect for student ideas, and strong encouragement of higher education. While it supported athletics and social activities, these did not define student success as they did at other schools.

Wisconsin High also recognized women as excellent scholars and class leaders and expected men to understand that. Sadly, racial diversity was minimal as it was in Madison as a whole. Our class of about 65 students had only one African American student. She was both a fine student and a student leader.

The four years at Wisconsin High provided a wonderful education during a period in which Cold War tensions increased. In May 1960, an American U-2 spy plane was shot down on an espionage mission over the Soviet Union. In August 1961, the Soviet Union built the Berlin Wall to separate west from east Berlin and increase military tensions. Young and dynamic John F. Kennedy, a well-publicized WW II naval combat hero, followed Dwight Eisenhower as President. Kennedy's inaugural speech in January, 1961 challenged young Americans: "Ask not what your country can do for you. Ask what you can do for your country?"

An inspiring part of the Kennedy program was the Peace Corps. It provided young (and not so young) Americans with opportunities to advance social and economic development in disadvantaged parts of the world and to make a "free world" statement against Soviet communism. Less publicized and glamorized was the fact that the military draft would continue and that peacetime military service might quickly turn to combat service. I registered with the Selective Service System in May 1962 shortly before graduation when I turned 18.

My high school academic record had been good, but not top of my class. Two classmates and close friends with stronger academic records than mine applied to Yale and were admitted. I wasn't. I was delighted for my friends and not badly distressed for myself. My family could not easily afford the elite school tuition, room and board. I also had a world-class public university two miles from home.

I enrolled at Wisconsin for $118 per semester tuition. I was able to pay that for two years from an Elks Club scholarship and my school year earnings from work in a campus cafeteria and the University printing office. Mom and Dad were happy to provide room and board.

My first two years at the University of Wisconsin were shaped by two features of the campus that gave me some of the benefits of a small liberal arts college experience. The first was the Integrated Liberal Studies (ILS) program. ILS provided an introduction to the humanities, social sciences, and natural sciences with a group of 150 classmates and a faculty of experienced and inspirational professors in those disciplines. As in high school, I thrived in history, political science and literature. I tried to hold my own in the hard sciences. My classmates were bright and energetic.

Beyond the classroom, I joined the Sigma Phi Society, a small and atypical social fraternity. Fraternities and sororities in the early 1960s were a major part of campus life. The film Animal House captured some of the realities of fraternity life at the University of Wisconsin in 1962. However, Sigma Phi was atypical in delightful ways. Most notably, we were housed a mile off campus in a house designed by world-famous architect Louis Sullivan as a private residence.

While social life was a part of the Sigma Phi attraction, most fraternity brothers were also serious students. One sign of this came from the campus sponsorship of a competition modelled on the nationally televised College Bowl program. Sigma Phi put together a team and somewhat to our surprise won the competition. The Sigma Phi House also became my first experience of living away from home.

The Cold War continued to warm during my first two years of college. Fall 1962 was marked by the Cuban Missile Crisis. The Soviet Union attempted to station missiles ninety miles from Florida in Communist Cuba. President Kennedy, who 18 months earlier had been embarrassed by a covert and failed attempt to overthrow the Cuban government of Communist leader Fidel Castro, was challenged by the Soviet Union's attempt to weaponize Cuba. President Kennedy placed a naval blockade around Cuba. Russian Premier Nikita Khrushchev and President Kennedy both recognized the danger of a nuclear war and delicately crafted a peaceful solution. Khrushchev stopped the missile installation. Kennedy secretly agreed to remove American missiles placed in nations bordering the Soviet Union and ceased further action to overthrow the Castro government. For 10 days in September, however, world peace had hung in the balance.

All young men at the University were enrolled in a one credit course to introduce them to the military and the ROTC. ROTC units at campuses around the country were one of the significant sources for new military officers who were not trained at one of the service academies or advanced to officer standing from the enlisted ranks.

I went slightly beyond the required introductory course by signing up for the Air Force ROTC program. I had taken my first airplane flights a year earlier and was attracted to a possible Air Force commission. As I recall, we met for an hour a week and had only classroom exercises. We were not in uniform and made no commitment to post-graduation service. The significant discovery in the program came in taking the physical examination. The exam revealed that my eyesight would disqualify me from a pilot's commission. After one semester, I left the program.

I finished my first year with a B average. I spent summer at work to build up my cash reserves. I resumed my second year of ILS and other classes little knowing how November 22, 1963 would mark all our lives. On that day, President Kennedy was assassinated in Dallas and Texan Lyndon Johnson took over the Presidency.

While JFK was President national security challenges had added Southeast Asia to the list of American military concerns. North Vietnam and domestic Communist forces (the Viet Cong) in South Vietnam challenged the South Vietnamese government and its modest military support from the United States. At the University of Wisconsin and other campuses some faculty and students began to question the American commitment. Protests and informal seminars added foreign policy to questions of African-American civil rights.

The summer of 1964 allowed the wonderful experience of a low-budget tour of Europe with two fraternity brothers and a friend from high school days. We flew to Paris and took the train to Wolfsburg, Germany. There we picked up a new Volkswagen at the factory and for two and one-half months explored Germany, Denmark, Sweden, Norway, the Low Countries, France, Italy and Austria camping at night and absorbing art, culture, food and drink. The trip shaped my career plans and hugely widened my perspective on the world.

One memorable day in August brought news about North Vietnamese attacks on American warships in the Gulf of Tonkin off Vietnam. The four of us had vigorous discussions of the rightness or wrongness of American policy and its possible implications for our futures.

We returned to the United States in mid-September to follow President Johnson's landslide victory over conservative Arizona Senator Barry Goldwater and his advocacy of an aggressive American policy against Communism anywhere in the world. While a few friends and classmates supported Goldwater, most backed Johnson's cautious support of the non-communist cause in South Vietnam and his emphasis on a Great Society at home that centered on improving the life of disadvantaged Americans and the provision of equal rights for African-American citizens.

My ILS learning and the European experience prompted me to double major in history and English. My grades improved and a good friend and PhD student urged me to consider graduate school and a possible career in university teaching.

Spring of 1965 provided the delightful co-curricular experience of my undergraduate years. The University was invited to compete in the nationally televised General Electric College Bowl. Students were informed that the regular campus College Bowl competition would provide a major part of the tryouts to select the television team. The Sigma Phis entered their team and were joined by 60 other teams. We have several winning early rounds but then were eliminated in a close match. Nonetheless, two of us were selected for the ten final prospects for the Wisconsin squad. A further interview with the team coach and a general knowledge test completed the selection process.

A few days later, I was informed that I had been selected as one of the four team members, but my Sigma Phi teammate had not.

The four of us (and our splendid alternate) then had a month to practice before our New York City appearance. We made no effort to study subjects we didn't know. Our focus was on practice rounds against good campus teams, some of whom doubtless felt that they should have been selected instead of some or all of us. Fortunately, we won the considerable majority of those practice matches. We also benefitted in the introduction to television provided by our Coach Professor Jerry McNeely who had substantial television experience. Jerry's major guidance was "relax and enjoy the experience."

What followed were five delightful weekends in New York City with all expenses paid by NBC and General Electric. This normally involved a Saturday morning flight (or flights) to New York City, a fancy dinner and a Broadway show or Metropolitan Opera performance on Saturday night and a Sunday of introduction to performing on live television before the televised College Bowl game that ran from mid-morning to the live broadcast at 5:30 p.m. Typically, the practice rounds (using questions from prior shows) gave us a good sense of our competition. Our first televised match found us starting slowly and trailing slightly at half-time. Then we dominated the second half and won the match. In three other matches, we started well and finished well. The competitive highlight was our third match in which our excellent opponent had lost a prior match on an error and was invited back for a second chance. They were smart, had prepared extensively and were eager to show that their four women could beat our four men. Their performance in the practice rounds showed that this was quite possible. The final round, with all new questions, was our round and we won a marvelous match with a combined score that was one of the highest in the dozen year history of the televised College Bowl.

Besides the fun of competition and the trips to New York City, the University was rewarded with $10,500 in scholarship dollars. We were also honored at numerous events celebrating our role as undefeated retired champions including a lunch with Wisconsin's Governor. We also became visible around campus and the state in a year in which the University's major sports teams were having poor seasons.

The year 1965 saw military matters take over the political agenda at the University as American involvement in Vietnam expanded markedly. Young, healthy male college students began to consider a future that might demand military service either before or after graduation. Deferments from the draft for students pursuing college degrees were generally granted, but little was certain. I recall one effort by the Selective Service System to require candidates for educational deferments to take a general intelligence test to prove their fitness for college work. That filled the campus sports complex one Saturday with young men eager to show they met the qualifications. It gave all of us a further opportunity to reflect on our post-graduation future.

Those months also increased campus opposition to the War and the draft. I remember that the College Bowl team was solicited for a public expression of support for the War. We explained that there was no "team position on the War." Our team captain was an Army ROTC senior commander. Another team member was an outspoken opponent of the War. The other three, myself included, were mixed in our views. Some campus leaders expressed unhappiness that the team was not solidly pro-War. Those divisions, however, were very predictive of what the next half dozen years would look like.

In retrospect, my greatest benefit from the College Bowl experience was an invitation from Journalism Professor Clay Schoenfeld to help him with a book he was writing on the role of summer sessions on American campuses. In addition to his journalism teaching, Clay was also Director of Summer Sessions on the Madison campus and a popular newspaper columnist on Wisconsin hunting, fishing and other outdoor activities. In his undergraduate days prior to WW II Clay had been a visible student leader and a strong objector to American participation in another World War. The country and the world had changed in 1941 and by 1943 Clay was a combat veteran on the Italian front.

The decision to say "yes" to the job offer was an easy one. It tripled my blue-collar salary. The research and writing experience on The American University in Summer was a marvelous one as I learned from a master of the crafts.

The work, however, was only the second-best memory of my senior year. A casual blind date arranged by mutual friends introduced me to Linda, a Chicago area junior, very bright and enchanted by the visual arts. After my European summer spent exploring thousand-year-old cities and their art landmarks, we had a lot in common. The blind date moved to a steady relationship within several months of the Fall semester.

That both clarified and complicated my post-graduation planning. One of my teaching assistants urged me to consider doing graduate work in history. My overall grade point average probably doomed an application at one elite school but did earn me admission and an attractive financial aid package at a less prestigious, but upcoming campus. My back-up was always the University of Wisconsin History Department, with its longstanding reputation for excellence. That combined with the opportunity to spend Linda's final undergraduate year in Madison seemed a very attractive option.

Fate intervened. Wisconsin informed me that while I would probably be admitted to the program, my application papers had somehow gone missing when selections for scholarships were being considered. Corrections couldn't be made and I would need to work my way up from second rank status among new graduate students. That had limited appeal and I began exploring officer commissions and postponing further schooling until after, and if, I survived military service.

As those discussions were going forward in the Spring of 1966, I stopped by the Wisconsin Law School and was lucky enough to connect with Professor of Law and Academic Dean Gordon Baldwin. I was given a wonderful introduction to the benefits of a legal education. Gordon was a military veteran and I think he understood my uneasy thoughts on American participation in Vietnam. Modest financial aid was offered and with Linda's support I said goodbye to a university teaching career. A fourth generation of lawyers in the Zillman family loomed. My draft board seemed quite comfortable with my continuing studies for three years in Law School, probably thinking that I might be quite attractive to the military upon my graduation from the Law School in 1969.

Law School proved an academic delight. Some excellent teachers and some fine classmates made for stimulating classes and a good group with which to discuss the large public issues of the Vietnam War and civil rights eras. Wisconsin Law was a pioneer in its emphasis on "law in action" tracing back to Wisconsin's role as a birthplace of the Progressive movement. Law in action considered both the law drawn from judicial decisions and the academic analysis of legal thinking and also from what were the impacts of the real world on law and the impacts of law on the real world.

The first-year experience in Law School and Linda's companionship provided a counter balance to the awful years of 1967 and 1968 as America became ever more entangled in Vietnam and the American people ever more divided over the issue.

A further energizing experience came with the summer after my first year. I was fortunate enough to get an offer to work with one of Madison's elite law firms (which in those days consisted of a dozen lawyers). They gave me a wide variety of experiences in the use of law and provided just the right balance of mentoring and letting the new kid blunder his way through the law and its human aspects. The latter could be as important learning as the precise language of statutes or Supreme Court cases. I recall one case in which a potential defendant-debtor was ignoring his creditor's request for payment of a clearly overdue bill. The frustrated creditor had finally handed the matter over to our firm who bounced it to me. I did a quick study of the cost of litigating the matter. I then explained to the debtor that the cost of the lawsuit (which he was almost certain to lose) would be far more than paying the bill. In a few days, the check was in our client's hands.

A further delight of the Summer of 1967 was the arrival of my first-year grades. My law school record made me eligible for membership on the Wisconsin Law Review. Law Reviews were the reward for excellence in American law schools and a fact well-known to employers of young legal talent.

The Law Review was hard work for the honors earned. Second and third year members of Law Reviews were expected to publish most of the top scholarly journals in the legal profession. Second year students were expected to write a publishable piece of legal research and to help with the methodical process of checking every statement in an article against the judicial decision, statute, regulation or scholarly article that supported the author's statements. Oh, in addition, the Review students were also expected to take and pass the regular classes that advanced them to graduation in three years.

In the Spring of our second year, our class prepared for its turn at leadership of the Review. Half a dozen of the 15 members of our class would take on the responsibility of soliciting and evaluating articles submitted for Law Review publication. The authors ranged from young academics to world famous scholars of law and the social sciences to distinguished legal practitioners and members of government. More often than we expected articles from excellent authors needed considerable work before they were ready for publication. We attempted to be delicate in our dealings with authors. But our thorough citation process enabled us to say: "Sorry that not is what the Supreme Court said" or "I think we know what you want to say, but it isn't communicated to the reader who lacks your expertise. Could we try this?"

The further part of our work was with our second-year student authors. Our third-year Note and Comment editors worked closely with the authors as they researched and wrote their work for publication. A fascinating part of this experience involved a classmate's very capable, and very new, study of environmental pollution and its treatment as a legal problem. A considerable debate arose: "Is this law?" The editors decided it was, the author was later recognized as the Review's outstanding writer. Within half a dozen years environmental law was as hot a legal subject as anyone could want.

Five members of our class sought election as the Editor-in-Chief of Volume 1969. All presented strong credentials from their Law School work. I was fortunate enough to win the election. Quite probably, I had Clay Schoenfeld to thank as the American University in Summer was in print with Donald Zillman as the junior author.

Even before the Law Review election, Law Review membership had made me an attractive candidate for employment with major national law firms. I started job hunting with interviews with firm members visiting the Law School and then accepted invitations to visit the firm all expenses paid. It was a marvelous time to be an academically strong law student.

The Law Review election committed the senior editors to spend their summer at the Law School preparing the next issues of the Review. That was the start of production of 1,265 pages in four issues of the Review. I recall only limited sadness in having to withdraw from the 1968 summer job market. The job market for 1969 looked every bit as strong and our resumes would be enhanced with our Law Review leadership positions.

Beyond Madison, the year 1968 was a memorable one. In January, the Tet Offensive in South Vietnam by the Viet Cong and North Vietnamese forces resulted in American battlefield victories but left the sense that long-term success in the War looked doubtful. American popular support for the War waned. In March, President Lyndon Johnson announced he would not seek re-election and would dedicate full efforts to ending the War. In April, civil rights leader Martin Luther King, Jr. was murdered in Memphis. Over the next two months, Senator Robert Kennedy, younger brother of the murdered President, appeared to be advancing to the Democratic nomination for President on a platform questioning the wisdom of the War. Then in June, just after winning the influential California primary election, the younger Kennedy was murdered. Nationwide protests suggested the American nation was falling apart.

During 1968 and 1969, Linda finished her bachelor's degree and took a professional position in the University's Institutional Studies Office. With support from our parents, drawing on their own Depression and wartime experiences about "life always being uncertain" we decided to get married. On June 8, 1968, just days after the second Kennedy assassination, we were married by Linda's minister brother and prepared to face what life might bring.

My last year of Law School was a fascinating combination of leadership of the Law Review, completion of my classwork for a JD degree, scouting for jobs and assessing my military future. The Editor's job was a fine combination of writing and editing, and exercising leadership over capable colleagues many of whom were wrestling with their own military, personal and professional futures.

Job hunting continued the second-year interviewing process. Linda and I had both decided we wanted to expand our experiences beyond Madison. With some regrets, we informed our Madison summer of 1967 employers that our immediate professional future would be outside Wisconsin. The Law School Placement Office again offered first contact with prestigious national law firms. Trips to interview in New York City, Chicago, San Francisco, Los Angeles and Phoenix provided an eye-opening look at legal practice around America and resulted in half a dozen offers to affiliate as an associate.

On the advice of several of my professors I also explored the prospect of a one-year judicial clerkship in the federal court system. The clerkships provided a marvelous post-graduate education in helping distinguished federal judges with their work. One of my professors connected me with The Honorable James Marshall Carter on the United States Court of Appeals for the Ninth Circuit based in San Diego. The Circuit served California and much of the western United States.

Linda and I visited Judge Carter on one of our trips west to interview law firms. The Judge impressed me immediately. He was a life-long Californian who had advanced from federal prosecutor to trial judge to judge on the 9th Circuit Court of Appeals. The Judge was an imposing figure as befit his credential as a college football lineman. He said he had heard good things about me from my faculty mentors. But, would Linda and I be interested in a legal career in California? Our visit in the middle of Wisconsin winter made that an easy "Yes."

A tougher question was what did I think about the Vietnam War, anti-War protests, and "new left" politics in general? I answered honestly that while I wasn't a protester, I did have serious reservations about the wisdom of the War. I was ready for this to disqualify me. But either my candor or the judge's own views did not stop him from making me an offer to serve as one of his two clerks for the 1969–70 term. The Judge did ask about my military status but he suggested that a year's deferment from the Selective Service was possible. The Judge also confirmed that law firms that made me offers would be quite likely to renew their interest in a candidate with a court of appeals clerkship added to his resume. I accepted the Judge's offer and Linda and I began to imagine our lives 2,000 miles from our home towns.

The next item on our agenda was military obligations. With the assistance of parents and academic mentors like Clay Schoenfeld and Gordon Baldwin we started sorting out options. In this I joined thousands of my contemporaries at this unsettled time in American history.

The least appealing option was immediate enlistment at the lowest rank and pay for two years in one branch of service, probably the Army. Even before Judge Carter's offer to clerk that had little appeal as a matter of career disruption, physical hardship or risk, separation from Linda and voluntary commitment to a cause that I doubted.

The next option was to wait for my Madison draft board to induct me and to continue with my career until they did, if ever. That raised some of the same concerns as voluntary enlistment. However, my good mentors reported that my law degree would probably keep me desk-bound in a legal office rather than in combat in Vietnam.

The last option was to use the Selective Service laws and regulations to craft exemptions from induction that would last as long as needed to avoid any military service. Variant one was the physical or mental disqualification.

Some disqualifications were obvious and would not be questioned. Examples would be blindness, loss of a limb, or an ongoing struggle against a potentially fatal disease. Others were not so obvious. President Donald Trump's alleged "bone spurs" will probably be regarded as the stereotype of the "game the System" physical exemption. Closer to home I recall a fraternity brother who carefully checked the standards for an "overweight for height" disqualification. He spent three months gorging on pasta dishes to gain the exemption. These exemptions often required a degree of collaboration with health care providers quite aware of the draftee's objectives and willing, and sometimes eager, to help with the draft evasion.

The second exemptions were for particular educational or employment opportunities. Numerous draft evaders changed their peacetime career plans to take a job or enroll in an educational program primarily to gain an exemption or deferment. Once the prospect of induction had ended, the need for the educational or employment ended with it.

The third exemption was for conscientious objectors to either some or all military service. The statutory exemption that was originally intended for small numbers of members of traditional "peace churches" expanded considerably in the last days of the Vietnam War.

Shortly after my Law School graduation in June 1969, the Madison Selective Service Board reclassified me in category 1-A, available for induction. I appealed that classification noting my year's employment with Judge Carter. The Judge had written the Board requesting a deferment for one year noting the "tremendous burden of work [on the Court] and the assistance of law clerks is absolutely necessary to get the work out." It would be "extremely difficult, if not impossible to secure another law clerk." The Judge further expressed his views that "Zillman will make a far better law clerk than a soldier" and hoped that a deferment until the end of the clerkship was possible.

During this time I completed an application for a place in the Navy's Officer Candidate School (OCS). My discussion with the Navy indicated that if I were selected, my law degree would probably have me assigned to legal work for the Navy. They promised an answer by December 1969. In early Fall I took my draft physical examination in Los Angeles. A day with the medical personnel confirmed my belief that I had no physical deficiencies that would prevent drafted military service.

The Madison Board was unpersuaded by the request for postponement of induction. The Members of the Board felt "that you may be replaced in the position of law clerk and that completing your service obligations would be more in the national interest." Judge Carter was not one to take "no" for an answer. In October, he wrote a two-page letter to Lt. Gen. Lewis Hershey, the national director of Selective Service. He reported that the Ninth Circuit was "far behind in its work" and that it would "be impossible to replace Zillman with another clerk" before February, 1970 at the earliest. Zillman's induction "would seriously interfere with the work of our court."

As we neared the half-way point of my service with Judge Carter my military plans continued to evolve. The Madison Board agreed to defer my induction until mid-winter. In early December the Navy notified me that I was not recommended for selection to the OCS program. They did not detail a reason for the denial but did note that the Navy OCS program "is extremely selective. Currently selectivity is at an all-time high. This results from the fact that unprecedented numbers of college graduates are presently applying for Navy OCS."

In the course of my discussions with the Madison Draft Board I received a notice that my file had been "damaged by vandalism at the local board office." I was asked to resubmit any medical statements that I wished the Board to consider. I had none, but the letter reminded me of the toxic politics of the Vietnam War and Selective Service in my home town.

A further memory of the process came after I was settled in as an Army JAG officer. A member of the JAG officer selection board that considered my case reported the Board had been uneasy about Judge Carter's one sentence recommendation of my work for him in a letter he had sent to his friend Major General Decker. The Board members, familiar with multi-page letters of gushing praise for other applicants, wondered whether Judge Carter was damning me with faint and brief praise. An intimate of both Judge Carter and General Decker assured the JAG selectors that this was a first-class endorsement from a man of few, but compelling, words.

By June, 1970 our military plans were settled. I had accepted the JAG commission with enrollment starting in September. That left the summer open for Linda and me. She took the opportunity to complete one year of her work with the California Department of Education and to receive the financial benefits that a full year of service provided. I finished my clerkship with Judge Carter and then with the Judge's assistance signed on for a summer of work with San Diego Defenders, Inc.

Defenders had established a reputation of one of the nation's outstanding firms providing defense attorneys for criminal defendants who could not afford a lawyer. The work with Judge Carter had given me a look at criminal law at a high level and at the end of the criminal law process. Defenders introduced me to the start of the criminal law process with a very human look at the workings of the process. Defenders' lawyers would be appointed to represent a criminal defendant when the arrested defendant would make his or her first court appearance and explained that he or she could not afford a lawyer. The United States Supreme Court had made clear that defendants in any serious criminal case had a constitutional right to a publicly funded lawyer if they could not afford one.

I would often meet my clients in the County jail a day or two after their arrest. They faced a variety of charges from physical attacks to stealing property to the sale and use of drugs. Drug crimes in particular had increased greatly in the last decade in southern California and many casual drug users faced felony prosecutions.

In theory, any criminal charges could give rise to a contested trial in which the government prosecutors would set out their evidence and the public defender would contest the facts of the charge or the legality of police conduct in gathering the evidence or both. A jury or a judge sitting without a jury would then weigh the evidence and rule whether the government had proven its case "beyond a reasonable doubt."

In practice, the large majority of cases would not be decided by trial but by a plea agreement negotiated by the government attorney and the defense counsel with the approval of his or her client. The clients admitted the violation of the law. The prosecutors and the police had complied with the Constitution and the laws in gathering their evidence against the defendant. The defendant's hope was to keep jail or prison time as brief as possible. The prosecutor would hope to avoid the work of a trial and the possibility of an acquittal while still requiring the defendant to pay a penalty for his or her wrongdoing.

Even in the two months of my Defenders' service I encountered a considerable variety of criminal conduct and criminals. Some, often drug offenders, were first time offenders. Others were frequent offenders who knew the realities of criminal law and procedure far better than I did. The young prosecutors with whom I negotiated "plea deals" were often told by their experienced superiors: "Don't worry, we'll get him the next time" if the rookie's mistake had allowed an acquittal. I suspect they also endorsed Judge Carter's bon mot that many defendants "were too stupid to be a criminal."

The heavy workload of the criminal courts in San Diego gave me the opportunity to represent two dozen clients, to get my first experiences negotiating with other lawyers and arguing in front of judges, and of observing the criminal process. It excited me that I would probably be able to continue that work in the military criminal justice system.

In early September, Linda and I said goodbye to San Diego friends and mentors, packed our Volkswagen, assured our dog we were not leaving him behind and headed north and east on a 5,375-miles trek to Fort Lee, Virginia and the start of my military service. We headed up the Pacific Coast as far as Seattle with stops at William Randolph Hearst's San Simeon and the California wine country. At Seattle we turned east towards the Rocky Mountains and Yellowstone Park and the Badlands to Madison and other Wisconsin stops. After brief reunions, we continued across the Midwest with an attempted visit with a Madison friend who was serving as a professor at Kent State University. Earlier that summer Kent State in Ohio and Jackson State in Mississippi had seen riots on campus and the death of students protesting the Vietnam War and racial discrimination. Our last major city stop was Richmond, Virginia, just up the road from Fort Lee, the headquarters of the Army Quartermasters Corps. On September 15th we checked in at Fort Lee. Our Army career was about to begin.

The Army Judge Advocate General's Corps' decision to directly commission lawyers as captains recognized that the new officers brought a maturity to their new position that wasn't true of most newly enlisted men and junior officers. It also recognized that the new JAGs were critically needed to do Army legal work and that delays in getting that work started were wasteful. Yet, the new JAGs were also commissioned officers and some training for that position was necessary.

The plan to achieve these multiple goals was a three-week course at Fort Lee in military basics. This would be followed by two months education in military law at the Army's Judge Advocate General's School (TJAGSA) in Charlottesville, Virginia. On Sunday, September 20, 1970 we reported to Fort Lee for our initial instructions. Paper processing, physical exams and vaccinations filled our first two days as soldiers. Wednesday began with the issuance of field equipment and lectures on the structure of the military, the expectations of a commissioned officer, military courtesies (how and when to salute) and inspections. Thursday lectures include voice and command and physical conditioning. Friday started weapons training with M-14 rifles and ammunition. The final hours returned to physical training.

The second week offered lectures on leadership, first aid and further physical training. On Wednesday we moved to nearby Camp A.P. Hill for weapons training, firing qualifications, and daytime and nighttime simulated combat. Physical training, primarily running or marching was relatively easy given my prior distance running experience. Target shooting was more of a challenge but with the help of the training officers, I managed to meet the qualifying standards. The simulated night firing experience was the most stimulating session. We weren't sure that the "live firing" was with blanks rather than bullets, but we had the good lawyer's sense to assume the worst and prepare for it. We returned to Fort Lee in good condition with a second week completed.

Our third week began with lectures on nuclear effects and chemical and biological warfare. We went from the lecture hall to the gas chamber exercise.

We were instructed on wearing a gas mask, standing in a gas filled room, and then removing the mask briefly before exiting into welcome clean air. I remember the satisfaction of seeing one of our classmates with considerable prior military experience gasping for breath as he emerged while I emerged seemingly unaffected. I didn't tell him that my prior exposure to tear gas had come in confrontations between student protesters and the Madison police. The rest of the week consisted of more drills, inspections and out-processing. A brief Thursday morning graduation in Army dress greens finished our course.

One of the most valuable pieces of news we received while at Fort Lee was the notification of our permanent assignments. I was pleased to learn that I was headed to Fort Dix in New Jersey with four other classmates. Fort Dix was a major east coast training base and likely to provide substantial criminal law work for young JAG lawyers. The chance to continue my work with Defenders was most appealing.

The three weeks at the Quartermaster School was hardly the equivalent of basic training for a new enlistee. We started as commissioned Captains and thus outranked the capable and experienced lieutenants who were our instructors in the classroom and in the field. Nonetheless, we appreciated the education in military culture they provided and the guidance in the use of weapons that someday might be essential.

We were then off to Charlottesville. For several decades, the University of Virginia had welcomed TJAGSA to its grounds. The grounds were the legacy of Thomas Jefferson, the Revolutionary War immortal and the third president of the United States. Jefferson's glorious home, Monticello, overlooked Charlottesville, and local lore had it that Jefferson still lived in Charlottesville a century and a half after his death.

The University of Virginia Law School was a two-minute walk from the beautiful heart of campus. TJAGSA was across the parking lot from the Law School. The Law School Library and the well-endowed University of Virginia Alderman Library provided a remarkable scholarly base for a military installation. Relations with University faculty, staff, and students and the Charlottesville community were largely cordial, a sharp contrast to what relations in Madison and elsewhere would have been in 1970.

The JAG School's major responsibility was to educate the 1500 licensed lawyers serving in the Army JAG Corps around the world. We were 100 members of the 58th Basic Class in the history of the School. Our 10-week program was designed to provide a basic education in military law to newly commissioned JAG captains. Also attending the School during our stay were experienced JAG officers taking the nine-month Advanced JAG class that mirrored a civilian Master's Degree in Law. The School also hosted a variety of short courses in specialized areas of military law.

The faculty of the School was composed of about 25 experienced JAG captains, majors, lieutenant colonels and colonels. Most were experienced in military law practice and were selected for good teaching skills. They were assigned to one of four sections that covered the military law specialties that JAG officers were expected to encounter in their first and subsequent assignments.

The largest section was the Criminal Law Division. While almost all law school graduates had taken criminal law and procedure courses in law school, few had serious exposure to the distinctive role of criminal law in the military. Federal statutes had created a Uniform Code of Military Justice (UCMJ) that defined both substantive and procedural law that governed members of the military. The substantive law identified crimes with which military members could be charged. Many were crimes—murders, assaults and crimes against property—similar to crimes in the civilian community. Other crimes were distinctive to the military and had no civilian parallel. Examples were absence from duty, disobedience of orders, and other offenses against military good order and discipline. A civilian failing to show up for work could be fired. A soldier facing the same charge could face criminal punishment, including imprisonment.

Much of the rest of the UCMJ detailed the procedures that would govern the handling of an alleged violation of one of the substantive offenses. The evolving UCMJ had attempted to balance the interests of the military command in maintaining good order and discipline in the forces and the interest of soldier-defendants in fair treatment for alleged criminal violations. Both the Constitution and the acts of Congress addressed fairness and impartiality in the handling of a military criminal case. A particular concern was improper "command influence"—the involvement of the defendant's superior officers in the criminal case.

Military criminal cases were tried by courts-martial in which the charges against the defendant soldier were considered and decided by a panel of officers or senior enlisted men who were not involved in the facts of the case. Alternatively, a defendant could elect trial by a military judge alone. The military judge was a trained JAG officer typically serving as a full-time judge for a period of time. After the trial was completed if the defendant were found guilty, several levels of appeal by the convicted defendant were allowed. The highest level of military appeal was the Court of Military Appeals, a three-judge panel of civilian jurists. In rare cases, the United States Supreme Court could grant a final review of the case.

In 1970, two decades of reported cases from the Court of Military Appeals and the lower Courts of Military Review had built a substantial body of decided cases to accompany the statutory provisions of the UCMJ. This was the raw material of learning about military criminal law for the young JAG officer.

The second division of the School was the Civil Law Division. Its work focused on non-criminal matters that would be a regular part of JAG work at most military installations. Here much of the law came from statutes and regulations written by Congress or branches of civilian government or by the military itself. A common example were laws that governed military pay and benefits. A commander might request a JAG opinion of whether, if at all, a law applied to a soldier. The analogy was to the office of a State Attorney General or a county or city attorney from whom a government officer might seek legal guidance. Alternatively, a soldier could request a JAG officer's help in clarifying his or her legal status. The analogy was to a legal aid officer for parties unable to afford a private attorney.

A second set of civil laws involved claims for money damages for conduct of members of the military that caused death, injury or property damage to another party. The prominent act of Congress that addressed many of these claims was the Federal Tort Claims Act (FTCA). This 1946 statute removed much governmental immunity from such claims and set up administrative and judicial procedures for handling such diverse claims as motor vehicle accidents, harms to real property and professional malpractice. As with the Uniform Code of Military Justice, a substantial body of federal court case law helped to define aspects of the law of torts in the military and other federal entities.

The third TJAGSA division addressed government contracting. The size and scope of the military of 1970 required the purchase of an enormous number of goods and services by the armed forces ranging from vehicles to weapons and ammunition to food. The statutory and common law of contracts and property and statutes directly governing the military provided work for JAG procurement officers.

The fourth Division was the International Law Division. The large presence of the American military around the world required the JAG attorney to deal with a variety of international treaties and agreements and matters of foreign nations' laws. These could be as significant as violations of international laws of war or as trivial at the application of German motor vehicle law to the American soldier driving a jeep in Munich.

Our 58th Basic Class was composed of exactly 100 officers. Ninety-nine were male. One was female. One was South Korean. Virtually all were Law School graduates from the classes of 1969 and 1970. Most were married. Only two had prior military service. One void in the class were graduates of the nation's elite law schools. There were no graduates of Harvard, Yale, Columbia, Chicago or Stanford Law Schools. About 10 were graduates of next tier schools like NYU, Michigan, Virginia, Wisconsin and Texas. The majority of new JAGs had attended the public university law school of their home state. About 40 members of the class were graduates of a southern law school.

TJAGSA looked like a continuation of the three years of law school with the added stimulation that the day's class might be covering what the young captain would need for the practice of law in the next few months.

On balance, I found the quality of TGAGSA teaching as good as civilian law school. The recent law practice experience of the faculty gave a good real-world aspect to the classes. There was some discussion of issues raised by the Vietnam War but both students and faculty recognized large military and foreign policy matters were well above our pay grades. Regular exams included both short answer and essay questions. A few instructors took pleasure in hinting "expect this to be on the exam." The unstated expectation was that all one hundred of us would meet minimum academic standards and go on to practice in the Army JAG Corps.

The School provided a variety of social gatherings at which officers from young captains to career colonels mingled comfortably. The Charlottesville community also provided diversions with University of Virginia football and basketball games and cultural activities to pleasant eating and drinking establishments. Linda and I had the good fortune to find housing with a delightful couple of native Virginians who were further guides to the culture of the community. We also discovered the fun of Virginia estate auctions at which we acquired pieces of antique furniture that still grace our home half a century later. Our favorite auctioneer livened his sales pitches with such native phrases as "some kind of nice."

The most consequent day of the TJAGSA experience involved a meeting with JAG personnel from the Pentagon to review duty assignments after our December graduation. I went in expecting to affirm that I was quite happy with my TJAGSA education and my anticipated Fort Dix posting. Instead, I was told that the current editor of the Military Law Review, published at the School, had been reassigned to a post in Ethiopia. It was hoped that I might take over that position. My civilian self, spoiled by elite law firm blandishments, responded that I was looking forward to continuing criminal defense work at Fort Dix. The officer responded: "Captain Zillman, we really need you to take this position." My new military self snapped to attention. "This is an order, Captain Zillman, not an offer." I went home to report to Linda that our lives had changed again.

An immediate consequence of the reassignment was our housing. The TJAGSA assignment gave us the reasonable expectation that we would serve our remaining military service in Charlottesville. Since there was no on-post housing at the School, the possibility of buying a first house was tempting. After some scouting on the local market, we found a small, but appealing, two-story property a mile from campus and the JAG School. The $15,000 sale price seemed within reason. Shortly before graduation we became homeowners.

Our Basic Class graduated in early December. I had the good fortune to be named Distinguished Graduate of the class based on my academic achievements. I suspected the JAGC Personnel Office had gotten wind of that likely ranking. Added to my prior Wisconsin Law Review experience and my federal court clerkship that made me a good prospect for running the Military Law Review. I smiled as I recalled Judge Carter's observation to the Selective Service System that I would be a better lawyer than a soldier.

As 1971 dawned, I settled into the Plans and Publications Division of TJAGSA. Over the last three months I had already connected with most of the faculty and a good number of the other officers and civilian employees at TJAGSA. My colleagues were capable and affable. For the most part they were pleased with their Charlottesville assignment. The career officers felt good performance in their duties would enhance their prospects for promotion. My fellow draft-induced volunteers felt TJAGSA combined a pleasant posting with the chance for enhancing post-service career opportunities. It also offered the chance to pursue a University of Virginia Law School LLM degree with the encouragement of the TJAGSA leadership. Eight of my colleagues from the early 1970s would go on to careers in civilian law school teaching.

I had the rare advantage for a young officer of taking a job that I knew better than most of my superior officers. They welcomed me and our relations were as colleagues rather than superior–subordinate. I sensed that they had instructions from the Commandant of the School to improve the quality of the Review. The models were good civilian law reviews. Those reviews sought thorough, original and non-partisan scholarly articles on a wide range of topics relevant to the military. I set to work.

I was quickly reminded of one difference between the Wisconsin Law Review and the Military Law Review. I signed a letter to one of my superior officers as "Editor-in-Chief" (my title at Wisconsin Law). I was gently reminded that while I might have had 25 staff members at Wisconsin under my leadership, at TJAGSA I was one on a staff of one. No pompous title was needed.

Each issue of the Review began with a statement of purpose: "The Military Law Review provides a forum for those interested in military law to share the product of their experience and research. Articles should be of direct concern and import in this area of scholarship, and preference will be given to those articles having lasting value as reference materials for the military lawyer.

The Military Law Review does not purport to promulgate Department of the Army policy or to be in any sense directory. The opinions reflected in each article are those of the author and do not necessarily reflect the views of The Judge Advocate General or any governmental agency."

The statement freed me of any need to clear articles with higher authority before publication. References to "scholarship" and "research" and "lasting value as reference material" also enabled me to politely decline any reflections of old (or young) soldiers that were not grounded in solid citation to existing statutory, treaty, regulatory or judicial precedents.

The statement of purpose also reflected that the two hundred or more civilian law reviews in publication were not rich in writing about military law. The topic of military law was not well known to their student editors. It was the rare editor who was a military veteran or who had taken a course in military law. A considerable portion of law faculty members also had no experience in the military. Probably, the majority of faculty and student editors in 1970 were lukewarm, at best, and hostile at worst, to a neutral treatment of military issues. As a consequence, the Military Law Review was one of the few scholarly journals that took a serious interest in military legal issues. It was also a place, or the place, where a JAG officer would want his or her thoughts published to impress senior officers, military contemporaries, and civilians involved in military legal matters.

That guidance helped me to make a careful analysis of the duties involved in publishing a quarterly journal of 200 to 250 pages per issue. The actual work involved (1) the solicitation and selection of between six and ten articles of quality per issue; (2) the editing of those articles with the collaboration of the author to assure reasonable brevity, appropriate neutrality and accuracy of the author's work; and (3) working with the publisher to provide a final manuscript that was ready for publication. In addition to work on specific articles, I handled any other requests that related to the Review.

As I reviewed recent issues of the Review, I found that the TJAGSA Advanced Class students produced quality articles as part of their year-long program. The best articles combined thorough library research with the young officer's practical experience in the area of military law. With my University of Wisconsin Law School exposure to "law in action" this was a delightful combination. In addition to the Advanced Class writings, the Review also attracted articles from other JAG officers and civilian authors with experience or interest in some aspect of military law. These contributions would often begin as an invited lecture at the JAG School. With some additional research and analysis, a Military Law Review article emerged.

One additional source of articles was my own research and writing. A likely topic was recent United States Supreme Court cases addressing military issues. Here I was able to both describe and analyze the case and to predict its likely impact on subsequent military law.

At first, I was a bit uneasy about being both author and editor. Fortunately, I could share my work with my TJAGSA colleagues and respond to their insightful comments. I had the good fortune to share an office with the School's other publications officer. He was a fellow draft-induced JAG volunteer, who had left large firm practice in Cleveland to serve his military obligation. His publication was the Army Lawyer, a monthly publication with a focus on timely, short articles with immediate relevance to the JAG officer's day-to-day practice.

That was the large part of my work for over two years. During those years I also had my first exposure to classroom teaching as my writing and research built my expertise in tort law and constitutional law in the military. In my Basic Class work I had the chance to observe some excellent classroom teachers. I tried to model my teaching on the best elements of their work.

Gradually, I moved to a teaching position in the Civil Law Division and passed on my Law Review duties to a new editor. While I did not fully appreciate it at the time, three-and-one-half years at TJAGSA provided me with a strong addition to my previous resume when I considered a possible civilian teaching position after active duty.

My teaching time at TJAGSA also coincided with a decision by the Judge Advocate General's Office and the TJAGSA Commandant to reach out from the School to the variety of JAG reserve and National Guard units around the continental United States. This allowed teaching faculty at TJAGSA to visit those units and to provide lectures and discussions on current issues to the members of the units. In practice, this put School faculty members on week-long trips to three cities or military installations to do the teaching and outreach.

The travel was a delight. I talked to crowds ranging from half a dozen to fifty or more. The unit commanders were gracious hosts who appreciated the School's outreach. I was wined and dined and advised on local cultural opportunities for my spare hours in their communities. Thirteen trips included San Francisco, Los Angeles, New Orleans, Dallas, Wichita, Cleveland, Houston, St. Louis, Denver and Madison. In addition to the teaching, I also became acquainted with leading American cities and military bases. A typical trip allowed visits to city art galleries and zoos in my spare hours.

The trips were a great learning experience for a neophyte law teacher. Each audience was different. Each classroom was distinctive. I recall stopping teaching until airplane overflights had passed. It was particularly stimulating to converse with law school contemporaries, both officers and enlisted men, who had taken different paths to performing their obligated military service than I had taken.

A further benefit of the TJAGSA assignment was the opportunity to complete a Master's Degree in Law (LLM) at the University of Virginia Law School. The TJAGSA Commandant encouraged TJAGSA faculty to undertake the LLM program. It both enhanced the qualifications of the faculty for their military teaching and demonstrated to the Virginia Law School faculty the quality of personnel at the JAG School. The Commandant provided the necessary time to prepare for and attend classes. The GI Bill paid for my tuition. How could I not say Yes?

The majority of my University of Virginia Law work was with the strong international law faculty who had a close relationship with Yale Law School's pre-eminent international law program. However, the class that most intrigued me was one taught by Professor Mason Willrich exploring the new field of energy law. Professor Willrich had practiced with a major energy public utility. He brought to the class a wonderful perspective on the "real world" of topics such as oil and gas exploration, electricity production, transmission, sales and environmental issues that were raised by almost every energy development. This had great appeal to my Wisconsin Law instincts to study "law in action," not merely law as written in court opinions, statutes and regulations and scholarly texts.

Beyond the classroom and library aspects of my TJAGSA tour, my active duty provided experiences, both large and small that shaped the rest of my life. These were matters I probably would have missed had I not served in the military and, most probably had moved from my clerkship with Judge Carter to large law firm practice in New York City, Chicago or California.

My first distinctive experiences were direct exposures to the American military in the early 1970s. The Army JAG School was certainly a unique posting. Its fifty or so personnel were largely officers who shared military and lawyer's work and perspectives. Most of the older officers anticipated a twenty year or longer career as an Army lawyer. The dozen or so first term JAGs, like myself, were draft-induced volunteers with little or no anticipation of further military legal service after their obligated tour of duty. Fortunately, and thanks to good leadership, there was not a sharp divide between careerists and short-timers. For the most part, each group respected the others and recognized their talents and shortcomings. The younger of us learned both military and legal lessons from our more experienced colleagues.

I came to appreciate the military culture that honored group dedication to "the mission" ahead of individual achievement and an appreciation of the different talents of colleagues. We socialized as a group that included spouses as parts of the team.

One life-long lesson of the military culture was an appreciation for physical fitness. A Criminal Law Division major introduced me to his favorite sport of weightlifting. Others encouraged me to return to distance running as that exercise became an essential part of military physical fitness.

Team sports were also important for building group morale. We played volleyball and basketball informally on the University of Virginia courts and more formally in the Charlottesville City leagues with reasonable success. Our prominent JAG basketballer was the Chief of the Criminal Law Division, who would eventually reach the rank of Major General. He had a wonderful ability to secure young captains some extended lunch hours to play ball.

My favorite memory in JAG basketball was a Saturday morning pick-up game against a group of young and good University of Virginia undergrads. By chance, the college classmate of one of our JAG captains was visiting his friend for the weekend and joined our squad. He was a bit late getting to the game in which the University of Virginia folks were sensing they had an easy victory. Phil showed up just in time and extended to his 6-foot 8-inch height. A worried look crossed a few UVa brows. "Don't worry" we said "he's just a second stringer." Phil Jackson played nicely under control for us and gave us a competitive victory. We congratulated our opponents and resisted the temptation to tell them that our "second stringer" had that role on the NBA Champion New York Knicks. Several decades later Phil Jackson became the legendary coach who led Michael Jordan and the Chicago Bulls to six world championships.

A further part of the military culture came with the expectation that TJAGSA officers would serve the grim duty of conveying death notifications to the next of kin of deceased service members in the Charlottesville area. The process was well defined. Notification of the death of the soldier would come from the Pentagon to the Commandant of the School. The Commandant would then assign two officers to go in dress uniform in a military vehicle to the home of the deceased soldier. We were to identify ourselves to the next of kin, typically spouse or parent and briefly announce the terrible news. We were to ask whether we could notify others, often the family religious leader. We were to convey the regrets and gratitude of the nation for the sacrifice of the deceased. We would report that other officers would provide further details. We were not to go into details of the death. We were assuredly not to discuss the wisdom of the Vietnam War or military service in general. We then departed.

A single episode also introduced a group of young JAGs to duties more commonly assigned to the National Guard. Heavy rainfalls had flooded the James River with major damage to the river town of Scottsville, about 40 miles south of Charlottesville. We drove down on Saturday morning in our fatigues and reported to law enforcement officers. They assigned us to help in cleaning up a badly flooded grocery store. Once we grasped that "the waters were up to here" just a few days before, military instincts kicked in. Our commander assigned duties. We set to work to help restore life to a battered town. Only later did it register that our Army status and dress gave the store owners comfort that might not have been accorded to a group of strangers from the civilian community.

An attractive part of TJAGSA duty was the connection with the world outside the United States. One source of that experience was the presence of foreign JAG officers at the School, typically in the JAG Advanced Class. Here again, sports played a role. One colleague was a Pakistani major who happened to be a fine (and much better than me) tennis player. We were matched up and had an enjoyable first match. At the end, we shook hands and promised to play again. Then my new friend remarked: "You know, I've never had to retrieve my own tennis balls." Cross-cultural education took place in both directions. In upper class Pakistan, ball retrieval was the duty of men of lower social status. I explained that my experience was the exact opposite. I suspect the story made its way to Pakistan with the message that not every American officer was born with a silver spoon in his mouth. As our friendship developed, I asked my friend whether his stature as a lawyer or an Army officer was more prestigious. If asked the same question, I would probably have thought briefly and chosen lawyer. In Pakistan, the answer was clearly Army officer.

The JAG experience allowed two trips on military leave to Europe. One trip introduced Linda and me to "space available" travel on military flights. We presented our leave orders to the air base at Dover, Delaware and were awakened that night with a knock on our door that a middle-of-the-night flight was leaving for Germany. We hurriedly packed and were shortly on board an Air Force transport carrying cargo and a few soldier passengers. After what seemed a long flight with no windows to watch the water and land pass below, we were in Germany and shortly bound for Great Britain by train for a fascinating exploration of Merry Olde England.

A year later a more organized trip with two TJAGSA colleagues let us circle northern Europe by car. We took advantage of our military status to visit elements of the substantial American presence in Germany. Here my education was greatly advanced by the presence of Norm Hamelin, a Basic Classmate and his German born wife. Norm was a natural for representing America in work with NATO allies. Visits with the Hamelins and other American soldiers on that trip reminded me that Vietnam was only part of the military's responsibility in the early 1970s. In fact, in terms of overall importance to American military and diplomatic work, the Soviet Union–American relations during the Cold War were more significant.

A further benefit of my active duty was my first significant exposure to the American south. My prior time below the Mason–Dixon line was limited to a trip to visit my uncle in Dallas at 10 years of age and our several family visits to Civil War battlefields.

Charlottesville was assuredly a distinctive part of the South. The local leaders and the tourist offices were happier to emphasize it as the home of Thomas Jefferson rather than its connections with the Civil War and Reconstruction. The University of Virginia was Jefferson's University. His gorgeous home, Monticello, was located on a hill a few miles from downtown. Charlottesville had avoided some of the more violent and contentious aspects of school desegregation, sit-ins, and continued anti-black violence of the 1950s and 1960s. Yet beneath the surface and reality of "southern hospitality," were reminders that this was a very different part of the United States from what I had experienced in my mid-western upbringing.

An experience remains in memory half a century later. A dinner invitation arranged through mutual friends brought us to the elegant old home of a long-time Charlottesville native. He probably expected that my military status carried with it a relative degree of conservatism. Our host quickly made clear his views on racial integration, protests against the Vietnam War, and northern liberalism. Linda and I tried to be polite guests, but it was a long evening.

Experiences outside Charlottesville further educated us on differences between north and south. The first was a Summer 1971 trip to Durham, North Carolina for a track and field competition between Olympic caliber athletes from the United States and black African nations. Performers and performances were memorable. Ticket prices were minimal and designed to encourage a strong turnout of black North Carolina residents. The spirit of the warm, sunny days was congenial and uplifting with spectators, black and white, mingling and honoring all participants in a spirit of excellence and equality. Stereotypes crumbled.

A year later, a subsequent weekend break to the Carolinas gave a different impression. As we crossed the Virginia–North Carolina border we were greeted by a large commercial quality billboard with the message: "Welcome to Klan Country."

By late 1972, the world had changed considerably from 1969–70 when military obligations directed our life. The American role in Vietnam was clearly ending. American troop withdrawals had accelerated. In January, 1973 America essentially declared an end to American participation in its longest, and least successful war. The stated premise was that the South Vietnamese government could sustain itself against the Communist forces of North Vietnam and the Viet Cong. The unstated premise was that if it could not, the Americans would not return.

One military era had ended and another was taking shape. My draft-induced JAG colleagues began to plan their lives after our military obligations ended. The JAG School and the University of Virginia experiences were leading me to consider a career in civilian law teaching. It was ironic that in 1966 I had abandoned thoughts of doctoral program in American history and with it the career as a Professor of History when I enrolled at the Wisconsin Law School. Now the possibility of a faculty appointment at one of the two hundred accredited American law schools seemed a real possibility.

In retrospect, examination of our lives after military service should have involved a careful exploration of plans for the rest of our lives. A first option might have been to continue a career as a JAG officer. My work at the JAG School had given me a good overview of that career and a solid record in my first three years of service as measured by the written performance reviews prepared by my superior officers. Several of those mentors at TJAGSA would go on to hold generals' ranks in the Corps.

I would certainly have needed to move to other than purely academic work in the Corps to advance in rank with or ahead of my contemporaries. Possibly, I would have needed to secure a Vietnam tour of duty before American participation in the War ended. That tour or a stateside relocation probably would have given me experience as a military prosecutor or defense counsel that would have eventually led to command experience supervising younger JAGs. The University of Virginia Law School experience in international law might also have moved my JAG career in the direction of a Pentagon or European assignment.

In truth, neither Linda nor I gave much thought to that option and I suspect that our superiors understood that other capable JAGs were clearly hoping to have a twenty-year or more JAG career. The end of the Vietnam War would reduce opportunities for all officers including young JAGs. Rightly or wrongly, we draft-induced volunteers were unlikely to be persuaded by the strongest of recruiting appeals.

The second career prospect was to resume contact with the large law firms that had recruited us vigorously in 1968 and 1969. Several of them did contact us with a "now that your military obligation is almost over, would you …" letter or phone call. We also would have felt comfortable in reconnecting with the firms.

There certainly would have been benefits to such a career decision. Salary and prestige would have been attractive. I would have had to recognize that I might have been behind Class of 1969 law graduates who had avoided the draft and gone straight into firm practice. However, my federal clerkship, Virginia advanced degree and Army experience might have made me an attractive young recruit and counted for some credit in determining my initial position and salary.

With few second thoughts, however, we moved in a different direction. In early 1973, we began seriously considering a career in civilian law teaching. My JAG work had introduced me to teaching and research. I had enjoyed both. Several of my civilian mentors had contacted civilian law schools with teaching vacancies and offered my name. An encouraging number of responses came back and JAG duty and the Virginia LLM provided a resume as attractive as if I had been in civilian law practice for the past three years. The call of the academy was strong and we followed it. Two pleasant on-campus interviews during 1973 resulted in offers of a professorship upon release from active duty. In practice this allowed a May 1974 release from active duty in time to begin the 1974–75 academic year as an Associate Professor of Law at Arizona State University Law School. That launched a half century of rewarding work in public higher education.

A significant part of my civilian teaching continued my TJAGSA work. The LLM experience launched me into the emerging field of energy law at a time that Middle East developments put the subject on the front pages and the evening news. My work with civilian suits against government offices and officers made tort law another logical subject. Military law with its focus on the constitutional structure of the American military and civil–military relations also made constitutional law an appropriate subject. Over the years, I would occasionally start a constitutional law class with the questions: "How many provisions of the Constitution directly address Social Security, funding of K-12 education, or protection of the environment?" "How many provisions specifically address the military?" The answer to the first question is "None." The answer to the second is "Seventeen." Energy, tort, constitutional and military law have been the heart of my research and teaching.

As it turned out, I did not sever all ties with the military when Linda and I gathered $1,700 in cash for my Army severance pay and promptly raced to a nearby bank to deposit the largest sum of money either of us had ever possessed. From there, a more leisurely trail took us to Tempe, Arizona and Arizona State University Law School. We arrived on a mid-June day with the temperature in the hundred and teens to begin our next career.

Shortly after settling into civilian law teaching, The Army came calling again with an offer I could refuse without fear of federal prosecution. The TJAGSA had a number of Individual Ready Reserve (IRR) positions and I was offered one. As the title suggests, the IRR was focused on individual officers with special skills who could spare two weeks in summer to bring their skills to a military installation. My teaching and research time on active duty fitted me for this position at TJAGSA. I did explore two matters before signing on. Was there serious work for me to do in Charlottesville? Was I free to end my service at any time? The answer to both was Yes.

I started another dozen years of military service and pay. The IRR provided frequent teaching opportunities in the short courses that brought JAG officers and others to Charlottesville in summer. The IRR called on my writing and research skills to draft Army manuals and publications in the Military Law Review and other journals. It also provided a delightful reunion with Charlottesville and old JAG colleagues and introduced me to new ones. From Arizona State's perspective, it enhanced my teaching, scholarly output and service. And, one year, it provided the hottest running race in my long career in which a heat-dazed fellow runner collided with a light pole and was carried off in an ambulance.

I did IRR duties until 1986 and received a promotion to major. Then, summer law school duties at the University of Utah and consideration of law school deanships discouraged further summer military duties. I was honorably discharged after 16 years of active duty and IRR service.

Deanship exploration ended successfully in 1989 when I accepted the post of Dean of the University of Maine Law School in Portland to start in the 1990–91 school year. Before that commitment was set, I reconnected with the Army when I was offered the post of Distinguished Visiting Professor in the Department of Law at the United States Military Academy (USMA) at West Point, New York. The West Point assignment was for the Fall Semester of 1990 with the understanding that I would spend some weekends in Portland preparing for Dean duties at Maine Law that would begin on January 1, 1991.

USMA or West Point had been the training ground for Army officers since early in the nineteenth century. Among its graduates and legendary future leaders were Ulysses Grant, Robert E. Lee, John J. Pershing, Douglas MacArthur, Dwight Eisenhower, Matthew Ridgway and George Patton. The four-year West Point program combined academic studies (with a focus on science and engineering), leadership training and athletics.

The Law Department combined teaching in law with service as the legal office of the Academy. A few senior JAG officers with lengthy service at West Point were joined by young JAG captains and majors to provide the classroom instruction. The Distinguished Visiting Professor, typically a civilian law school instructor, provided a civilian perspective for both JAG instructors and cadets.

My colleagues at West Point briefed me on my duties. I would teach two classes of fifteen cadets each. The students were members of the First Class (the equivalent of civilian university seniors). The class was an introduction to law as it applied to the military with an emphasis on the role of young officers in implementing that law; administrative law governing such matters as personnel evaluations, promotions, discipline short of criminal prosecution for soldiers; personal injury and property damage (tort) law in which the United States or the soldier might be either the injured party or the party causing the injury; and aspects of international law such as legal control over military activities in foreign nations.

The class was required for all first-class cadets and was taught by most of the Department faculty. That provided a rare opportunity for a civilian law professor to have a dozen or more faculty colleagues teaching the same material at the same time and sharing responsibility for the frequent student examinations in the subject. The opportunity to regularly brainstorm my teaching with colleagues was a delight of the course.

In addition to the required Law course, the Department also taught and administered a major in law that encouraged cadets to delve more deeply into legal matters. An unstated premise of the major was that a modest number of cadets might then go on to a JAG career. I had the fun of teaching an hour or two of those classes in my areas of research.

My final teaching opportunities came in teaching to my faculty colleagues in some of my areas of scholarship. This provided the chance to share my ideas with young and senior military lawyers who had specialized in legal practice in these areas.

In short, I found the chance to connect with faculty colleagues one of the most enjoyable experiences in my 50 years of law teaching.

My colleagues had also briefed me well on what to expect from the students. They had worked their way up from raw plebes (freshmen) to firsties (seniors). Many had survived and thrived and were now the student leaders of the Academy. Their success in the classroom, in leadership training and intercollegiate or intramural Academy athletics, and sometimes all three, had earned them the right to rest on their laurels before they would receive both their college degree and their officers' commissions before going into Army leadership. They were respectful, but not overawed, by academic types.

I was also informed of a USMA custom that reflected the hugely busy schedule that cadets carried. If a cadet felt sleep coming on in class, she or he was instructed to stand at attention until the urge to sleep passed. The instructor was advised that this was not a sign of boredom with class or the teacher. The instructor was not to call on the standing student.

Suitably prepared, Linda and I took another cross-country trip from Salt Lake City to the Hudson River of New York with stops to visit with old friends along the way. On our last day of travel, life changed. We turned on the radio to learn that Iraqi dictator Saddam Hussein had just invaded and quickly taken over neighboring Kuwait. A major Middle Eastern oil producer and military power had just absorbed another major oil producer and now staked a claim to control much of Middle Eastern petroleum. We looked at each other with a sense of "what adventure have we gotten into?"

We reported to the Law Department and were soon checked into Academy faculty housing just a short walk from the Law Department and the lovely center grounds with a marvelous overlook of the Hudson River. On one of our first days, we witnessed the return of the new plebes from a 12-mile march which ended their initial training exercises.

While much of the Fall term of 1990 repeated USMA activities many decades old, Saddam Hussein had guaranteed that this would be a unique year. President George H.W. Bush and his advisers faced a difficult challenge. Saddam Hussein's military was emerging from a bloody eight-year struggle with neighboring Iran that was shaping Middle Eastern relations. That had implications for Saudi Arabia (the world's largest oil producer, but hardly a military power), Israel, Russia, much of Europe and the United States.

The United States was 15 years removed from losing its war in Vietnam against less formidable military powers than Iraq. A new generation of military leaders had attempted to rebuild the American armed forces. West Point and the Naval and Air Force Academies were key parts of the rebuilding. How would their graduates perform?

The soon-to-be graduates who were our students were well aware of what faced them. With a decade of combat and 58,000 deaths in Vietnam as the recent American combat experience, few cadets and their parents were not aware that death on the battlefield might face them in the year after their graduation.

President Bush, a combat hero in World War II and an experienced diplomat, quickly made clear that Saddam's conquest of Kuwait "would not stand." He recognized that he would need a wide range of allies to make clear to Saddam that he had little support around the world. While the United States would lead the military effort, it would need a diverse number of allies.

Cadets and faculty at West Point closely followed developments in the build-up of Allied forces in the Middle East for war against Iraq or diplomatic negotiations that might persuade Saddam Hussein to withdraw from Kuwait without the need for war. Several memories from Fall 1990 at West Point remain vivid half a century later. One was a low-level flyover of the Academy by A-10 jets. These planes would be a key part of any American battle against Iraqi tanks in the desert.

A second memory was a briefing to Department of Law faculty given by the commander of the Judge Advocate General's Office based on briefings from higher headquarters in the Pentagon. The message was that the combination of American air power, tanks and artillery, and well-trained combat infantry would be able to dominate Saddam's forces. At a minimum this would liberate Kuwait and do serious damage to Iraqi military forces. At a maximum it could capture Baghdad and capture or kill Saddam Hussein.

The third memory was of an early evening command performance for all cadets in the largest assembly hall on the grounds. The speaker was a four-star general from the Pentagon who gave a similar briefing to the one that we had just received. We watched as the entire student body marched to the auditorium in combat fatigues to learn what the first months of their commissioned service might be.

Further memories of West Point involved the gradual diversifying of the student body and the Army. To be sure, in 1990, the average cadet was a young, white, heterosexual male. But that was changing. Racial integration had progressed considerably since the Vietnam War. Blacks, Hispanics, Native Americans and Asian Americans were all represented in the cadet student body. Inside or outside of class I did not encounter evidence of racial prejudice. I sensed that any plebes who had entered the Academy with such prejudices had them changed as they trained, studied and socialized with members of different races. It doubtless helped that the outstanding varsity football player of the year was African American. Likewise, at the top of Army leadership was General Colin Powell, who would soon reinforce his credentials as a diplomat and military leader in the war against Saddam Hussein. The superb military sociologist, Professor Charles Moskos, a drafted veteran himself, observed in the late 1980s, that the armed forces were the one profession in America where blacks regularly bossed around whites. The symbol of that was the black senior enlisted man and drill sergeant in charge of recruit training.

Within the legal realm, the point was illustrated by a fellow law dean who was not a veteran. He reported that the national law school organization had directed that discrimination on the basis of sexual orientation would not be permitted in accredited law schools. Specifically, law schools would not open on-campus recruiting to schools that engaged in anti-gay discrimination. The Dean thought this was an easy statement of Law School virtue until eight members of the Black Student Association at his School visited to explain that the anti-gay discrimination by the Army was a matter of federal law not unthinking military bias. Further, all of the eight students hoped to secure a commission in the JAG Corps.

If many racial discrimination matters had been resolved against racism and for equality, gender discrimination had a good distance to go. Until 1976, West Point had been open to male students only. This was often justified by Congressional policy that excluded women from the combat arms of arms services. In 1976 Congress changed policy and admitted women to the Academy. A decade later when my students had started their schooling several things had become clear. First, some women were excellent candidates for Army commissions. Their academic credentials were equal to and often better than men. Second, some women were also excellent prospective leaders and athletes. Third, more military specialties were being opened to women who could meet qualifications that many men could not. Fourth, the nature of modern combat often made it hard to segregate combat from non-combat troops. Terrorists would not distinguish between combat infantrymen and military office workers or vehicle drivers or medical personnel when they planted improvised explosive devices or ambushed a small unit.

By 1989 gender integration at West Point had advanced but still had ways to go. Unlike racial integration, this was a subject that both male and female cadets felt comfortable discussing with a civilian instructor with a military background. The females often excellent athletes opposed their exclusion from any military specialties in which they could meet the same standards as men would need to meet. They also felt that women on average were better suited for certain military work than men.

Male cadets who were skeptical of some or all women cadets usually stressed physical skills. Women couldn't lift as much weight or run 100 yards as quickly as the average male cadet. I would encourage them to think of how to treat the woman who could meet male standards. Equally important, how critical were some of these skills to what the military officer was expected to do. A third reminder was that women were now providing about 15 percent of the total Army force. They were not taking jobs that qualified males could take. They were allowing the Army to maintain strength without having to open the ranks to males of doubtful educational, physical, and character qualifications.

As mentioned, a third realm of discrimination was against gays and lesbians. In 1990 legislative policy as clear. Gays and lesbians were not eligible to serve. In reality, some gays and lesbians had served quietly in the military for decades. They often suffered intense prejudice and could be dishonorably discharged at any point in their service. Their best defense was to keep their sexual orientation to themselves and make themselves indispensable to their unit. I recall a splendid gay TJAGSA colleague who managed to complete his obligated tour of duty in the early 1970s and went on to a distinguished career as a federal administrative judge before falling victim to the AIDS virus. TJAGSA rumor had it that a major who was strongly opposed to gays in the service complained to the Commandant. "What are you going to do about that?" he asked the Commandant. "Not a thing," the Commandant replied. "He's the best man in the command," making clear that that included the unhappy major.

My West Point classes included discussion of the future of gay–lesbian discrimination in the services with a review of the Equal Protection Clause in the Constitution. One of my sections seemed quite comfortable with a change of policy. If a gay or lesbian soldier could do the work, they were entitled to the same rights as a heterosexual soldier. The other section divided sharply. Opponents of gay/lesbian service worried over damage to unit moral, inability to provide leadership, and character inadequacy. Further exploration suggested that it was male homosexuality that really troubled them. The female who appeared to have male characteristics was probably seen as a better soldier than many non-lesbian women and men.

A range of other experiences also made the West Point semester a fascinating variation from Law School teaching. One delight was the connection with athletics, both varsity and intramural. Some competitive athletic performance was expected of all cadets and performance was usually at a higher level than the civilian university intramurals I knew from my undergraduate and faculty days. Injuries were common and it was a common sight to see cadets on crutches moving around the grounds. Equally delightful were the varsity sports, especially football. The 1990 Army team played well, but lost a few close games that kept a good season from being a great one. Happily, they defeated their legendary rival, the Naval Academy.

I had several varsity athletes, male and female, in my two sections. One happened to be an excellent running back who would finish in the top ten in the annual balloting for the Heisman Trophy for the outstanding college football player in the nation. Halfway through the semester, I needed to notify him that his initial quiz scores put him in danger of failing the required law course. We had a good discussion and set out a plan for improvement. I couldn't help but reflect that the outstanding football player at any other Division One school would not have faced a serious risk of failing a required course and being disqualified from further inter-collegiate sports. Happily, my student–athlete (an honestly earned title at West Point) raised his academic game as well as his athletic one. He attained a solid passing grade and helped beat Navy.

A personal athletic delight came when faculty were invited to join cadets in their required timed two mile run along a paved trail by the Hudson River. A faculty colleague and fellow distance runner and I joined about fifteen cadets in our heat. We went off at a controlled pace among the top five in the race. One cadet quickly dashed to the front. My colleague and I were ready to concede first place. By the half-way mark the gap was narrowing. We held our pace. Our competitor started to struggle and we moved on to first and third places in the race. Credit training ahead of youth and raw skill.

As the semester wound down, war with Iraq seemed increasingly likely. Saddam Hussein remained firm in his resolve and was happy to express his view that the United States was only bluffing. Even if it wasn't, the Vietnam War perceptions indicated that Iraqi forces were superior to the Americans.

Classwork finished in early December and we headed to Portland to start my tenure as Law Dean. Shortly after the start of the new semester, I was invited to be a speaker at a campus gathering to discuss the forthcoming war. The majority of speakers and audience members were skeptical about war in general and this war in particular. A good number also seemed in doubt about American forces' capability to defeat Saddam Hussein's forces on their home ground. The Vietnam legacy lived on.

A Kuwaiti national presented a good argument for the rightness of the Allied cause and the harm already done to the Kuwaiti people. I presented the case for an Allied battlefield victory that I had heard at West Point. Within a week the war began. The Allies quickly established aerial supremacy and my mind went back to the A-10 flyover at West Point. Allied forces then made a flanking attack on the Iraqi forces in the desert. In four days the Allies had liberated Kuwait and done major damage to Saddam's military forces. Allied casualties were under one thousand. President Bush then made the strategic decision to stop short of capturing Baghdad and killing Saddam Hussein. The War was over and the American military had reasserted itself.

Our West Point year ended with a return to the Academy for June graduation. President Bush was the graduation speaker on a gorgeous late Spring day. He was introduced by the Superintendent of the Academy in a speech that praised the American effort as a model of civil–military relations. The President had shaped the overall war goals in brilliant exercises of diplomacy. The actual fighting was then placed in the hands of the armed forces with a clear line of command. After the victory on the battlefield, the President and the civilian leadership then stopped short of total victory noting the risks of losing allies and sharply increasing casualties.

The return to USMA also allowed five of my TJAGSA colleagues to shape plans for a book, Constitutional Law for the Citizen Soldier, that would serve as a text for the future offerings of the required USMA Law course. Within two years we were in print.

In the years that followed, I drifted away from military studies. My academic focus shifted to energy law and a wonderful affiliation to a group of about twenty international academic colleagues who became the Academic Advisory Group of the International Bar Association. Meetings of the AAG around the world shaped biennial publications on energy law issues for publication by Oxford University Press. By coincidence a March 2003 meeting took place at Oxford just as President George W. Bush was preparing to overthrow Saddam Hussein. I joined most of my colleagues in doubting the wisdom of this exercise of American military power.

Section IV

PERSPECTIVES ON TODAY'S MILITARY

We conclude our studies and personal recollections with a variety of observations. CHAPTER A draws on Section II and provides a historical study of the role of the draft in the American military in the twentieth century and its replacement in 1973 with the All-Volunteer Force.

CHAPTER B summarizes the heart of the book—our eight shared recollections of military service and its influence on our lives. We were all young men influenced by the prospect of military service prompted by the draft during the Vietnam War and the middle years of the Cold War. A half-century of young Americans men since then have not experienced that exposure to military service.

CHAPTER C moves the focus to the present day. We look at the current American military and the challenges facing it and America. We examine factors that might call for a larger and more diverse military in the third decade of the twenty-first century. We also examine opposition to mandatory military service that might not have been present half a century ago. What factors could impel the American people to support or oppose a return to conscription?

CHAPTER D moves to legal questions. If popular opinion supported a possible return to the draft, the burden would shift to Congress, the President, and the Supreme Court to answer tough questions about the specific features that would be required in law if the country were to reimpose mandatory military service. The primary burden is on the Congress to answer most of those questions. But it is a certain that whatever Congress settles on, constitutional challenges will follow that would inevitably reach the Supreme Court.

CHAPTER E examines the wide range of issues facing America in its immediate future. We review the extraordinary events of 2020–22. How do they impact decisions about American foreign and domestic policy and the raising of its armed forces?

We write from the perspectives of our active military experiences detailed in Section III and from our reflections on those experiences today. Our experiences since the end of our active service have included academic study of the military, membership in veterans' organizations, and thoughtful consideration of American military, foreign policy and public policy issues. It was conversations among the eight of us that we were the inspiration for this book.

Chapter A

THE DRAFT AND THE ALL-VOLUNTEER FORCE

What are the lessons of America's experience with mandatory military service as we approach the second quarter of the twenty-first century? Almost a half century has passed since the end of the draft and the beginning of reliance on an All-Volunteer Force in 1973. That period can be contrasted with the 35 years (1917–18 and 1940–73) in which America mandated at least the possibility of military service for young men. All of the authors of this book served in the military in the final decade of mandatory military service. Let us compare the two eras.

The Draft Eras

America relied on mandatory military service to fight WW I, WW II, most of the long Cold War with the Soviet Union, the Korean War and the Vietnam War. The first four conflicts involved combat or potential combat against powerful enemies with military capabilities similar to that of the United States. WW I and WW II ended in victory for America and her Allies. The Cold War helped to avoid a shooting war between the world's two major nuclear powers and helped set the stage for the collapse of the Soviet Union in 1989. The Korean War, which began with an invasion of South Korea by Communist North Korea, had limited objectives of preserving the status quo between the two Koreas. It achieved that goal, albeit at considerable cost.

Only the Vietnam War ended in a failure of American objectives as Communist North Vietnam gained control of all of Vietnam two years after the United States withdrew its military support of the South Vietnamese government. The war's unpopularity in its later stages prompted candidate and President Richard Nixon to favor ending the draft and replacing it with the All-Volunteer Force. Flawed as he was, Nixon properly sensed that popular sentiment about the war was driven in considerable measure by objection to the draft. As the risk of being drafted abated participation in antiwar protests waned.

The All-Volunteer Force Era

The 50 years of the All-Volunteer Force has seen fewer serious military challenges to the United States than during the draft eras. The collapse of the Soviet Union in 1989 through 1991 can be attributed in part to America's willingness to continue its leadership of NATO and other multinational efforts to limit possible Soviet expansion. The major armed conflicts of this era centered in the Middle East and Afghanistan. It fell to an All-Volunteer Force to respond to Iraq's invasion of Kuwait in 1991 and the September 11, 2001 terrorist attacks on the United States.

Operation Desert Storm in 1991 was the most successful use of American armed forces of the half century. President George H.W. Bush led an international effort to overturn Iraqi dictator Saddam Hussein's conquest of Kuwait, his threat to other Middle Eastern states and the Middle East's provision of petroleum to much of the world. A well-coordinated military and diplomatic effort liberated Kuwait and badly damaged Iraqi armed forces but intentionally stopped short of conquering Iraq or overthrowing Saddam Hussein's regime. American fatalities were less than 200. Even briefer military actions earlier in Panama and Grenada also achieved victories—albeit minor ones—for American armed forces.

General Colin Powell, Chairman of the Joint Chiefs of Staff during Operation Desert Storm, died at age 84 in 2021. His obituary in The Economist observed: "His rules for going to war, which other people called the Powell Doctrine were colored by [his Vietnam Experience]. Had everything else been tried? Was it in the national interest? Was there a clear objective worth risking lives for?...Did America have the resources to do the job fast and well? Had the consequences been considered?...Did allies and the American people, support it? And was there a strategy for leaving?"

Since 1991, the United States and its All-Volunteer Force have won some battlefield victories but have also suffered both military and foreign policy losses in the 20-year "Global War on Terror." In American eyes that "war" began with the Al-Qaeda attack on New York City and Washington, D.C. on September 11, 2001.

American forces disrupted Taliban and Al-Qaeda control of Afghanistan within months after September 11th and began campaigns against "Islamic terrorist" organizations in the Middle East and Africa. Major combat resumed in 2003 with President George W. Bush's decision to overthrow Saddam Hussein in Iraq. The Bush administration alleged that Saddam had concealed weapons of mass destruction. The allegations largely proved to be false. The Bush Administration did achieve the objectives of a conquest of Iraq and the capture and eventual (botched) execution of Saddam.

THE DRAFT AND THE ALL-VOLUNTEER FORCE

What followed, however, was an American occupation of Iraq and Afghanistan at the cost of several thousand American and Allied deaths and enormous wealth in 20 years of "endless war." Those deaths were dwarfed by civilian deaths. The Afghanistan engagement ended in August 2021 when President Joe Biden followed through on President Donald Trump's promise of a rapid withdrawal of combat forces. Within a remarkably short period after the hasty final phase of the evacuation the Taliban had seized control of most of the country. The Afghan government and armed forces offered little effective resistance.

A modest American military force provided essential help in withdrawing over 130,000 American civilians and military personnel and many Afghan supporters of the American cause. However, the chaotic scenes at the Kabul airports were a painful reminder of the frantic evacuation of Saigon in 1975 that marked the end of American involvement and the eventual Communist takeover of South Vietnam. The Taliban victory resulted in a second "lost war" by American forces.

The Next Fifty Years

Even before the loss of the Afghanistan War, the United States faced potential conflicts with China, Russia, North Korea and Iran. All four are far more serious potential military opponent than Saddam Hussein's Iraq, the Islamic State (ISIS), or the Taliban. China, Russia and North Korea are nuclear powers with increasingly powerful conventional military power. Iran hopes to add nuclear weapons capability to its significant military forces. War with even one of these four nations could demand a far larger military force than the present Army, Navy, Air Force and Marine Corps. That combined force is smaller than the American Army alone at the height of the Vietnam War. Starting with Operation Desert Storm in 1991, a significant mobilization of American forces required the activation of a sizable portion of the reserve forces and the National Guard. Depending on the nature and tempo of the threat, those realities could demand a return to conscription if America wishes to retain its role as the world's major military power with a world-wide operational capability.

Even if America could be certain of no larger wars than the conflict in Ukraine in the decades to come, a return to mandatory military service could offer benefits to both the nation and to the men and women who would be called to duty. The military of today increasingly needs educated and skilled soldiers, sailors, fliers and marines. Conscription could help staff the armed forces with necessary talent where it was needed.

Some draftees or draft induced volunteers would serve in the traditional combat forces—marksmen, artillerists, fighter pilots, naval gunners, etc. Increasingly, more of the conscripted members of the new military would be using their talents in such fields as engineering and science, cyberwarfare, conflicts in outer space or familiarity with foreign cultures and languages.

We explore these issues in greater detail after we review the lessons of our experiences as drafted or draft influenced members of the military. We use the term "draft-influenced" to cover the wide range of incentives for military service beyond waiting for and complying with a notification of induction. A familiar "draft-influenced" opportunity for several of us was the college or university ROTC. ROTC allowed a student to combine academic study with a military training program sufficient to entitle him to receive an officer's commission at the same time as his academic degree. The ROTC program often allowed substantial financial support to the prospective military officer.

Chapter B
OUR SHARED EXPERIENCES

Our personal accounts describe the range of experiences that our military service provided. We eight were not a "band of brothers" who shared military experiences in a single command at the same time. Rather, we were a group of civilian friends either before or after active military service. In recent years, we have shared our thoughts on that service and its relevance to the present day American armed forces.

We served in the Army, Navy, Coast Guard, Marines and Air Force. Our services were in the United States and overseas, combat and non-combat. Yet, they provided experiences that we shared and that we agree on half a century after our service ended. We identify a dozen of those common features.

1. Pride in our military service: Whether our service was in front line combat or stateside desk duty, we look back on our years in uniform respectfully, even if not always fondly. Our service gave us a strong sense of what it meant to be an American.
2. Service as a maturing experience: Unlike most first civilian jobs, our military service was often far from home and parents, mentors, classmates and friends. Often it involved doing initially unfamiliar work. It did not allow the abandonment of that work without criminal consequences.
3. The lifelong value of physical conditioning and/or competitive athletics: Regular exercise or competitive sports remained, for most of us, an attractive part of our life in our post-service careers.
4. Early opportunities for leadership: Military service, particularly at the officer level, typically required service in leadership positions. This often involved working with multi-million dollar equipment under challenging conditions. We did this work in our early twenties often far sooner than we would have in our first post-graduation civilian employment.
5. An unease with the way military service is praised today: We performed our military service during the latter part of the Vietnam War and Cold War eras when a substantial portion of privileged young men avoided military service of any kind. A significant and visible minority of them

sharply criticized the military. Often the criticism was directed at the uniformed military members themselves rather than at their civilian leadership. Those of us who did serve found much to admire about military leadership, but also things that did not impress us. In the America of the 2020s, we are unenthusiastic about mindless "thank you for your service" adulation of the military from those with no personal experience with it.

6. The exposure to Americans of different races, religions, and geographic regions: The military of the 1960s and early 1970s was hardly free of the discrimination that infected the America of its time (and still does today). But, unbiased advancement through the military ranks was more likely than in most civilian employment.
7. Exposure to the world beyond the United States: The majority of us served at least part of our active duty outside the United States. That provided a wider view of the world than most young men of our age received. Even those of us whose service was all in the United States encountered foreign military members in our duty stations, in our basic and advanced training classes, and in visits with fellow veterans stationed in Europe, the Middle East or Asia.
8. The military as the shared national experience: As the United States has become increasingly divided geographically, politically, and culturally, it is valuable to have national experiences that connect 335 million Americans. Military service was that common experience.
9. Value of the draft as a check on the excesses of civilian leadership of the military: With all young male members of civilian society potentially liable for military service in the 1960s and early 1970s, potential draftees, their parents, civilian employers, and friends remained far more attentive to the wisdom or stupidity of national military policies than they are today.
10. The benefits to veterans of the GI Bill or other post-service benefits: Such veterans' benefits encouraged a productive transition to the civilian work force after the veteran's military service. In addition, the benefits to individual GIs helped provide a better trained American work force.
11. The experiences of our spouses and children from our military service: Most of us shared our active duty service with a spouse. They were very much a part of our service experience and often bore the burdens of our duties. Young children also shared some part of the experience. Both spouses and children faced the burdens of military service but they also learned from those experiences. While our children have not chosen voluntary military service they have pursued a wide range of successful careers.

12. While we honor the veterans of the All-Volunteer Force, we disagree that they have provided a more capable military than the draft era. The draft era provided a wider selection of military members who were more diverse and often more capable than those of the All-Volunteer Force. The wider range of potential military members from the draft era made for a healthy diversity of the American armed forces.

Chapter C

THE CONTEMPORARY AMERICAN MILITARY

The American military of the 2020s is drawn from a variety of sources authorized by federal and state law. As Section II indicates, throughout American history different laws and policies have governed different parts of the military. The members of the today's American armed forces are drawn from the following sources.

Officers are the product of the service academies—West Point for the Army, Annapolis for the Navy and Marines, the Air Force Academy in Colorado Springs, and the Coast Guard Academy in New London. A substantial portion of the Academy graduates are expected to serve a career in the service of twenty years or more. The best of the graduates will serve as generals and admirals 30 years or more after their academy days.

A second primary source of new officers are the ROTC. These programs are hosted at universities around the country. They appeal to students wishing to attend a civilian university with its wide variety of degrees and, at the same time, to have military training that qualifies them for an officer's commission following graduation. Government support of ROTC programs and students can substantially reduce the cost of a college education.

Other programs allow talented enlisted personnel to advance to an officer's commission. A final path to an officer's commission allows a direct commission from a professional position in civilian life to perform similar military duties. Doctors, lawyers and chaplains are examples.

Enlisted personnel today enter military service through voluntary enlistment. The terms of enlistment typically commit the enlistee to a fixed term of full-time military training and service (usually two to four years) followed by a further period of obligated reserve service. The reserve duty typically requires weekly duty in a reserve unit and several weeks of annual summer service. The reservist is also subject to recall to full-time active duty. After the reservist has completed the obligated term of service, he or she can continue as a reservist for many years, qualifying for retirement benefits at age 60.

A further essential piece of the modern federal military establishment is the National Guard. The Guard combines state government control and national government control of the service member. The states' National Guards perform a wide variety of missions under the direction of the state governor and legislature. Some duties, such as riot control, mirror national military duties. Others, such as natural disaster response (floods, fires, hurricanes, tornadoes and health emergencies) will supplement services performed by local and state officials.

The National Guard's connection to the federal military establishment has evolved over American history. For most of the last century National Guard membership has committed the Guard member to possible federal military service.

During the Vietnam War era, the national government chose not to rely on activation of the Guard and reserve for wartime service. That burden was placed on draftees or draft-induced volunteers. Guard or reserve status freed the Guard member from being drafted into active federal military service. With the end of the draft and the beginning of the All-Volunteer Force, it became clear that Guard or reserve membership subjected the individual to the real prospect of being called to full-time national active duty in the nation's wars. Often this has resulted in multiple calls to duty in combat service around the world.

A final portion of the military are civilian employees of private businesses that are under contract with a branch of the military. These personnel are not uniformed officers or enlisted personnel in a branch of the armed services. However, the civilian employees often perform duties as dangerous as members of the armed forces, serve closely with members of the uniformed military, and suffer injuries and death like uniformed members. Often the private contractor's employees are military veterans who bring special skills or experience that exceed that of the average uniformed service member. When serving with an armed force in the field in time of declared war or a contingency operation, these individuals are subject to the military justice system.

We now examine three factors that might encourage a return to drafted military service. Section E takes a specific look at the last two years of developments with an impact on the American military.

The Need for a Larger Force to Fight Conventional Wars

As mentioned, the strongest incentive for a return to compulsory military service would be the need for a much larger American military than has been needed over the last half century. Journalist Bob Woodward quoted

Chairman of the Joint Chiefs of Staff Peter Pace on the consequences of a failure of a five-brigade "surge" (increase) of American troops in Iraq in 2007. If the surge failed, Pace said "you are forced to conscription, which no one wants to talk about...To mention a draft was to invite the ghosts of Vietnam into the tank."

In 2021 total United States active duty military personnel were reported at 1,346,400. They were supplemented by 799,500 reservists and 337,525 National Guard members. What are the current international threats that might prompt a return to the draft in order to increase the size of the American military. Five potential enemies stand out.

China: China's population of 1.3 billion makes it by far the largest of potential American enemies. The quality of Chinese armed forces has improved markedly over the last two decades. China now has the largest military in the world. Its Navy is the largest in the world. Its Air Force ranks second only to the United States. It is the third largest nuclear armed force in the world.

In the last two decades China has also asserted a military and foreign policy that views itself as the dominant power in East Asia and the rapidly emerging dominant world power. President Xi has asserted the dominance of the Chinese Communist Party and his leadership of the Party for the foreseeable future.

In the last decade Communist China has asserted broader control over Hong Kong. China's actions have undercut many of the democratic values that date back to the British rule over Hong Kong.

China has also regularly asserted that Taiwan with its sophisticated technology-based economy is effectively a part of mainland China. Taiwan's population of 25 million is dwarfed by mainland China's one billion, three hundred million. China has also asserted control over the South China and East China Seas.

Within China itself, China's treatment of the Islamic Uyghur population has attracted widespread condemnation for its denial of human rights of the Uyghurs and the placement of hundreds of thousands of Uyghurs in concentration camps. The United States and other nations refused to send national leaders to the 2022 Winter Olympics in Beijing in protest of the offenses against the Uyghurs in Xinjiang. The United States Congress has also passed legislation forbidding the sale of goods made by Uyghur slave labor. China has angrily responded to the intrusions on its sovereignty.

Russia: Russia has a population of 156 million making it the largest European nation, but with less than half the population of the United States. Russia's population is declining and its economy depends heavily on the sale of its fossil fuels for export.

Under the aggressive leadership of Vladimir Putin, the Russian military rebuilt after the collapse of Russian military power with the fall of the Soviet Union from 1989 to 1991. Putin's Russia has sought to revive Russian leadership over the "near abroad"—current independent nations that were formerly part of the Soviet Union or part of Eastern Europe "behind the iron curtain." Russia has taken strong objection to efforts of the NATO to add some of these nations to its membership.

In 2014 Russia seized Crimea with its considerable Russian population from Ukraine. Western opposition to the annexation was strong but did not extend to military action. Russian-Ukraine relations turned to outright war with the Russian invasion of February 2022 discussed in Chapter E International Affairs. Events beginning in February 2022 in Ukraine, discussed shortly, moved closer to war between the United States and Russia.

Russia also continues to threaten other portions of eastern Europe that were formerly under the domination of the Soviet Union. Examples are three NATO members, Estonia, Latvia and Lithuania. Beyond the "near abroad" Russia has asserted a major role in the Middle East especially after the American withdrawal from Afghanistan. Russia remains the second dominant nuclear power in the world. It has also appeared to be responsible for, or at least encouraging, major cyber attacks on a wide variety of American governmental and corporate institutions.

North Korea: North Korea has an estimated population of 26 million, barely half the population of South Korea. North Korea's economy is meager compared to South Korea and is largely dependent on China. Its leader Kim Jong Un is the third member of his family to assert lifetime rule over the country.

North Korea initiated the Korean War in 1950 with its invasion of the south. The War ended in stalemate and North Korea has continued to be a significant military power. It is an expanding nuclear power posing an immediate threat to South Korea, Japan and Taiwan. It may soon have a capability to strike with nuclear weapons around the world, including the United States. It has a significant conventional army that threatens its near neighbors, most notably South Korea.

Iran: Iran has a population of 85 million making it one of the major powers in the Middle East. Iran has maintained a hostile relationship with the United States and Israel for nearly half a century. Its armed forces are among the most powerful in the Middle East. It continues to be a major player in Middle Eastern energy policy.

For several decades Iran has threatened to become a nuclear military power. During the Obama Administration a multinational agreement with Iran offered to remove significant economic sanctions on Iran in return for Iranian agreement to end or delay its efforts to become a nuclear military power. President

Donald Trump regarded the nuclear agreement as a terrible deal for the United States and ended American participation in the Agreement. Iranian leadership in the last two years has reasserted Iran's hostility to western interests.

Islamic Terrorists: The attacks on the United States on September 11, 2001 prompted President George W. Bush to identify the Al-Qaeda attackers (the majority of whom were Saudi citizens) as "Islamic terrorists" and the terrorists as a worldwide threat to the United States and other nations around the world. The term today could apply to both organized groups and "lone wolf" or small groups of individuals. dedicated to violent attacks on citizens and governments. For a brief time, the ISIS organization seized control of considerable territory in Iraq and took on aspects of a traditional state. Currently, Islamic militants are active in many central African nations.

A war with any one of the four nation states would be a more significant challenge to the United States than any posed since the fall of the Soviet Union three decades ago. The prospect of alliances among the four nations against the United States and its allies raises a far greater challenge. Probably no nation today envisions playing the role of Germany or Japan in the 1940s and intentionally engaging in war to gain world-wide military dominance. But the United States and its allies may need to increase their military strength to persuade potential adversaries not to resort to war. And, the Russian invasion of Ukraine in February 2022 has stimulated a significant response from the NATO alliance.

War with one or more of the potential American adversaries would quite likely dramatically increase the number of American armed forces needed to defeat the adversaries. The analogy would be to World War I and World War II in which conscription and draft-induced "volunteering" were felt essential to achieving American war objectives.

Today's More Sophisticated Military Needs

The American military of the 2020s and beyond will need large numbers of technical and other specialists rather than only combat troops. The typical draftee might no longer be only the high school graduate or drop out with few technical or professional skills. Rather the armed forces today need existing specialists in engineering, modern science, technology, cyber warfare, foreign languages and cultures and other skills. Today, some of these specialists are provided by private contractors who often draw on military veterans for their workforces. While the military could provide basic training in some of these fields, it would be far more valuable to draft college educated and/or technologically experienced personnel already skilled in these fields. Those draftees would be immediately valuable to the military services and could help in the training of raw recruits or existing members of the forces.

The events of 2020–22 that we discuss shortly indicate the likely need for skilled members of the military (active duty, reserves and National Guard) to assist with domestic (and possibly foreign) disasters that overload civilian capacities. The first example is the two-year (and continuing) COVID-19 pandemic, which has overtaxed hospitals and medical personnel around the nation.

Skilled military doctors, nurses and others trained in medicine can be ready to respond quickly to such emergencies. Other military personnel can serve as drivers, cooks and law enforcement officers. The draft-encouraged recruitment of such personnel could place the nation in better condition to handle such health emergencies.

A second lesson of 2020–22 came from the wide variety of natural disasters throughout America. All of those disasters could be blamed, at least in part, on climate change.

Trained military personnel were useful in these and other natural disasters. Emergency responders in military uniform would also be invaluable in many other situations from big cities to rural communities.

A Need for Shared National Sacrifice and Greater Citizen Familiarity with the Military

As our eight profiles indicate, the draft of the 1960s and 1970s exposed young American males from all social classes and from all parts of the nation to the possibility of military service. It continued the tradition of the World Wars and the Cold War. The prospect of drafted or draft-induced service that faced young men of those eras also gave their spouses, parent, mentors, friends and employers a direct stake in American military policy.

After 50 years of an All-Volunteer Force, that connection between the average citizen and the American military is disturbingly limited. A disproportionate number of new servicemen and women are children of veterans of military service. Many of them have grown up around military installations. Those installations are disproportionately located in the south and inland west. Soldiers' parents rarely come from the upper middle class, let alone the most privileged five percent of the population. Today's military volunteers are rarely graduates of elite preparatory schools or universities. Young men and women from those elite backgrounds have limited knowledge of the military. Their parents (and possibly grandparents) and other relatives, teachers and employers are also quite likely not to seen military active duty or even to have faced the prospect of drafted military service. Even if they view the military as one of the most esteemed parts of American society, it plays no part in their lives.

National government leadership is also short on members with even brief military service. The Pew Research Center reports that 91 members of the 117th Congress are military veterans. Sixty-three are Republicans and twenty-eight are Democrats. That amounts to 17 percent of both the House and the Senate. That is the lowest number of veterans since World War II. Between 1965 and 1975 at least 70 percent of members of Congress had seen military service. In 1980 18 percent of all American citizens had seen military service. By 2018 that number was down to 7 percent.

Washington Post columnist E.J. Dionne reflects on the decline in members of Congress with military experience. He quotes Democratic Representative Jason Crow about the need to execute "a radical change in our society in the way we distribute the burdens of conflict." Fellow veteran Republican Representative Michael Waltz sees the small number of veteran legislators as being a "big part of explaining the record amount of dysfunction" in today's Congress.

The Presidency has also seen a decline in veterans. Harry Truman, Dwight Eisenhower, John Kennedy, Richard Nixon, Gerald Ford, Jimmy Carter, Ronald Reagan and George H.W. Bush all served in the military, many with combat service. Since the 1992 election of draft evader Bill Clinton over WW II combat veteran George H.W. Bush, non-veterans have been more successful in winning Presidential elections than veterans. In 1996, President Clinton defeated wounded WW II combat veteran Bob Dole. In 2000, George W. Bush who was seen as evading active duty or Vietnam service by doing reserve duty in Texas, defeated Al Gore, who had seen active service in Vietnam. In 2004, the younger Bush was reelected over Navy combat veteran John Kerry. In 2008, Barack Obama, who was too young to have faced the draft, defeated Vietnam combat pilot and prisoner of war John McCain. Most recently, in 2016 Donald Trump was elected over Hillary Clinton despite Trump's avoidance of conscripted service on the basis of alleged "bones spurs".

The Supreme Court for all practical purposes lacks any justices with significant military service. Prior Courts have included the membership of Chief Justice Earl Warren (WW I service as private and lieutenant), Justice Hugo Black (WW I field artillery captain) and William Brennan (WW II Army colonel). Retired Justice Anthony Kennedy served in the California Army National Guard. Retired Justice Stephen Breyer did six months of active duty training and eight years of Army Reserve duty from 1957 to 1965.

Current Justice Samuel Alito is the single present justice with any military experience. He was in the Army ROTC in college. That included six weeks of basic training at Fort Knox.

In recent years several of the authors have had the experience of attending such diverse functions as athletic events, church services, and Rotary Club meetings that recognized November 11th Veterans Day or July 4th. We were asked to stand to be honored for our military service. Despite the considerable numbers of draft era attendees at such events, few veterans stood to accept the well-intentioned congratulations.

That division in society influences those who serve today. Many current service members correctly see themselves as removed from the more privileged classes and the leadership of American society. The Biden Administration has recognized the large number of suicides among active duty and recently discharged service members. Secretary of Defense and veteran Lloyd Austin cited 30,000 suicides among veterans who served between 2001 and 2021. The highest rate of increase in suicides were among Army and Marine Corps members. Secretary Austin found these findings "troubling" and "not going in the right direction."

The dangers of division showed up in the numbers of active duty military personnel and veterans who participated in the insurrection to seize the U.S. Capitol on January 6, 2021 following the 2000 election. Before and after their arrests some justified their actions as "following orders of their commander in chief Donald J. Trump." Trump continually raised the claim of a "stolen election" despite rejection of that claim by dozens of court decisions and findings by state election officials. All found that there was no significant fraud in the 2020 Presidential results that made Joe Biden President.

Gene Fidell perceptively reflects on "extremism in the [current] ranks." He feels that the "services need to find [constitutional] ways to screen out bad apples at the accession stage, separate them promptly administratively [if in the service], and punish them where their conduct hits one of the punitive articles of [the Uniform Code of Military Justice]." This may be easier said than done!

Within a week of the American withdrawal from Afghanistan in August 2021, the Taliban takeover of the country, and the perception of another lost war, the Department of Veterans Affairs felt it necessary to message "[v]eterans from all eras" the following: "You are not alone. Veterans may question the meaning of their service or whether it was worth the sacrifices they made. They may feel more moral distress about experiences they had during their service. It is normal to feel this way....At this moment, it may seem that all is lost, like your service or your sacrifices were for nothing." A page-long enclosure offered "Strategies for Managing Ongoing Distress."

Chapter D

DECISIONS FOR THE GOVERNMENT ABOUT A RENEWED DRAFT

A return to some form of required service will require congressional approval. The Constitution in Article II, Section 1 gives Congress "all legislative powers." Section 8 gives Congress the power "To raise and support Armies" [para. 12]; "To provide and maintain a Navy" [para. 13]; and "to make rules for the Government and Regulation of the land and naval forces" [para. 14]. While the President "shall be the Commander in Chief of the Army and the Navy" that does not give him or her the power to draft citizens into the military.

The Legality of the Draft

The Supreme Court and the lower federal courts have power over cases arising under the Constitution and laws of the United States. The Supreme Court firmly and unanimously upheld congressional power to enact the 1917 Selective Service law in 1918 rejecting challenges to the legality of the draft from around the country. The Court was clear in rejecting claims that the draft was equivalent to slavery or involuntary servitude forbidden by the 13th Amendment. Decisions since then have emphatically reaffirmed the legality of military conscription.

Gender Classification

No conscription statute has required women to be subject to the draft. In 1981 in *Rostker v. Goldberg* the Supreme Court was asked whether this blatant gender discrimination violated the Due Process Clause of the Fifth Amendment. The Court preserved the legality of the male only draft registration by noting that the goal of the Selective Service Act was to secure combat troops. In 1981, women were not eligible for combat assignments. Hence, the Court concluded that a "male only" draft was constitutional.

Forty years later, women constitute 15–20 percent of the armed forces. All military positions (including combat ones) are open to qualified women. Thus, today both men and women can legitimately object to a "male only" draft. Men who do not want to serve in the military could claim that they would bear an unequal burden of military service. Women serving or wishing to serve could claim men are treated as favored members of the service. Given the wide range of alleged discriminations against women in the armed forces, Congress would be hard pressed to retain a "male only" draft. Even with its usual deference to congressional authority in military matters, the Supreme Court would have a hard time sustaining the "no women draftees" policy now that women have become an integral part of the American armed forces.

Mandatory Public Service Beyond the Military

A particular challenge for Congress would be whether to extend the draft to public service beyond just the armed services. Various programs of the federal government might be candidates for that treatment. Giving the draftee the option of performing his or her mandatory public service in the Peace Corps, Americorps or another non-military federal (or state government) program might broaden the appeal of public service to potential draftees, their parents and the general public. It might also lessen objections from citizens and voters who objected to military service or to specific conflicts in which the military was engaged. It would also make public service (including military service) an expected and appealing part of growing to maturity in America. Part of the appeal of mandatory service could be the considerable financial benefits to young people who serve. The forgiveness of student loans to college students who performed mandatory public service would mark a return to the generosity of the GI Bill in the post-WW II era.

Conscientious Objection to Military Service

A further challenge to Congress returning to the draft would be the treatment of men and women with conscientious objection to military service. The 1917 draft act excused persons with "conscientious objection" to military service based on religious belief. The statute exempted members of "any well-recognized religious sect or organization…whose existing creed or principles forbid its members to participate in war in any form and whose religious convictions are against war or any participation therein." In 1917 most legislators supporting the exception recognized the long-standing national admiration for the Quaker faith and its pacifist beliefs. Mark Sullivan's "Over Here" reported that "All told some 3900 men were recognized by the Army as individual conscientious objectors" during World War I.

The expansion of the draft to include peaceful civilian service might remove the need for a statutory conscientious objector exception to military service. In the latter days of the Vietnam War conscientious objector claims extended well beyond membership in one of the traditional "peace churches." These claims posed difficult challenges to draft board members and the courts reviewing refusals to serve. If multiple civilian public service options were available to a draftee, no one could claim their rights were violated.

Administering the Draft

The 1917 Selective Service Act relied on a War Department estimate that the nation had nearly two million men aged 18 and 19 and an additional 3,775,376 between 20 and 24. They drew their estimates from the 1910 Decennial Census. How would the America of 1917 select 500,000 or one million men for the first draft?

Army Chief of Staff Peyton March, writing after the war, reported: "I learned that Secretary [of War] Baker was personally responsible for the method adopted by the War Department of forming draft boards from citizens of the different communities...instead of organizing them [by] military men...The decision of Secretary Baker's not only popularized the draft system, it really made the draft."

The local draft board would remain an essential part of Selective Service for the rest of the twentieth century. General Enoch Crowder, who led the military's administration of the draft in WW I, summarized the draft as a "plan of decentralized civilian machinery with centralized supervision under the military."

Secretary Baker had no military experience. His reputation was earned in civilian government. Treasury Secretary William Gibbs McAdoo described him as: "A small man physically. Baker looked boyish in the company of the tall and bulky generals who were usually around him." As such, Baker capably represented the civilian perspective on military issues.

President Woodrow Wilson also had no military experience. But both Baker and Wilson were persuaded that conscription would send a powerful message to Germany as well as to the citizens of the United States. They had the good fortune of having Congressional support from Republican ranking member of the House Military Affairs Committee Julius Kahn. Democratic Chair of the Senate Committee George Chamberlain summarized the need for conscription: "Now that we are engaged in war with one of the greatest military powers in the world, the adoption of the principle of universal service becomes all the more imperative...This nation can make no headway unless we adopt a system of waging war which will enable us to utilize to the fullest possible extent our entire resources in men and material..."

Six weeks of vigorous debate in Congress over the draft in Spring 1917 surfaced two critical issues. The first was whether the draft was essential to see that the burden (or privilege) of military service was not borne primarily by the elite of society while the lower classes and/or recent immigrants would avoid military service. The draft was needed to compel the "slackers" to serve. The second was the treatment of African-Americans ("Negroes" in the polite parlance of 1917). Mixing of white and Negro soldiers in military units was criticized by both Northern and Southern white legislators. Southerners also feared that giving Negroes military experience would threaten white supremacy in the South.

Approximately 4,600 local draft boards were constituted around the nation. While some board members had performed military service themselves, almost all were better identified as prominent local citizens who probably lived within fifty miles of their prospective draftees. Many of the draftees or their family and friends knew at least one member of the Board. The Board members knew their communities.

Secretary Baker later reported that more than one-third of the draftees asked for infantry service. The next choices were light artillery, heavy artillery, and aviation service. Summarizing the registration in December of 1917, Baker observed: "No other country in recorded history ever did such a thing, and it was done by us so easily, so simply, and so completely as a matter of course that it passed by without adequate notice of its significance..."

A very different America would confront an attempt to reinstate the draft in the 2020s. The later stages of the Vietnam War had seen prominent draft evaders come from the middle and upper classes. The burden of drafted service fell on less fortunate Americans with a disproportionate share of draftees coming from African American and other minority groups. The legacy of WW II, Korea, and the Cold War had left most Americans familiar with and supportive of the military. George Marshall, Dwight Eisenhower, Matthew Ridgway and Douglas MacArthur were heroic and popular figures in the civilian community. Today a local draft board, possibly run by local political figures, would probably be less appealing than one run by the military.

Popular Views on a Return to the Draft

The prior section describes some of the factors that could stimulate Congress to legislate some form of mandatory military and other public service.

Possibly, Congress and the President could lead the initiative as they did prior to American entry into WW I and WW II. But, today public opinion may need to lead, or at least encourage, government at a time of badly divided and partisan government. Opposition to a return of the draft would come from a variety sources.

The first would be public opposition to worldwide American leadership that requires a considerable commitment to a strong and large military that would probably need to rely on the prospect of mandatory military service. The experiences in Vietnam, Iraq and Afghanistan have not been happy ones; they would scarcely encourage widespread American military involvement overseas.

While worldwide military involvement may appear necessary, it also draws resources away from local and national needs. Education, social services, infrastructure and citizen equality can all suffer from the diversion of limited American dollars to overseas military activities.

The second would be objection to a deprivation of liberties of the drafted service personnel. Two years of fighting the COVID-19 virus has been hindered by resistance from citizens objecting to the denial of their "freedoms" and "rights." If receiving a vaccine shot is an invasion of liberties, how much more invasive would be a government requirement of two or more years of mandatory military service?

A third objection would come from considerable portions of military leadership. The last years of the draft in the Vietnam era were unhappy ones for much of military leadership at both junior and senior levels. The prospect of a return to those days would not be popular.

A fourth objection to a renewal of the draft would come from military contractors who have taken over many of the roles previously held by uniformed service members. The contractors would be calling on political support in Congress to preserve their businesses.

A fifth objection might come from the younger Americans who would bear the burden of a return to mandatory military service. They would recognize that, unlike in the post-WW II decades, two generations older than them had not faced mandatory military service. Absent the equivalent of a Pearl Harbor attack, why should they now bear the burden of military service that their parents and grandparents avoided?

Chapter E

THE EXTRAORDINARY EVENTS OF 2020–22

Decisions on military policy and the need for a draft will be shaped by events that go beyond purely military concerns. No one could have predicted the tumultuous events the country and the world have faced since the start of 2020. We conclude with a brief review of those events and their implications for decisions on American foreign and domestic policy, the missions of the armed forces, and a possible return to the draft.

The COVID Pandemic

At the end of 2019, both American government officials and a few well-informed American citizens were encountering a mysterious virus that soon became known as COVID-19. The virus had first been recognized in Wuhan, China. Its precise origins remain a matter of speculation. What is more certain is that Chinese officials were reluctant to report the virus to international health officials even though doing so would have allowed prompt global efforts to control the spread of the disease.

By March of 2020, the virus had reached much of the rest of the world including the United States. The first fatalities had occurred. Horribly, COVID had begun to take on political connotations. Scientific and medical experts were nearly unanimous that the virus posed serious risks and that the prompt actions needed to be taken. The Trump Administration, with an eye on the presidential election, downplayed potential COVID harm, predicted the virus would run its course by Easter and adopted a skeptical view of scientific expertise. President Trump and administration officials were almost contemptuous of urgings by scientists to avoid large "spreader" gatherings and the values of wearing masks.

By mid-summer of 2020, infections had spread around the country and considerable deaths and hospitalizations were being reported. It appeared quite likely that things would get worse before they got better. Analogies to the 1918–19 "Spanish" influenza epidemic began to circulate. President

Trump suggested that local and state governments bore major responsibility for handling the epidemic. He did, however, support efforts to find a vaccine that could prevent COVID infections, or, at least, lessen the seriousness of the disease.

By the November election the COVID virus had impacted the life of most Americans. Deaths reached the hundreds of thousands. President Trump's response to it had reflected, at best, a lack of vigorous leadership at a time of national emergency. Democratic candidate Joe Biden's victory at the polls was influenced by Trump's ineffective response to the pandemic.

Upon assuming office in January 2021, President Biden was blessed with the news that several vaccines to control the virus had been developed at extraordinary speed. Biden and his medical advisers took responsibility leading the fight against the virus. In a remarkably short time millions of shots were ready for American's arms. State and local governments and private employers joined in the injection efforts. By late Spring of 2021 it appeared that while infections and deaths were still daily news, things were moving in the right direction. Exhausted health care workers hoped they were seeing the light at the end of the tunnel.

Two factors beyond the President Biden's control then combined to continue the emergency into 2022. First, the politics of the pandemic continued as a significant minority of the population refused to be vaccinated. Portions of the group claimed that their rights were being infringed by mandatory vaccination orders. Second, the emergence of the omicron variants of the virus allowed a continuation of widespread infection.

The total economic cost of COVID ran to the billions of dollars. Businesses shut down. Employees lost their jobs. State and local governments lost tax revenues and faced increased social costs. Inflation plagued the nation. Massive federal relief programs helped to mitigate harms that had threatened to rival the Great Depression of the 1930s.

Climate Change and Natural Disasters

Political disagreement over science and its consequences was also sharpened by startling natural disasters around the country. Most scientists attributed the harms in part to climate change. Record setting events ranged from tornadoes to wildfires to extreme heat or cold to hurricanes.

Within two years, Americans experienced a statewide disruption of electric power in Texas, a tornado that crossed six plains states, wildfires that destroyed over 1,000 homes in the Boulder, Colorado area and a tornado that crossed 70 miles of Iowa in Winter 2022. Often these disasters came out of season or were of greater than usual magnitude. The property damage was sufficient to destroy entire small towns and to force emergency evacuations of thousands of citizens. Police, firefighters or Forest Service personnel were overwhelmed. Military personnel, often National Guard members, were an essential addition to handling the disasters.

Race Relations

The Black Lives Matter (BLM) cause gained national visibility starting in 2020. A number of lethal encounters, primarily between white police officers and African American citizens, were captured on video and widely circulated on national media. BLM protests of the killings took place around the country and were met with counter protests defending law enforcement officers and opposing movements to "Defund the Police."

A gathering in Washington, D.C. near the White House in June 2020 dragged the military into the debate. Chairman of the Joint Chiefs of Staff General Mark Milley joined a gathering near the White House at the behest of President Trump. General Milley, in uniform, soon discovered the gathering was a political rally in which the President sided strongly with the police and against BLM protesters. The next day Millley apologized for participating in a political rally and damaging the military's duty of political non-partisanship.

Political Disruption

The Trump Administration's handling of the pandemic and the economy gave rise to Democratic victories in the Presidential election and elections for both the House and Senate in 2020 and 2021. Even before Election Day President Trump was predicting that election fraud would cause him to lose a "stolen election." The final election numbers gave Joe Biden a solid 306–232 victory in the Electoral College and an impressive popular vote victory of over seven million ballots. Both margins were far larger than those margins for John Kennedy over Richard Nixon in 1960 or George W. Bush over Al Gore in 2000. Bush's margin in the decisive state of Florida was a razor-thin 537 votes. Both Nixon and Gore contested some results through the accepted measures of vote recounts by state and local officials and court challenges. Both losers accepted the results and made clear that their opponents were the legitimate Presidents-elect.

Donald Trump did not. He continued his claims of voter fraud in court challenges and requests for state officials to recount votes in his favor. A recorded Trump phone call to the Georgia Republican Secretary of State asked the Secretary to "find" him another 11,700 Trump votes, just enough to give him victory in Georgia. The Secretary refused. The Electoral College in mid-December validated the Biden victory. Trump, nonetheless, continued his claims of a stolen election and encouraged his supporters to gather in Washington, D.C. on January 6, 2021 when the House of Representatives would confirm the Electoral College vote.

What followed would put January 6, 2021 in the history books along with September 11, 2001 and December 7, 1941. Trump supporters rallied near the White House to hear the President urge bold action at the Capitol. Many supporters then marched to the Capitol. Violent confrontation followed with Capitol Police and District of Columbia law enforcement officers being overwhelmed by protesters who stormed legislative offices, sought to harm members of Congress and Vice President Mike Pence, damaged government property, and injured hundreds of law enforcement officers. Six deaths resulted. President Trump, who remained at the White House, took no prompt action to stop the "insurrectionists." Gradually order was restored with the help of National Guard members. The House reassembled late at night to complete the validation of the Biden election. Two weeks later Joe Biden and Kamala Harris were inaugurated President and Vice President. Donald Trump did not attend the ceremony and flew to his Florida estate.

As unprecedented as the events of January 6 were, the events following defied two centuries of political expectations. A second impeachment of President Trump failed to gain the required two-thirds support in the Senate. A House "bipartisan" investigation of the January 6 insurrection gained only two Republican members. Those two members were then censured by the Republican Party leadership. A variety of state and federal actions continued to gather evidence of President Trump's role in the challenges to the election and the events of January 6. Additional proceedings investigated aspects of Trump's financial dealings.

International Affairs

Developments overseas since 2020 have posed the most direct challenges to American military and foreign policy. We've earlier noted the August 2021 withdrawal of American forces from Afghanistan and the almost immediate recapture of leadership by the Taliban. The Trump and Biden withdrawal from the "endless war" was widely seen as an American calamity and another "lost war." American international leadership suffered. Autocratic leadership around the world rejoiced.

China hosted a joyless Winter Olympics in February 2022 in Beijing. COVID concerns barred much foreign and domestic attendance. It also confined athletes and coaches to isolation from the rest of Beijing. Chinese Communist Party discrimination against the Uyghurs was the subject of much objection. The United States and other western democracies refused to honor the Olympics with the presence of their national leaders and other diplomats.

North Korea continued missile tests that reinforced the friction between that nation and its near and far neighbors including the United States.

The most troubling of all disturbances were Russian President Vladimir Putin's threats to its neighbor Ukraine. Starting in late 2021, Putin assembled nearly 200,000 Russian troops on three sides of Ukraine. Putin also made bold demands on Ukrainian allies, most notably the United States, to recognize Russian dominance. The prospect of the "the largest European War" since 1945 appeared very possible.

On February 24, 2022, fears turned to realities. Russian troops and weapons entered Ukraine from the east, south and north (through Belarus). Most probably, President Putin expected, or at least hoped, that a second Afghanistan would result with Ukrainian government leaders fleeing the country, Ukrainian government military action being limited and feeble and the Ukrainian nation ready for, or at least accepting, a Russian takeover.

Instead, Ukraine resisted vigorously. Russian troops were killed by the thousands. Russian planes, helicopters, tanks and other vehicles were destroyed. The Russian presence clearly was coming in the face of brave Ukrainian resistance and the escape of four million Ukrainian women and children after Russian attacks on civilian targets. Heroic Ukrainian President Volodymyr Zelenskyy remained in Kiev rallying his people and urging western nations to oppose the Russian invasion. President Biden led a worldwide rallying of nations against the Russian invasion and war crimes. All of NATO supported the Ukrainians and opposed the Russians. Germany cancelled the Nord Stream pipeline between Russia and Germany. Germany also massively expanded its military budget. Neutral Sweden and Finland began to explore NATO membership. Even traditionally neutral Switzerland supported Ukraine, as did 150 members of the UN General Assembly.

As of mid-summer of 2022 the outcome of the War remains unclear. But, Russian hopes for a quick victory have failed. The invasion itself and its conduct have harmed Russia's reputation around the world and subjected it to multiple violations of international law. They have also unified most of Europe against Russia and revitalized NATO. Finally, at a time of extreme division in American politics, Vladimir Putin's conduct has united Americans of both political parties and placed a strong military prepared to fight modern wars high on the congressional agenda given the current volatile global picture.

INDEX

Adams, Brook 5
Adams, Henry 5
Administrative Procedure Act 35
All-Volunteer Force 155–58
American military 163–70
Army Bill 10
Atomic Energy Act (1946) 20

Baker, Newton 10–11, 13–15
Baldwin, Gordon 124
Benecke, Louis 115
Bergdahl, Bowe 35
Biden, Joe 157
Black Lives Matter (BLM) 179
BLM: *see* Black Lives Matter
Brooklyn Dodger 97
Bryan, William Jennings 7
Bush, George H. W. 156

Carnegie, Andrew 5
Carter, James M. 127–29
Caruso, Enrico 14
Castro, Fidel 120
Chambers II, John 10
Charlottesville 142
Chiang Kai Shek 20
China 166
Churchill, Winston 20, 116
Civil War of 1861–65 5–7, 12, 107, 115, 117, 142
Cleveland, Grover 7
climate change 178–79
Cohan, George M. 14
Cohen, Eliot 6, 23
combat 21
conventional wars 164–67
Coolidge, Calvin 15
COVID pandemic 177–78
Cox, James M. 15
Crowder, Enoch 13

Daley, Richard J. 40
DAR: *see* Daughters of the American Revolution

Daughters of the American Revolution (DAR) 59
Davis, James 23
Defense Language School 101–2
Dolbeare, Kenneth 23
Dole, Bob 21
Draft Act 9–15; administering 173–74; gender classification 171–72; legality of 171; mandatory public service 172; military service, conscientious objection to 172–73; popular views on return to draft 174–75

Eisenhower, Dwight 118
Ellis, John 20
Evans, Harold 20
extraordinary events (2020–22) 177–82; Black Lives Matter (BLM) 179; climate change 178–79; COVID pandemic 177–78; international affairs 180–82; natural disasters 178–79; political disruption 179–80

Fallows, James 23
Federal Tort Claims Act 134
Ferdinand, Franz 8
Fidell, Eugene R. 29–36; as co-founder of NIMJ 35–36; as consultant in fisheries law 35–36; duty in Boston 33–34; education 31–32; experience 29–36; family background 29–31
Foote, Shelby 5
Fussell, Paul 19–20

Gardner, Augustus 12
General Bridge Act (1946) 34
Germany 7–9, 14–16, 18–22, 30, 85, 89–90, 102
GI Bill of Rights 56, 85, 107–8, 113, 116–17, 139, 160
Goldwater, Barry 22
Greenberg, Aaron 29

Harding, Warren 15

INDEX

Harries, Meirion 15
Harries, Susie 15
Hay Bill 8–9
Hershey, Lewis 128–29
Hillman, Elizabeth L. 35
Hitler, Adolph 16
Hoover, Herbert 15–16
Hughes, Charles Evans 9
Hussein, Saddam 156–57

Inouye, Dan 21
international affairs 180–82
Iran 166
Islamic terrorists 167

JAG (Judge Advocate General) Corps 31
James, Henry 5
Jefferson, Thomas 142
Johnson, Hiram 11
Johnson, Lyndon 22, 126

Kennedy, John F. 119–20
Kennedy, Robert 126
Kerry, Bob 21
King, Martin Luther, Jr. 126
Korean conflict 1, 107
Korean War 21–22
Kudirka Incident 34

Lehman, John 23

MacDougal, Gary 85
Mackie, Tom 37–58; active duty 44–55; family background and experience 37–39; high school and path forward 40–42; post-active duty life 55–58; road to military service 41; summer jobs 40; trainings 43; university life 42–44
magnetic anomaly detection equipment (MAD) 65
Mao Tse Tung 20
Marine Corps Reconnaissance Units 47
McBee, Mick 42, 59–72; active duty military career 63–66; civilian career 66–70; college ROTC 61–63; early experiences 60–61; family background and experience 59–60; family military experiences 59–60; Flight Indoctrination Program (FIP), participation in 63; military service 66–70; NROTC scholarship 59, 61–62; other observations 70–72; post-active duty military connections 66; Selective Service System and 61–63; Sigma Phi fraternity membership 62
McKinley, William 6
McNeely, Jerry 122
Mead, Gary 14
Military Establishment 10–11
Military Justice Act (1968) 33
Military Selective Service Act (1967) 23
military service 1–2; American 163–70; citizen familiarity with 168–70; conscientious objection to 172–73; contemporary 163–70; draft eras 155; raise of 3–24; shared experiences 159–61; shared national sacrifice 168–70; sophisticated 167–68; training 9
militia obligations 4
Millett, Allan 4
Morgan, J. P. 5
Moskos, Charles 22
Mussolini, Benito 16

National Guards 6, 8–11, 23, 164
National Institute of Military Justice (NIMJ) 35
NATO 156
natural disasters 178–79
Naval Oceanographic Facilities 92–93
Neutrality Act (1939) 16
NIMJ: *see* National Institute of Military Justice
Nixon, Richard 23, 155
North Korea 166

Operation Desert Storm (1991) 156

Pace, Peter 165
Peace Corps 119
Pershing, John J. 12
political disruption 179–80
Powell, Colin 23, 157
Presley, Elvis 22
Public Law 309 (February 28, 1919) 15
Putin, Vladimir 166

Quayle, Dan 23

renewed draft 171–75
Revolutionary War (1775) 3–4
Rickover, Hyman 77
Robinson, Jackie 97
Rockefeller, John D. 5
Rockefeller, John D., Jr. 14
Roosevelt, Franklin D. 14–16

INDEX 185

Roosevelt, Theodore, Jr. 6
Roosevelt, Theodore, Sr. 5, 10, 12
Root, Elihu 5
Rostker v. Goldberg 171
ROTC programs 163
Rudman, Warren 21
Russian military 166

Salvesen, Arne 73–86; education 73–74; as Engineer Officer of the Watch 83; in Germany 84–85; at Mark Controls Corporation 85; Naval Aviation training 75; NROTC scholarship 74; shipboard life experiences 74–86; USS Enterprise, nuclear carrier 79–86; at Zimpro waste treatment plant 84–85
Salvesen, Leif 87–97; active duty life in navy 94–95; family background and experience 88–91; life after active duty 95–96; at Oceanographic Naval Facilities 92–93; reflections 96–97
Schoenfeld, Clay 123
Scott, Hugh 10
SeaBees 38
Selective Service Act (1940/1948) 19–21
shared national sacrifice 168–70
Shunk, Adeline Matilda 37
Spanish-American War (1898) 6
Stallone, Sylvester 23
Strieby, Paul 99–106; in Army Language School 101–3; for Boot Camp 101; experiences 102–6; family background and experience 100–101; at Fort Meade, Maryland 105; military education 101–3; military service 101–6; in RC-135 (RIVET JOINT) missions 103
Strouse, Jean 5
Swanson, Joe 90

Taft, William Howard 6–7, 10
Terwilliger, Wayne 97
Tewhey, John 107–14; duty at F.E. Warren Air Base 108; in E.C. Jordan Engineering firm 108; education 108–10; family background and experience 107–10; first Air Force assignment 110; fourth Air Force assignment 112–14; military career 107–14; ROTC and 109; second Air Force assignment 110–11; as second Lieutenant in US Air Force 109–10; third Air Force assignment 111–12
The Judge Advocate General's School (TJAGSA) 132–40
Tronex Technology, Inc. 85
Trump, Donald 128, 157
Tucker Act 35

UMT: *see* universal military training
United States Military Academy (USMA West Point) 145–51
universal military training (UMT) 9–10
Universal Military Training and Service Act (1951) 21

Vietnam war 1–2, 23, 30, 59, 62, 64–65, 71, 95, 102, 107, 109, 124, 127–29, 131, 135, 140, 142–43, 148, 151, 153, 155
volunteers 5–6, 8–11, 21, 66, 70–71, 136, 139, 143, 158, 164, 168

Washington, George 4, 7
Watts, John 85
Westlund, Cliff 73
William, Henry 5
Williams, Ted 21, 22
Wilson, Woodrow 7, 9–12, 15
Woodward, Bob 164–65
World War I 1, 14–17, 19–21, 107, 167, 173
World War II 1, 21, 29, 37–39, 52, 60, 71, 107, 147, 167, 169

Yardley, Jonathan 23

Zillman, Christian 115
Zillman, Donald 115–51; in Air Force ROTC program 120–21; as Army JAG officer 129–45; birthday 116; disqualifications 128; family background and experience 115–17; IRR service 145–48; in JAG basketball 140–41; Law School experiences 124–27; memories of West Point 146–49; schooling 118–19; Selective Service System and 119; Sigma Phi Society and 119–20; summer 1971 trip to Durham 142; TJAGSA duty 129–45; tour of Europe 121; university education 119–24
Zimpro 84

www.ingramcontent.com/pod-product-compliance
Lightning Source LLC
Chambersburg PA
CBHW021142230426
43667CB00005B/223